UP IN HERE

T0119742

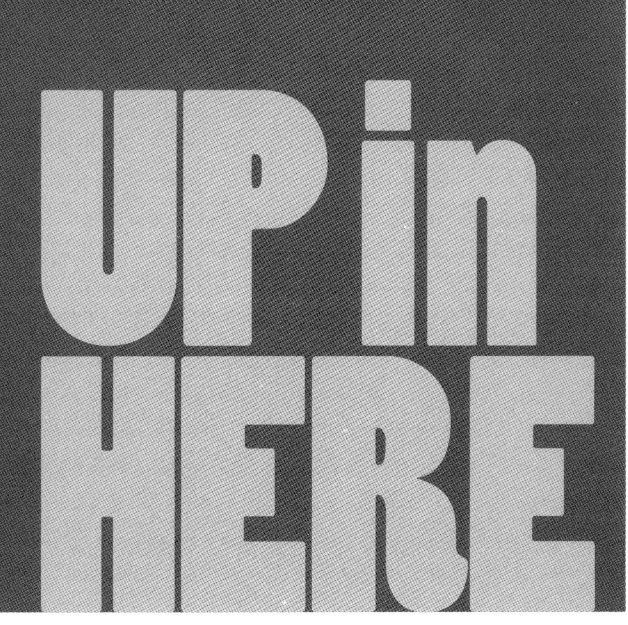

JAILING KIDS ON CHICAGO'S OTHER SIDE

MARK DOSTERT

UNIVERSITY OF IOWA PRESS

Iowa City

University of Iowa Press,
Iowa City 52242
Copyright © 2014
by Mark Dostert
www.uiowapress.org
Printed in the
United States of America

Design by Richard Hendel

No part of this book may be reproduced or used in any form or by any means without permission in writing from the publisher. All reasonable steps have been taken to contact copyright holders of material used in this book. The publisher would be pleased to make suitable arrangements with any whom it has not been possible to reach.

The University of Iowa Press is a member of Green Press Initiative and is committed to preserving natural resources.

Printed on acid-free paper

Library of Congress
Cataloging-in-Publication Data
Dostert, Mark, 1971–
Up in here: jailing kids on Chicago's other side / by Mark Dostert.
pages cm
ISBN 978-1-60938-270-4 (pbk)
ISBN 978-1-60938-288-9 (ebk)
1. Juvenile delinquents—Illinois—Chicago.
2. Juvenile corrections—Illinois—Chicago.
I. Title.
HV743.C5D67 2014
365′.420977311—dc23 2014006251

For Mom and Dad

NOTE ON NAMES AND METHODS

This is nonfiction. There are no composite characters or events. Every juvenile and coworker has a pseudonym. More important than any real names are the stories they tell. Some of the dialogue I have recreated from writer's memory as best I could. Most though I recorded on the cellblocks shortly after it occurred or on my train rides home. From first draft to publication, this book's revision spanned nearly ten years, but all the original dialogue remains as first recorded on blank white pages in a folder that I carried in my duffel bag every shift.

PROLOGUE

My job is to let Ruben out of his cell. Through the door of steel-framed Plexiglas, I watch the shirtless, brown-haired boy gathering soap and shampoo from the scant personal effects off his blue fiberglass desk. I open the door. When his five shower minutes are up, I will lock him back inside this brick and steel chamber—no larger than a modest walk-in closet.

"Here's where it went in," Ruben touches a pockmark under his sternum, replying to my question about his wildly scarred front torso.

I stare at the punctured skin but say nothing. The pudgy fourteen-year-old then twists his left arm behind him pointing to another pink, dime-sized discoloration, this one below his left shoulder blade. "Here's where it went out."

Ruben pivots back to face me. My eyes drop with his eyes to the start of a vertical scar flanked by suture dots running mid-chest to navel. A sickle-shaped mark also disfigures his left rib-cage. He adds, "I had exploratory surgery to remove bullet fragments."

Until he explained all the scars, I hadn't envisioned doctors digging lead out of Ruben. I'm new on this job. I shift my feet and try to meet Ruben's eyes, hoping that he will linger in his cell doorway and talk with me. If he stays, I'll think that my noticing his maimed chest is helping him cope with the idea of someone attempting to kill him.

"What happened?"

"Gang-related activity," Ruben answers and walks off, past me and down the cardboard-colored brick hallway toward the shower area.

From a gangland veteran I expect edgier slang, not medical terminology echoing doctors and nurses nor legalese parroted from court hearings or police interrogations. I can muster no response to keep Ruben close. No chance for another question. I have many.

Before working at the Audy Home, I knew only two people ever hit by gunfire—a next door neighbor wounded in the Korean War and a friend injured in a hunting mishap. A few more weeks here and I will lose count of the boys answering my query about their limp or conspicuous blemish with: "I got shot." At first, profiles of each bullet victim freeze in my head, carving themselves out like memorial statues. Then the names, faces, and disfigured flesh patches blur into a single mass of resignation, the boys' and mine. I quit asking about scars.

Five years before meeting Ruben and his scars, I climb into a minivan with several other students at a Moody Bible Institute parking lot. I'm a senior. We've spent a cloistered day at our cramped campus, mere blocks from the Magnificent Mile and Lake Michigan, studying the Scriptures and how best to explain them to others. The end of this minivan ride will provide that opportunity: our weekly Practical Christian Ministry at the Audy Home. Soon we cross the cement-banked Chicago River well beyond where city officials dye the canal green on St. Patrick's Day. Driving southwest, buildings shrink and grow shabbier. After a stretch of Halsted Street absent any of its famed jazz clubs, comes the West Side Center for Disease Control. A few hundred yards ahead to our left stands a five-story steel and glass quadrangle—the Audy Home.

At more than half a million square feet, the facility dominates the block. Tinted windows and every steel surface painted the hue of tar render most of the structure an invisible mass blotting out the dusky cityscape west of us. Lights illumine only the revolving entryway and the rectangular second floor office windows. We rotate through spinning doors. No one staffs the walk-through metal detector inside. Two after-hours deputies camped behind a tall counter barely glance up at my classmates and me, much less search us. They must doubt our posing any contraband risk. We ascend a cement staircase with a metal railing and join a handholding circle with other volunteers and Chaplain Rick, a blind man wearing oversized pitch-dark glasses. Wavy black hair falls down his forehead to his eyebrows. His ample hair and impenetrable shades turn his face into a veil. I wonder what it means that he can't see us. Other volunteers, all black but one, are male and female Chicagoans of varying ages and occupations. There are a dozen of us in total.

Wayne, a self-described floor buffer in his mid-thirties, eventually tells me, "Hey, I have three X's on my back. I'm lucky to have any job." His back and shoulders, wide as a stove, could accommodate the entire alphabet. I'm curious but don't prod about his felony or his number of penitentiary years or "what was it like" to be in prison. I do envy Wayne. At twenty-one years and four months of age, I've never sniffed or shot drugs, smelled marijuana, sucked on a cigarette, swallowed a full can of beer, or said "Damn" loudly enough for anyone to hear. I have no criminal record, not even a speeding ticket. The youth detained on three floors above us, I worry, will heed Wayne's bass-voiced admonition to live lawful lives more readily than mine. Strapping Wayne is black and from the South Side of Chicago. I grew up on the south side of the Red River, in Bedford, Texas.

The group prays out loud that God will help these young people understand how Jesus can save them, but I pray secretly that even though I look nothing like Wayne, the boys won't scoff at me. My skin is light, maybe pale. My hair is sandy. Nine out of ten Audy Home kids have dark hair and skin darker than mine. Half were born to teenage mothers. Three quarters pledge gang allegiance.

This place is actually the Cook County Juvenile Temporary Detention Center. Inmates, ages ten to sixteen, await trial on charges like first-degree murder, attempted murder, rape, carjacking, assault, armed robbery, and narcotics offenses. To most staff and inmates, it remains "the Audy Home" after the Arthur J. Audy Children's Home—a juvenile lockup built in the 1920s that also sheltered abused and neglected youngsters. County bulldozers razed it fifty years later when this five-hundred-cell stockade opened. The new complex houses only boys and girls arraigned in legal cases and functions solely as a jail, but everyone calls it a home.

When I was the inmates' age, church pews made for my second home. I credit God and the Bible I read on those pews for the fact that I haven't done whatever bad things Wayne did or whatever bad things the juvenile delinquents we soon will meet did.

Stacks of paperback Bibles in our hands, Chaplain Rick directs us onto an elevator up to the residential floors. On the fifth I exit alone. I wish I could tag along with Wayne, but Chaplain Rick sends us solo. Overhead fluorescent panels glare. Walls on either side of me are beige bricks halfway up, then convert to what resembles bulletproof glass. Every twenty feet is a vertical steel stud painted Mississippi mud brown. The floor tiles are thin and lighter, the shade of toffee.

I poke my head into an open cellblock door. Boys in their midteens slap aces and spades at five or six round plastic tables in the shoe box–shaped room's middle. The block's composition matches the adjoining hallway—more glass, more shellac-coated steel, more tan linoleum floor, and more russet bricks. The inmate tally is at least twenty because more boys idle in chair rows at the block's left end behind a glass partition where a television transfixes them. I square up with the black man wearing no uniform hunkered near the door at a huge metal desk equipped with a flat panel of knobs and switches. The knobs and switches conjure up little purpose in my mind, like the man, who only sits and monitors.

The man doesn't nod, so I do, anxious that he might warn the boys with a frown that I preach a white man's gospel irrelevant to the street and the slammer.

From him I glance toward the inmates at the tables and say, "Anyone for Bible study?"

Four juveniles stand. Surprised and relieved, I smile and stroll with them down the corridor to another round table, this one with chrome-legged chairs in an unstaffed room just big enough for the furniture and us. Cellblock chairs are exclusively plastic to lessen their lethalness if swung or chucked. In our special room though, no inmate elevates a forearm or fist at me, much less a metallic chair. I don't need Wayne. Being in jail must turn bad kids good.

Each Monday night, fall and spring semester, we perch on our deadly chairs for half an hour and ponder the Golden Rule and God so loving the world and a Samaritan bestowing mercy upon his enemy. The boys tilt their chins in consent. They speak in turn. They bow their heads to pray and be forgiven. They never curse or complain or badger me to do something fun or whisper about my smuggling them a bag of hot chips or a Milky Way. They ask questions, and to my relief, never the question my impending theological degree hasn't answered—Why didn't God give them my life with a dad who played baseball catch with me about as often as I asked him to and a mom who said "I love you" so many times that I lost count? As with Wayne, I don't ask the inmates why officers arrested them. From the newspaper or a radio flash, I may know of their alleged crime. Kids murder kids in this city. A Great Awakening tent revival preacher founded my college. An eye, I believe, like those clergy of old likely believed, merits another eye. In our interpretation, the Bible requires that if you kill someone, then the rest of us must kill you. So in my head I believe in the death penalty, but, outside my head, I don't want Illinois to kill any of my Bible study subjects.

After graduation I return to Texas, resolved to pursue an advanced degree in history—now convinced by my Bible college studies and volunteering at the Audy Home that time and place root our feelings and thoughts about God and the Bible. I have much more to learn, but soon I am pondering Chicago again while watching Michael Jordan's Bulls against Charles Barkley's Phoenix Suns in the NBA Finals. When Jordan and company triumph, I think of the neighborhood around his team's aging arena, hardly a mile north of the Audy Home. Last summer, fans there streamed out of neighboring flats and housing project high rises to torch cars and bust storefront windows after the home team won the same championship trophy. As the Bulls clinch this victory in Phoenix, outside their arena, riotous fans re-inflict Chicago with celebratory damage. But I'm wondering if any of my former friends, many now released from the nearby jail, can claim anything worth celebrating in their new free lives.

My first grad class is a seminar on Europe during the Great Wars. Required Internet access somehow lands me at the *Chicago Tribune* electronic archives where my focus falls back on the city's criminally accused children instead of historiographical arguments about a seemingly bygone Europe of three-quarters a century ago. Robert "Yummy" Sandifer, age 11 with an uneven Afro and a sweet tooth, dies when older gang comrades, two teenage brothers, shoot him in a pedestrian tunnel to thwart his informing police how they puppet-stringed him into gunning down another child, a girl. Two preteens drop a five-year-old, Eric Morse, from a fourteenth-floor project window, allegedly for refusing to help them steal candy. Four of these kids, one now dead, have spent nights at the Audy Home, possibly my volunteer nights.

From the *Tribune* website, I also learn about Teachers for Chicago, which apprentices college graduates to become certified Illinois schoolteachers. As a teacher, I could befriend students, perhaps kids growing up to be kids like Robert and his assassins and the two unphotographed boys who sent little Eric over that window ledge. I could care for them like I had my Bible study subjects—quizzing them about their lives each afternoon when school lets out, tipping them off to the Bulls next free telecast. I won't apply to PhD tracks or chase jobs at private high schools like my graduate school contemporaries. Teachers for Chicago will accept me, I'm convinced, but I also contact Missionaries of Charity, a combined food pantry and after-school program. I'd be honored to work even indirectly for Mother Teresa, who founded the center during her visit to the Henry Horner Homes, a public housing complex once as populated as some American suburbs, across the street from the Bulls' since-demolished Chicago Stadium. I know of this nonprofit from *Wall Street Journal* reporter Alex Kotlowitz's bestselling book, *There Are No Children Here*, which chronicled two brothers living in these very projects during the late 1980s. The violence they witnessed prompted their mother to inform the author that despite their ages, nine and twelve, the brothers had "seen too much to be children."[1]

Sister Marilyn from Missionaries of Charity soon notifies me, "We do not employ anyone, but volunteers are welcome." Chicago Public Schools then writes that my transcripts show too few hours in math, science, and civics. I'm nearing a Master of Arts in history, but Chicago's school district won't train me to teach history to its middle school students.

I scour the *Trib* job listings again and discover that the Cook County Juvenile Temporary Detention Center needs children's attendants. I haven't seen any inmates in three years but still remember names—Jerome, Terry, Antwan, Marvell, Sergio, Curtis, Melvin, Lemmuel, Luis, Thaddeus—when my computer screen in Texas tells me that the Audy Home is hiring. Kotlowitz has deemed its ground floor courtrooms, where the older brother in his book stood trial for a vehicle break-in, "not a friendly place."[2] How could it be friendly when judges hear seventy-five cases a day and workloads bury the juveniles' public defenders and probation officers? I write for an application. Like I had the visitation rooms, I can at least make those cellblocks upstairs friendly places. I can do more than lounge behind a bunker desk and monitor.

Cook County Human Resources sends me a flyer. A children's attendant:

> Provides direct supervisory care for juveniles in custody at the Juvenile Temporary Detention Center. Helps maintain order, cleanliness and decorum in the living units and other areas. Prepares juveniles for various group and individual activities such as religious services, classes, recreational programs and court hearings. Responsible for the well-being and safety of juveniles during tour of duty.

Attending children doesn't sound insufferable: remind the inmates to clean their cells, model how to address their judge in complete sentences, and coax down occasional flaring tempers. My Bible study subjects never raved about any brawls or security wrestling kids to the floor. The handbill also lists the minimum qualifications:

1. 21 years of age
2. High School diploma or General Education Development test certificate
3. Negative drug screening report
4. No past criminal record of conviction for a felony or misdemeanor
5. One year of experience within a field of social or community service working with adolescents
6. Negative report from the Illinois DCFS Child Abuse Registry

All the red tape scrutiny pleases me. Cook County government's precaution to protect its detained children must confirm their harmlessness while jailed. Most must be polite and crave friendship like those who joined me in those little rooms to crack open the Bibles I brought. Applications cannot be mailed, so I fly to Chicago to submit one.

A letter then instructs me to return for a written exam. I pass the test and in several months assemble with twenty-seven remaining applicants in an arc of chairs stretching across a conference room on the facility's second floor. We're not far from Chaplain Rick's office. One other candidate is white. Two or three may be Hispanic. Everyone else is black like Assistant Superintendent Fred Davis, a lumbering man in his late fifties, who paces in front and addresses us. "Your job won't be to come in, sit down, and watch the kids. Your job is to help the children become better people than they were the day they walked in here." Davis is the only Audy Home employee I've spotted in a suit. The lecturing tone, instead of what I feel should be an opportunity pitch, appears to be Davis's effort to ward off those here to score what they perceive as a plum position—just sit and watch and get paid. What he says still heartens me. Helping children is what I'm all about.

Davis and the panel of supervisors and caseworkers finish their presentation and instruct us where to report for individual interviews. I find my room. Davis himself and a short supervisor with a tangle of gold chains covering the buttons down his shirt-front walk in. Davis and the squat man, black too, take chairs across a desk from me.

"Mr. Dostert, do you have any questions for us?"

"Yes. How many kids will I be responsible for? And how many coworkers will I have?"

The men advise that if hired, I will be teamed with one attendant to manage up to twenty-four juveniles, but there is a handle—the Faraday Alarm. Davis gestures a sinking motion with his arm bent at the elbow, "You pull it if things get really crazy."

My security-officer-on-the-cellblock-with-me theory, which I've harbored since first reading the job description, evaporates. A lever. No whistle or mace or pepper spray or hand cuffs. Not even a badge and uniform. One attendant later sums it up: "All you have is your mouth." To me, *children's attendant* never sounded like *jail guard* in the written summary. I construed the position as Cook County's humanitarian innovation to install counselor-types on the cellblocks who would humanize and *attend* to the inmates' social and emotional needs while real guards lingered nearby just in case. I'd simply missed those guards while a volunteer.

Next come their questions. The most vexing: *What would you do if you saw a kid take an apple from another kid?*

"Were they arguing over it? Did they both think it was theirs?"

Davis scripts words into the hypothetical kid thug's mouth: "You're a chump and I'm taking your apple."

Thirty years separate me from Davis, who was pulling shifts here during my birth year. He wields the secret to reproaching such fruit-mugger murder suspects and expects likewise from suburban Texan me. Davis's scenario rings surreal, considering that I'd never even ordered the inmates to be quiet while reading the Parable of the Seeds or assigned specific chairs because they bickered over who sat where during my explaining Jesus's Sermon on the Mount.

"I think I would consult the rule book and enforce the consequences for theft."

"Let's say you own your own facility. You make the rules. How would you handle it?"

My instinct is to order the bully to return the other boy his Red Delicious. But the solution can't be that obvious. Stolen apples didn't materialize while studying the children's attendant job summary. I figured official security would deal with any blatant pillage. I stir in my chair and look at Davis and the supervisor.

They wait.

"Well, I guess I would tell the kid to give the apple back."

Simple enough to be nonsensical. I have no other ideas and feel like a dope. I've answered a trick question with its sucker answer.

"*You are hereby notified that there is a vacant position as a Children's Attendant I and you are eligible for appointment*," a mailed notice reads. Two months have passed, and this statement is sterile and disconnected from the children's attendant that I aspire to be, even if a minority of inmates will attempt thievery. But Cook County wants to hire me. Assistant Superintendent Davis and his bowling ball–stomached partner overlooked my unsophisticated answer to the apple question. I can't help wondering if there exists a quota for white employees and if the other white guy's apple question stumble simply eclipsed mine in naïveté. In June's final week, I carry a sleeping bag into the subterranean Chicago apartment of a friend from college. I'm staying here until I rent my own place. Orientation for new children's attendants begins today, but I can't participate. I must submit another urinalysis. Three mornings and three missed sessions later, my drug test results arrive. At the Cook County building downtown, I autograph a stack of forms eight months and four plane tickets in coming, then board the Blue Line westbound and step off at Polk Street. University of Illinois at Chicago students, many seemingly med students, scurry toward the station, between classroom buildings, or to nearby breakfast eateries. In white smocks with book bags slung on their shoulders, they don't look at me. They're heading to lectures and labs and meetings and won't ever stress about stolen apples and yanking a lever if murder and carjacking suspects "get really crazy."

Several blocks beyond the campus at Hamilton Avenue is the jail. Columns of streaky grit run down the steel-plated sides, grit now visible because the building's once ink black exterior is snowy white. Six months back while waiting to begin the written test, a local candidate told me straight-faced that county officials had commissioned the paint job because seven of ten inmates are black—the facility had been a black jail nearly full of black kids. The Audy Home's new color isn't the only change from my volunteer days. Erected next door is an eight-level auxiliary building to accommodate more courtrooms, the juvenile probation department, and the Illinois Department of Children and Family Services (DCFS). The positioning exhibits a tragic pragmatism—young persons breaking the law often have inadequate parenting. A glass pyramid-shaped skylight tops the $95 million edifice, distinguishing it not only from the Audy Home's opaque decor but from countless shorter brick-sided, tar-roofed buildings in the adjacent city grid. Unlike the jail's shaded cell windows, sunlight penetrates clear windowpanes in the DCFS offices, where paper piles are heaped onto desks and floors. Certainly if a new juvenile court complex and new DCFS headquarters justify such extravagant means, then resources and programs on the detained juveniles' living quarters will be adequate for me to "help the children," as Assistant Superintendent Davis challenged during the interview.

I shuffle through the revolving glass door entry and wait in a line of attorneys, parents, guardians, and other visitors. Because the county has yet to issue me an identification badge, I must clear the weapons and metal detector manned during business hours by armed deputy sheriffs. Nothing beeps as I walk through the doorframe-like scanner. Upstairs, a supervisor behind the front desk, a peeling lobby-length wood counter, greets me. Then I follow him down two stair flights to the training department coordinator in her basement office. She wears a pantsuit and is the first white Audy Home employee I've noticed. Her last name is Eastern European, spelled with multiple c's and z's, some silent.

She insists that I call her Martha. Her face is plump, her body a giant pear. She stands out here even more than I do.

Martha waves me across the hall and into the classroom. Nine black men in their twenties and thirties in jeans, casual shirts, and sports-logoed caps sit at three long tables arranged in a U-shape. Their vibe says they came of age in the same neighborhoods as the juvenile suspects we must prevent from stealing each other's apples. I should start orientation a year before them, not three days following. I want another white face here, too. Continuing what I began under Chaplain Rick would seem more realistic with other white suburbanites dreaming my dream. *Here's a guy who will have to yank the Faraday alarm handle*, the nine black men must be muttering to themselves. "What up, Mark?" a square-faced trainee seated near the doorway lifts his chin. I mumble something back and slide into the empty chair near an unclaimed inch-thick handbook on the table, *The Policy and Procedure Guide for Group Services*. The word *Services* does encourage me. Other trainees mouth less perceptible greetings, appearing equally surprised.

The instructor, Supervisor Hilliard, is black too. Once a marine in Vietnam, he's in street clothes now. His voice is coarse teaching the module on a particular service: room searches. These inspections must be "systematic and thorough to yield contraband." I never fathomed the inmates I once knew, certainly not Jerome, who gave me his address so we could write each other after his release, smuggling weed or little cocaine rocks or dollar bills to barter for shreds of skin mag pages. No way would he file a plastic spoon handle into a dagger against his brick cell wall. Nor had I derived such duty from the job summary's requirement that I be "responsible for the well-being and safety of the juveniles." I thought "well-being" meant their moral awareness and healthy self-esteem engendered by someone taking interest in them. I took "safety" as my occasionally waving over the actual guards to reinforce my directions. My urine tests are long complete, but my nervous bladder fills. I have no vocational interest in jamming "a pencil or something" into the grooves of kids' window sills to flush out banned and illegal goods or commanding them to shake their sheets and blankets like dusting a throw rug. How can this make the boys "better people"?

I glance around the table. The other trainees emit no shock. No matter our title, we're jail guards. They know this. Supervisor Hilliard recounts one juvenile who ignited toilet paper bonfires. He and the block's attendants vainly combed the boy's cell after each incendiary incident. Then Hilliard marched the pyromaniac to the infirmary for what only nurses are authorized to execute—a cavity search. "They found a lighter in his rectum."

After seven employed hours in the building, I want to quit. Whatever good my benevolent intentions might yield, it's not worth it if I must be a guard first and a counselor second.

Hilliard wraps his session, and the superintendent, Jesse Doyle, enters the classroom. Though in his mid-forties, Superintendent Doyle shaves his head and his physique cuts that of a linebacker. He recounts a youthful rage that he "channeled into the martial arts," which instilled him with discipline and self-control. "Now it bothers me to walk in here and see coffee stains on the floor." Doyle's cheeks sag though, as if his face is too tired to smile. He hasn't smiled yet, which is odd to me, given his optimistic words about himself and the youthful, raging kids upstairs. What bliss it must be to wear a tie and blue suit, have your own office, and fret over coffee-stained floors instead of lighters in rectums and handcrafted weapons stashed in mattresses or windowsills.

The superintendent concludes and departs. I stand with my trainees and mill around the classroom, feeling obligated to mingle and pretend I'm thrilled at the prospect of searching cells for lighters and joints and shanks until pension time. Hilliard rests on a chair along a wall. I introduce myself and tell him about going to college in Chicago and volunteering here with Chaplain Rick. "Then I went back to Texas and did a master's program but decided I wanted to come back to Chicago to work with kids." My plans now sound absurd.

"They need work." Hilliard glances up and then blinks down at the shag carpet floor, never moving from his chair. Nothing about the juveniles needing people like me who want being a children's attendant to be more than a job. I'll soon learn that like a children's attendant, Supervisor Hilliard interacts with the juveniles far more than Doyle and Davis. Martha wanders back into the classroom. Not sure what to say to Hilliard, I turn to her for my schedule. The training department has tomorrow, Friday the Fourth of July, off. Orientation is over. I've received less than a full day of training. Monday, I shadow-shift on a real cellblock.

I move toward the door and shake hands with a trainee about my age. We match in height but his chest is much thicker.

"The kids are gonna try and make it harder on you because you're white."

"Oh yeah?" I'm too skittish in a room full of black men to argue: *Aren't these kids in jail? Shouldn't they do whatever we tell them, regardless of who the instruction comes from? Dozens of black inmates respected me four years ago under Chaplain Rick!*

On the subway back to my friend's North Side apartment, I'm aghast at having moved eight hundred miles to inspect bed sheets and rolled-up socks for matches and spoon handles, to rummage through the kids' cells to determine if they merit a cavity search. I key myself inside and pace the hardwood living room floor, alone. I don't know what to do, so I pick up my friend's phone and call home. I admit to my parents that I plan to resign. I was a fool for leaving Bedford, Texas, to be a children's attendant in Chicago.

"Yeah, Mark, I know it looks tough, but you gotta give it a chance. A lot of people move to different cities and take new jobs and don't like them at first. Give it a few weeks before you decide on anything," my father advises. He worked for thirty years in property insurance.

I know he feels terrible for me and would give a finger or an entire hand to assuage my unease, but the only children he's ever attended to are myself and my equally law-abiding brother. He has no clue about being a guard at Chicago's juvenile jail.

Dad asks about my immediate schedule. A different college

friend has invited me to Wisconsin for the holiday. "Go on up to Joe's for the weekend and then decide what you're gonna do."

In the morning I drive north, no resignation letter written. Quitting this soon will ruin my résumé for whatever alternative career plan I conjure up. Right now, I have to be a jail guard.

2

Monday morning I steer my Toyota Tercel off Joe and Beth's gravel driveway onto a double-lane road splitting cornfields and dairy farms. Knowing that I won't see this landscape again this afternoon or tomorrow or the next day, the barns and silos become beautiful. In minutes, I'm envying Wisconsinites on either side of me, whizzing down Interstate 94 to jobs in corporate Chicago, where they won't have to invade someone's living quarters, sleuthing for Flic-My-Bics or weed or handcrafted weapons.

At the jail, a supervisor leans across the front desk like a sage grandfather and says, "We're gonna put you with Mr. Walton." His expression says *I'm a Greenhorn I Have No Clue What I'm Doing* is stamped across my forehead. Three days of burgers and steaks supplemented with tennis and Frisbee in rural Wisconsin haven't eased the dread as my father hoped.

The supervisor and I hardly speak on the elevator ride to the third floor where there is no new paint job or other renovations from the tens of millions of dollars. He leads me over the same thin beige floor tiles, faint seams separating them. Darker bricks still compose the corridor's inner walls, floor to ceiling. To my right, the outer wall's upper half is glass, so I can see the barren concrete courtyard, seemingly the size of a football field, opposite the cellblocks. Twenty paces down the hallway, the inner wall to my left turns to floor-to-ceiling glass, so I can see into empty cellblock G. The supervisor opens the steel-framed glass door with his master key, and I step in behind him for my first full entry into a cellblock. The desk, or console, remains to the left of the door, squarely in the cellblock's middle. Twenty feet ahead stand eighteen cell doors, all brown steel-frames and most with

Plexiglas windows. In the brick space between cells nine and ten, just below the ceiling, hangs a round wall clock staring at the console. A wall of real glass partitions off the block's left end—the TV area. More bricks enclose the right end—the bathroom area. Familiar multi-colored plastic-coated fiberglass tables and chairs fill in the middle space common area, along with a battered green ping-pong table.

Walton, today's 6 A.M. to 2 P.M. children's attendant on 3G, saunters out of the TV area and the supervisor leaves. "Right now, all our residents are at school, except for room twelve. He's in Confinement," Attendant Walton begins without looking directly at me. Hair grays at his temples. He doesn't tower over me like some trainees in orientation, but a voice booms from his burly chest, deeper and more ear grabbing than my voice. We face the eighteen-cell row and the clock centered between cells nine and ten. For the children's attendant, time is everything. The boy locked behind door twelve is asleep on an emerald mattress laid over the floor. Judging from his size, I'd say he's fourteen or fifteen. Like a sponge against a mirror, his Afro top presses into the expansive, nearly door-length window. Attendant Walton explains that he committed a major rule violation and will remain there all day—*Confinement*. Time is a farce for this kid. He can't see the clock even when awake.

Attendant Walton moves behind me and picks up a stationary book off the console along with a clear plastic board about the size of a kitchen cabinet door. His hands are puffy, like those I imagine would belong to an oilrig worker. Walton still hasn't looked at me. Instead, his attention rivets on this tool of our trade—the plastic board—like a soldier marveling at a trusted sidearm cradled in his hand. Pasted to the see-through plastic rectangle are three columns of brass name tag holders.

"Let's go back here, Mr. Dostert," he motions toward the TV area past the half dozen tables with chairs hued like playground fixtures at McDonald's. The sky blue, canary yellow, lime green, and candy apple red furniture seem Cook County's apology for the living quarters' orgy-of-beige color scheme. Walton and I ease down onto cushioned low-back armchairs at the rear of the

TV area, positioned in front of the first cells. He sets the board on his chair arm.

"Here's all our residents right here."

Slid inside most of the nameplates are strips of tag-board, each with a name written in blue or black ink, a cell number, and an admission date to the facility, be it last week or last year. The plastic board is an oversized roll sheet. Walton taps a cigar-thick finger near the first name cards in the third column, numbers nineteen and higher, "We have eighteen rooms. So these residents right here are overflows." Block 3G has more inmates than cells. Overflows sleep on cots.

Attendant Walton's use of *residents* and *rooms* confuses me. Supervisor Hilliard used the terms too, as did *The Policy and Procedure Manual for Group Services*, which no one instructed me to bring today and isn't available here on 3G. It explains *residents* as: "children charged with committing a delinquent or criminal act, failing to appear for a court hearing, adjudicated pending disposition and/or placement, serving a disposition up to 30 days per offense or placed on a violation of probation pending hearing/disposition."[1]

Children sanitizes the more accurate labels—juveniles or inmates—that we're instructed not to call the boys. The manual does likewise with its reference to fifty kids brawling simultaneously in the courtyard as a *group disturbance*, not a riot. Administration must think that pretending the boys' legal predicaments aren't dire alleviates this depressing reality—months and years of their childhoods warehoused away where they can't change a television channel without sanction from one of us. Sleeping in a *room* must not scar a boy's soul compared to sleeping in a cell. Glancing into the rectangular brick-walled chambers, hardly wider than my arms' span, I can't deny that they are cells, damn it. And in cells live inmates.

To remind us that cell twelve's kid is in Confinement, a red tag with the letters CONF fills his slot. No one will let him out by accident. As if it's none of my business, I don't inquire about his Confinement-meriting offense. Confinement helps keep order, Attendant Walton explains. In the late 1960s Attendant Walton worked at the actual Audy Home, he informs me, where there were no cells in which to lock unruly kids—inmates slept on bunks.

Certain creased, dog-eared name cards include other capital-lettered codes. These designations aren't removable, like the CONF tag. One penned in red is: AT.

"The residents who are ATs can't be overflows. They have to be in a room," Attendant Walton says, with his eyes on the board.

All eight AT name cards occupy a slot somewhere between cells one and eighteen—none are overflows. A serious violation occurs if one bunks down on a cot.

"What's AT mean?"

"Automatic Transfer. They go to court at 26th and California."

I'm not familiar with "26th and California" either and Attendant Walton doesn't elaborate, but in college, I wondered how a Chicago street could be named California. Maybe a hundred years ago, this north-south thoroughfare marked the city's western frontier, removed from its industrialized, polluted core. It was out there on California Street or Place or Boulevard where Chicagoans migrated for a fresh start. Currently, it's where we forcibly relocate criminally accused adults to await trial pending life sentences and lethal injections. The Cook County Jail—dozens of dull, squared buildings—dominates multiple sides of the 26th Street and South California Avenue intersection. Ironic now is the name. The adult jail's southwest part of town, with its currency exchanges dotted around deteriorating brownstones and multi-level wooden flats, hardly resembles Bodega Bay's black sand beaches or Sonoma's redwoods and wineries or even Los Angeles County's ice plant–lined freeways winding into the San Gabriel Mountains. Eventually, I learn that an Illinois kid becomes an AT if charged with a felony while thirteen or older. When ATs turn seventeen (a legal adult in Illinois), they can no longer be housed with children at the Cook County Juvenile Temporary Detention Center. They must be incarcerated with men, because their court is prosecuting them as men, and thus they are transferred to the Cook County Jail. Right now, Attendant Walton only tells me about ATs and what pertains to us here on 3G—ATs must be in a room. I will learn more about Automatic Transfers on my own, like specific AT charges—First-Degree Murder, Aggravated Criminal Sexual Assault, Aggravated Vehicular Hijacking ("carjacking"), Armed Robbery With A Firearm, and narcotics or weapons possession within one thousand feet of a school or housing project.

Attendant Walton next points to a CW tag on top of several other name tags. "These residents are Close Watches, so they can't have a bed frame or any sheets in their room. And their room has to be right across from the console." Walton touches a name tag with the CW label. "He's got Dr. Jacobs thinking he wants to kill himself."

It's the confined boy, dead to the world in cell twelve. According to the roll board, his name is Calvin. When Calvin threatened suicide, Dr. Jacobs, our lone full-time mental health professional, deemed him a Close Watch and removed his bed sheets. Calvin's cell also contains no desk or chair or a bed frame for the mattress. His entire floor is exposed, save for what his mattress covers. Why might Calvin fume about suicide? Is this why he is still knocked out at nine in the morning? Is he too depressed to sit up and survey his world? I speculate about all the names on this plastic rectangle. How few know their fathers? Can any read at their grade level? Despite their obstacles, can I improve their life quality, their moral fiber, their self-esteem?

Trainer Walton doesn't reference kids by name, but rather by their room numbers: "the resident in room twelve." He says nothing about how to, as Assistant Superintendent Davis worded our mission, "make them better people." On those terms, Attendant Walton could seem a bad attendant. Nearing his thirtieth year of attending children, tomorrow's paycheck and an approaching pension may well be his primary motivation. I'm thankful though that he agreed to mentor me. If no veteran had, I might have no shadowing. My coworker would be flying solo with scant occasion to enlighten. Novice to the demands of monitoring and jailing, I could only watch like a dunce. The block might "go up," that is "explode." What I can't understand is why Attendant Walton in all his age and experience, in the lull of this empty cellblock, isn't unloading on me with everything he knows about each inmate—their positives, their negatives, their sore spots and soft spots, what I need to help them.

"Want a mint?" Walton extends a foil-wrapped roll toward me. He pops one into his mouth. "I get bad breath working here." Beside the interior decor, something else is constant from my volunteer days—the Audy Home smell. For me, whiffing it evokes a sterile, medicine-y hospital wing, yet somehow, a place of musty antiquation. Even with six hundred boys' perspiration and carbon dioxide to mask it, the scent we suck into our mouths everywhere in the building reeks strongest on the residential floors. I take one of Attendant Walton's mints. He sets aside the plastic board and opens the lined white paper journal—the logbook. He's already penned the name of every 3G kid into two columns. After each name, he notes whether or not the boy is an AT, Close Watch, in Confinement, and if he is scheduled for court today. "Everything that happens on the unit, you write it right here." Inspect the cells—log it in the logbook. The breakfast, lunch, or dinner cart arrives—log it in the logbook. Serve a meal—log it in the logbook. Resident returns to the block from court—log it in the logbook.

Cellblock life revolves around this logbook and plastic board. So far I've only seen one actual juvenile, slumbering Calvin in cell twelve and can't fathom how a stationery book and sheet of plastic will help me "help the kids" or even help me foil them from mugging each other for apples and shoving cigarette lighters up their asses. With Jerome and Terry and Curtis, it was just the Bible, them, and me. Now all these objects exist between us—bolted cell doors, a logbook, a roll board with myriad tags and labels. I'm working with everything but the kids.

The console phone rings. Attendant Walton sends me from the TV area to answer it.

"3G, Mark."

"Actually, Mr. Dostert," a supervisor says, "we call each other by last name here. Make sure the residents do too."

Attendant Walton has been addressing me as Mr. Dostert,

but it hasn't occurred to me to call myself Mr. Dostert. I hadn't picked up on this practice when the front desk supervisor called Attendant Walton "Mr. Walton." Administration must think that "Mister" dignifies better than "Attendant," given that we aren't certified as law enforcement officers like juvenile facility workers in other counties and states. Chaplain Rick never called me Mr. Dostert, nor had my Bible study subjects. I was Mark to them. Yet another hedge between the kids and me is my name. I didn't take this job to be a Mister to anyone.

At noon, 3G's 8 A.M.–4 P.M. attendant, a wiry and Jheri curl headed man, appears in the hallway with the other twenty-two residents, who unlike Calvin, are not in Confinement. They're home from morning school. Whether indicted for first-degree murder or spray-painting gang trademark pitchforks on the dumpster behind a Walgreens at 79th and Damen Avenue, federal law blesses any jailed young person with an education twelve months a year, so long as you behave on your cellblock and don't land in Confinement like Calvin.

Sitting with Attendant Walton in the TV area, I see the boys through the glass wall behind the console. Immobile, they pose outside the door in two single-file lines—all black and brown, mostly black, none white.

The 8–4 attendant keys the door open and directs them inside, one line at a time. In turns, each line of boys passes the console in a parade of skin tones ranging chocolate milk to gleaming coal. Several loom big as me, and I'm almost six feet tall. Asian letters, whose respective sounds I doubt very many of their carriers can enunciate, tattoo necks and forearms. Other uncovered skin displays reptiles and creatures of fantasy. And confined, Calvin doesn't sport the only Afro on 3G. The Audy Home seems to be without a barber.

No one smiles. Every kid wears ratty or new or half-ratty/half-new tan, gray, green, or blue trousers, and a white T-shirt. Some shirts hang loose on narrow shoulders. Other shirt fabric stretches over broad frames or vanishes into crevices of rolled waistline fat.

The inmates turn around and align shoulder-to-shoulder, backs to the cell doors facing the console. On each white T-shirt chest I notice one of three bird logos—an owl's face and two full-bodied fowls identical to those sported by the Baltimore Orioles and the St. Louis Cardinals baseball teams. However *jailbird* originated, here is more cruel irony—jailed kids donning shirts emblazoned with birds. Attendant Walton and I stay in the TV area. He writes more in the logbook. I watch the 8–4 follow the last inmate inside.

"Pull 'em up!" he barks. The boys bend and grab their pants' legs at the calf and yank them above their ankles. Faces grin, glare, and smirk. Some bleed apathy. Many check me out. They don't seem displeased that I am here, so I look away and turn back when they are refocused on the 8–4. His head rotates side-to-side, eyes probing, I assume, for pencils, dollar bills, Salem 100s, or folded up *Playboy* centerfolds bulging underneath their socks. Walton didn't prep me on this routine, a routine I never witnessed as a Chaplain Rick volunteer and never read about in the job summary. Obvious now is my accountability to search more than the boys' living quarters. I must visually inspect the boys' bodies after every trip off the cellblock.

"Shirts!" the 8–4 shouts from in front of the console. He wears jeans. My khakis and collared shirt make me feel like a dishwasher in a tuxedo.

The kids drop their pants' legs and hike their shirts over their beltless waistlines. They do what he tells them to, but the man is yelling at the air, as if his very act of articulating commands ensures the boys' compliance. It does. I hope it will for me too.

He scans the exposed trouser and boxer lines. Flesh falls over some waistlines; stomachs concave behind others. I wonder if any lighters are lodged where only nurses have chance to ferret them out. The 8–4 nods. Shirts roll down. "Shoes!"

The boys kick them off, hunch down, and pick them up. Holding them tops down, they look at him as he nods again. They whack the sneakers together like beachgoers brushing off before easing back into their cars. No contraband drops from the shoes and the boys toss them to the floor and wiggle their feet back into them.

"First four, TV area!" At the line's left end, four boys peel off and file past the glass partition to the thirty chairs arranged in five or six rows and sit. The 8–4 dispatches the next four and the next four until everyone rests in a chair. Then he joins us. Attendant Walton summons me to leave the TV area with him. I follow to the console. He has spotted the lunch cart in the hallway and opens the door to pull it inside. Angling his burly frame back around toward the TV area, Walton calls out, "Let me have my kitchen help." His tone is flat, empty of feeling to my ears, like he is uttering bad news. These two kitchen-help juveniles have earned this duty through cooperative behavior. They stand up and exit the TV area and come to us. Attendant Walton dishes up the plates and the boys arrange them in rows on the ping-pong table.

I go to the food cart—lightly breaded baked fish, greens, rice, a small bottle of Louisiana hot sauce, and a cellophane-wrapped precut chocolate cake in a flat cardboard box. Better than the prison schlock I expected. One of the kitchen helpers, Monty, a couple inches of Afro mounded on his head like Calvin, looks at me after Attendant Walton instructs him to portion out the precut cake pieces onto the plates. Monty holds a wide metal spatula. He is shorter than me, so our closeness doesn't intimidate me. I could overpower him. Almost like Attendant Walton, Monty doesn't look me in the face until he has reason—his unease with the cake-serving task. I reach out for the spatula. He hands it to me, and I do the first one with him watching. He says, "Thanks," and grins when he neatly wedges out the cake's second chunk. I'm here for this—to make kids smile. Monty and his partner position four finished plates at each of the six tables. Then Attendant Walton calls the remaining boys from the TV area and lines them along the cell doors—exactly where the 8–4 attendant put them for the after-school search.

"First four, right here," Walton points to a table. They comply and each boy pauses behind his chair, hands wrapped in back of him. Walton and his coworker do everything in fours. Walton fills the other five tables and then asks, “Someone wanna pray?” A kid shoots up his hand and Walton nods. The boy begins with his peers chanting in unison: “God is good, God is great, let us thank him for our food, in the power of Jesus name, Amen.” In a government institution, this stuns me. Perhaps the prayer is Attendant Walton’s gift opportunity for the juveniles to publicly repent for whatever dirty deed prompted an officer to yank them into a squad car and deposit them here. The boys’ piously submissive words remind me of church potlucks from my childhood, except these praying participants do not hold hands, and no moms arrived with homemade ice cream and pecan-studded brownies.

“Mr. Dostert, come with me this way,” Walton grabs the lone plate of food off the ping-pong table. Half buried in the rice is a plastic fork. I trail Walton to cell twelve. Awake now, Calvin is propped up on his elbows looking through his Plexiglas right at us.

Attendant Walton pushes his key into the shaft and pulls the door open. He leans down and hands the lunch plate to Calvin who scoots back on his stomach and digs into the food. Walton steps back. I’m still behind him. I hold up because he isn’t moving.

Grasping the edge of the door, Attendant Walton jerks it towards his nose but halts the door with the toe end of his shoe. “See there. Always do it like this,” he eyes the mud brown doorframe and then his foot. With no barrier between the door’s steel edge and me, a juvenile inside could shove it back and slice open my forehead. He motions for us to leave.

I fix a plate and eat behind the console while Attendant Walton returns to the TV area and pens more entries in the logbook. Maybe he is recording the fact that the new guy now knows about cell door danger, so if a juvenile gashes my face with one, Attendant Walton and Cook County won’t be liable.

“This table, scrape,” the 8–4 attendant points to one.

The four boys pop up and brush their lunch remains into a plastic garbage bag hung on the food cart’s edge. They stack plastic plates on the cart and toss plastic forks into a bin, the 8–4 counting each fork—potential shanks. The boys then line the wall to wait their restroom turn. The bathroom area has six toilets and three sinks, but unless one of us stands nearby, only one juvenile can enter. "Never let two residents be alone where you can't see them," Walton has already cautioned. "They can fight or molest each other." Everyone lingers along the wall in front of the cell doors. The 8–4 attendant dismisses other tables individually to "scrape." The kitchen helpers begin sweeping and mopping the common area. Once each juvenile is standing against the bricks and cell fronts, the 8–4 sends them into the bathroom one at a time. Still stomach-prone on his cell floor, Calvin squishes his forehead and nose and puffy hair against the Plexiglas. Squirming as close to everyone else as his door allows, he hammers out homespun rap lyrics. Lonely, he must want others to loiter at his window where he can see and hear them and they can see and hear him.

I don't know what Calvin did to be arrested or to be confined here on 3G, but Confinement strikes me as inhumane. I want to sneak the master cell door key, thick as a silver dollar, off Attendant Walton's belt and free Calvin to follow everyone to the TV area. The head-bopping rapper perpetrates no crime right now. I can't picture him ramming his steel doorframe into my face.

3

"Line up!" Attendant Walton hollers from the console. Breakfast is over, and the boys have done the four-by-four again scraping and then bathroom area visits.

Twenty-two androids stand up from their TV area seats, plod past the glass partition, and arrange themselves in two lines at the door. Attendant Walton will escort them to morning class—the 6–2 shift's main duty. The 8–4 did it yesterday while Walton waited for me with the cellblock paperwork lesson. No hustling me through the logbook and roll board again.

Old enough to be any inmate's grandfather and shorter than at least a third of them, Attendant Walton's control impresses me. The boys obey him with the demeanor of boot camp recruits waking up, remaking their beds, brushing their teeth, and dressing—not loving it, not hating it, just doing it. If Walton wields such influence, I should too, once trained. I'm younger, taller, stronger. My stomach is much flatter. I've lifted weights since my last year of high school. Skin color can't make that vast a difference. I was right not to quit after one day of orientation. The logbook, cell searches, and steel doors potentially heaved at my face will prove only minor distractions from my real mission—befriending Calvin and Monty.

Standing aside the back of Walton's line, something catches my eye from the right. It's Calvin, still confined and still a Close Watch, awake today and propped on his elbows again, tracking us from his cell floor. I turn fully around. Lodged across from the console so we can watch him, Calvin is sitting up on his green mattress, smirking like Confinement is a party, and he relishes missing school. I feel stupid about yesterday's pity. Being "played" is any children's attendant's Achilles' heel, I will learn. Attendant Walton hasn't batted an eye at Calvin.

"Step out," he commands, monotone.

Walton can't say it any other way. Jailed boys can't walk themselves to school. Nothing here to be happy about. The inmates copy his solemnity. But I wish to be their remedy, to cheer them up and rebuild their humanity, like when I modeled the cake serving for Monty, and he grinned. No chance right now though to help anyone beam.

An inmate up front pushes the door open. It is fashioned like the cell doors—a vertical glass rectangle framed with steel painted Mississippi mud brown, as if the cellblock is its own cell. The boys live in cells within a cell. I trail Walton and the two-line formation to the elevator shaft. The boys halt in place while he waves a black electronic key against a dark panel embedded in the brick wall. A red light, small as an eraser head, illuminates. With punch buttons, juveniles could slip off their cellblocks, activate elevators, and bolt east along Roosevelt Road toward the ABLA housing projects before we detect them absent.

Without incident, everyone steps into the carriage. Like suited corporate workers from different firms, the inmates say nothing during the ten-second ride downstairs. Some study their sneaker tops or stare straight ahead. I catch Attendant Walton's plain expression in an awkward exchange, like we're supposed to be ignoring each other too. I look away, and without intending to, meet eyes with an inmate. The kid frowns, and I'm embarrassed. I focus down or up, anywhere but someone's face.

One floor below and off the elevator, Walton points the boys into the Chicago Public Schools' Nancy B. Jefferson Alternative School. Revered as the "Joan of Arc of the West Side," Ms. Jefferson's nursing career propelled her to three decades of involvement in numerous social institutions, which included the school system, the police department, and the Mayor's Council on Women's Affairs. I see no sign with her name, much less an embossed shoulders-up profile, like the plaque for Arthur Audy mounted on a wall out by the front desk. The public never sees the school section of the jail. Instead of cellblocks, classrooms line both sides of this hallway. Every school area wall is complete brick—no glass here. Metal doors coated in the same brown paint barricade each hallway end. The bricks and floor tiles replicate the massive beige-out of the corridors and cellblocks upstairs.

Hundreds of juveniles in hundreds more bird-shirts and various colored khakis pour out of elevators in the hallway and crowd us in a wide human river. Some march in equally straight lines. But certain attendants lack Walton's command or do school runs much more loosely because their boys are wiggling and gyrating and throwing their hands and elbows around. I follow Walton and he gestures our boys in fives and sixes into different classes and then reverses back toward several chairs set along the wall—our post for morning school.

"Right here you want to make sure no resident leaves a classroom without a pass. And even if you hear all hell breakin' loose, we can't go in unless they call for help." Attendant Walton believes that we should be stationed inside the rooms to assist with order. "They don't do much teaching in there."

Some instructors can control and stimulate, I hear. Curious how many juveniles each teacher must manage, I'd glanced over inmate shoulders into classrooms. Fifteen, tops. Not bad for public school. But corralling student interest here must be quite the bitch. Students who last week may have pressed pistol barrels into strangers' foreheads may not press their noses into prepositions worksheets very enthusiastically this morning. Teaching here successfully though once demanded even more instructional creativity because until the mid-1990s, some classes were coed—two of the jail's thirty cellblocks house females. "Then some girls turned up pregnant," another attendant will tell me. A few classrooms have bathrooms. Male and female students were slipping into those bathrooms during class.

Leaning against the brick wall, minute after unbothered minute, Attendant Walton and I stop the occasional student leaving from the half dozen classrooms within our eyesight, but they all have passes—if not, a security risk punishable by up to five days of Confinement. For all the commotion of funneling six hundred juvenile delinquents down one, two, and three floors into classrooms, the hallway is calm with them in class. Right now, school area duty is easier than filling out the logbook.

Walton and I record nothing, document nothing, add and subtract nothing. There are no code tags on roll boards that break real Illinois laws if positioned in the wrong slots and acted upon. We only idle, watching—exactly what I took this job not to do.

I'll soon hear about school area brawls, but no hell breaks loose today, so for two and a half hours, Walton and I chat with other attendants who saunter by until a designated attendant, Coleman, blows a whistle and calls, "Third-floor boys!"

Two hundred juveniles spill out of classrooms and around this husky man with short hair brushed back into tight, shiny ripples that grant him a military vibe. Poised in the hall's middle, the school area is Attendant Coleman's cellblock.

Morning instruction has ended. No bells ring at this school—someone just yells. The four hundred inmates from the other two floors remain at their desks until the third-floor loads the elevators, clearing the hall. Flashing past me, non-3G faces twitch as if spotting a lizard crawling across the Alaskan tundra. This morning I put on jeans and a solid T-shirt. Why stick out for anything more than my hair and skin? But I'm still not blending in. Attendant Walton rises from his chair, and I veer with him into the swelling sea of bird-shirts and blaring voices. More heads twist at me and I hear: "Newjack"—slang for a rookie children's attendant who looks intimidated and snowed under. Walton must not have caught it or not caught it from specific mouths because he isn't reprimanding anyone but rather bearing ahead twenty yards and crossing the corridor. At an indistinguishable spot on the brick wall, he stops.

Our twenty-two inmates spurt from the corridor's jumble and dot themselves into one line. The hallway's width and seven other cellblocks lining up likewise prevents multiple, short lines. Attendant Walton counts roll with the paper roster he completed earlier this morning. Each kid answers a bored "Here."

"Let's go," Attendant Walton snaps out what sounds like a mild punishment.

We march to the elevator, and I tread close to Walton's sloped shoulder. He says nothing to me. My shoulder is harder and more muscled, but I'm feeling like an inmate, like I'm supposed to be following orders too because I'm oblivious about what orders to give.

Attendant Walton should articulate each move, command, and decision—exactly what will happen before it happens so I can learn how to execute a school run. I wouldn't know what to do and what to say to the juveniles if he wasn't here. Walton doesn't do or say much, yet the inmates are orderly. It can't be magic. He nods at the boys. They file into the elevator. Walton and I step in. His commands, spare and abrupt, might as well be a foreign language. And I want a translation, given the civility they solicit, but Walton is silent. The boys are silent. Inside the elevator I'm again looking at anything but faces.

Attendant Walton serves lunch and a different 8–4 attendant returns the inmates to school. Walton leaves when the 2–10 attendant arrives. I remain on unit with him. This new 8–4 returns the boys from school at 3:00 P.M. and like yesterday's 8–4 did, spot-searches them on the wall before depositing them in the TV area.

After a couple minutes, one of the attendants announces, "You can have rec."

Half the boys leave the television and plunk into chairs at the tables. Several dart up to the console where the attendant hands out card decks, rollup chessboard mats, and plastic sacks of playing pieces. This is why I spent $600 on plane tickets—the social interaction with troubled youth that I treasured while working for Chaplain Rick, not recording data, shifting tags on a roll board, and staring at bricks in an empty school hall. Seven tedious hours into the 8–4 shift, this is my first activity without commands. Maybe I can wax eloquent that chess requires thinking before acting—skills these boys will need for free world survival. *Better make sure that bishop on the other side of the board can't whack your queen, should you nudge her up a space.* Code for: *Don't take those dime bags again from your "guy" to peddle at the corner of 51st and Prairie because police will sling you right back here to the Audy Home.*

The boys move, so I exit the TV area where, before leaving,

Attendant Walton scripted his final logbook entries, noting how many inmates are Close Watches, in Confinement, still at court, and until a few minutes ago, at school.

I find a chair at a chess table with three inmates. No one glances up when I sit down.

Pitchforks, the primary symbol of the Gangster Disciples, brand Reginald's forearms. I know from the plastic roll board that he is an AT. He isn't playing. Shorter and stockier than the two competitors, Reginald's so-called nappy hair—an Afro with divots—also sets him apart. The two players' scalps are nearly clean-shaven, so a barber exists here somewhere. All three look no younger than fifteen.

The boys ease their pieces into different positions. I watch.

"I can't wait to get to the county! Man, I can't wait to get to the county!" Reginald blurts hoarsely while his peers stare at their game pieces perched atop rows of dark and light squares.

We haven't said anything to him. Soon I'll learn of Reginald's charges—two killings, hence his AT status. "The county" is new to me. Attendant Walton doesn't use the term. He barely explained Automatic Transfer.

The players maneuver, and I concentrate to refresh my memory of chess rules and strategy so one of these two won't cream me if I take on the winner. Reginald is constantly interrupting with additional blurts about "the county," so I refrain from chipping in about how chess renders you a more cautious and thus a smarter decision maker. The way the two players meditate on every move, they know this. Sadly, if convicted, one faces an adult-length prison sentence like fellow AT Reginald. Such contemplation skills may be too late in maturing. This first impression of Reginald makes me doubt he has ever fingered a chess pawn or bishop. He simply acted without thought and was arrested. The other two seem reflective like my Bible study friends. It's hard to think of them as criminals, as bad kids.

"I can't wait to see some G-shots when I get to the county," Reginald jumps in again. "I'm gettin' me some G-shots at the county, man!"

The players don't react, but I look over. Reginald lurches

up and ambles off to the TV area, blue khakis beltline slipping toward his buttocks and showing the band of his boxers.

I watch Reginald go, but they ignore him, as if such erratic, attention-lapsing behavior is no shock. "What's he mean by 'the county'?" I interrupt the game myself.

One lifts his eyes just enough to acknowledge my question and says, "He's an AT. So when he's seventeen, he go to 26th and California."

Two accused murder cases do make an Illinois sixteen-year-old an Automatic Transfer to the Cook County Jail.

"So what are G-shots?"

The other kid darts his eyes at his lap and smiles—a gentle mock of my ignorance. The game continues and they explain that G-shots are photos of women's genitalia.

Blabbery Reginald believes he can amass his own pornographic library once he becomes a man and moves to the county jail. Prospective pictures of women's genitals in his prospective possession must distract Reginald from the real-life possibility of men, the actual men at the county, men who have been men for many years, forcing him to look at their genitals in person, and then making him do something worse.

In a week, other inmates will tell me that birthday number seventeen waters Reginald's eyes, spitting out his farewells after a solid year of juvenile detention. Soon after, the AT chess player with whom I'd listened to Reginald's G-shots rant returns from his own court appearance. An adult pal, already seventeen, informed him during their secured room interval ("the bullpen"), before answering to their judges, that guards had punched Reginald around for flashing gang signs. So I doubt he has taken up chess at the Cook County Jail. At the Audy Home, we merely locked him in his cell when he tossed up a hand with particular extended fingers to signify his *nation*. I almost ask for word on raspy Reginald's collection of G-shots, surprised and troubled by my sympathy for a possible double-murderer, a possible double-murder salivating at a shot from a camera jammed between a woman's legs.

4

Attendant Walton leads me down two stair flights to the basement. With a regular key, he unlocks a metal door and heaves it back. Over the whoosh of soggy subterranean air, I hear them before I see them—basketballs jackhammering an orange double court. The dribbling noise is neither joyous nor leisure. The sound seems rebellious and hostile as if in pounding the dozen balls up and down hard enough, the boys could drill their way through the hard rubber playing surface and underlying cement to freedom.

From the doorway I look through all the dashing inmates, big inmates who are bigger than any inmate I've seen on the third-floor, and I spot a black attendant no more broad-shouldered than me, Pruitt. He sits a hundred feet across the gymnasium floor on a folding chair near the physical education teacher's office. Even from this distance, it's obvious that Attendant Pruitt, maybe thirty-five, thrives around the facility's scariest inmates. Nothing about him appears ruffled despite sharing the gym with only one other adult—the PE teacher zigzagging among what seems like three or four cellblocks worth of juveniles scattered over the two courts, both with an extra pair of goals and nets. The frail educator's mouth moves to issue directions, but no inmates' eyes or ears tic toward him. Attendant Walton points at Pruitt and sends me in.

I weave around the seventy-five sprinting bodies and pretend not to notice their faces: *No way! A white Newjack!* My jeans and cheap T-shirt provide even less camouflage down here. In the school hall, I was moving, as were the juveniles. Now we're trapped in the same room, noticing each other. The two or three white juveniles in the gym check me out too. As in the school area, inmate hair is braided into swinging ropes and beaded rows. Some heads are sheared to bristles. Brown and black hair shocks trail over other necklines. A good number of kids don Afros and tattooed throats, necks, and arms. Life-size teardrop outlines decorate lower eyelid corners. Other teardrops are solid. I've heard that an empty teardrop mourns a slain fellow gang member. A teardrop colored-in celebrates your gang avenging that death. No 3G boys flaunt such war medals.

Next to Attendant Pruitt between the two courts, I stop and introduce myself. Never really staring in any particular direction or staring at any particular cluster of inmates, he simmers a confidence that simply because he is here, the inmates are afraid to scream or threaten or laugh like maniacs or trip each other or kick off a gang fracas. And none do. The boys just race around and play ball and gawk at me.

Right away Attendant Pruitt coaches, "Make sure the kids don't huddle together and pace the walls shoulder-to-shoulder. It's gang representation. Make 'em sit down against the wall if they're not playing. If they're on the floor, they can't fight as good as when they're standin' up." He adds that if confrontations materialize during pickup basketball games or whatever exercises the teacher coordinates, we're to intervene.

I glance at the courts.

Several boys slouch against nearly every wall. I am curious how tracing a gym's perimeter could signify a specific gang. I'm thankful for Attendant Pruitt's explanation of gym rules, but I am more stressed about those gangs dueling than about how they "represent" themselves. Rather than inquiring, I confess my dismay at being what I now realize is a prison guard, nothing like a Chaplain Rick volunteer. This is not what I aspired to involve myself in here. *Children's attendant* is a damn lie.

"Yeah, in five years I've only seen seven or eight white guys work here. Most quit right away, some on the first day." His candor alarms me. I say nothing back. What a contrast with my childhood suburb where whites and blacks (the few that there were) conversed as if we all looked the same and thought the same. At the Audy Home, black is black and white is white. Inmates hating me is believable now, given their leers and jeers in the school area and the gym. I think of the fellow trainee's warning before my weekend in Wisconsin. As with him and Supervisor Hilliard, I want Attendant Pruitt to gush and reassure me that wayward inner-city kids need everyone's concern and care, and that yes, white Attendant Dostert, you belong here too.

Instead Pruitt adds, "Maybe you should have started off at a group home."

I did interview at the Lydia Children's Home on Chicago's North Side. During my dorm floor visit, I met one boy ten or eleven years old whose three fingertips were missing on one hand. His fingernails were half-size. A worker explained that the child's parents had nipped them off with a kitchen knife. I wanted to work at Lydia and befriend such children but couldn't have afforded apartment rent on the annual salary—less than $20,000.

"Yeah, I really didn't know what this was gonna be like." Otherwise, I'd have researched more foster facilities.

"The kids really aren't that bad, it's dealing with administration that's a pain," Pruitt lets on, as if to encourage.

Attendant Pruitt makes me jealous and dejected. I worry about the other commands I will need when attendants like him and Walton are not present. Will my commands be effective? I wish an aging, limping man in an office downstairs, Assistant Superintendent Davis, was my worst nemesis, rather than the gang-banging, felony-indicted youths an arm's length away. Davis seems harmless, and foolishly charitable, for hiring someone like me.

Attendant Walton assembles everyone for morning school, but one kid is sobbing. It's Monty—the boy pining for my assistance on day one, when Walton handed him the big spoon to divvy up the chocolate cake. A post-puberty crying male is disturbing, so I look away from his wet face. Shame nudges my upper body. I've ignored the young man—betrayed my original mission. Upset Monty doesn't distract Attendant Walton. We depart on time. I observe only the back of Monty's head on our way to the elevator, never detecting how long he needs to recompose.

After school and lunch, Walton gestures me behind the console to complete a referral form to Dr. Jacobs so Monty can be summoned for a consultation. Perhaps he should be a Close Watch too, and we need to confiscate his bed sheets.

Attendant Walton turns to me. "What was that resident's name?"

"Monty Preston."

From the roll board, I know Monty has been 3G-incarcerated for a month, but Attendant Walton can't remember his name, first or last. After four days, I know both. Unless a juvenile speaks without permission or ignores Walton's signal not to enter the bathroom area, he rarely pays one juvenile more attention than another.

I linger beside him at the console. Attendant Walton isn't nasty to the boys, but instead consumed with keeping record of who is where and why, and laying down orders to engineer forward the cellblock's machinery, chewing away the minutes and hours of our shift. I have yet to witness Monty misbehave. If I were the senior attendant on 3G, I would have motioned crying Monty to the console to ask what was wrong. Afternoon school could have waited a minute or two. Monty should know that someone is witnessing his grief.

There are other attendants who level much worse indifference than Attendant Walton. One wanders by during school area duty while Walton is down the hall. Standing in front of me, he brags about having once slapped a juvenile. This man is closer to three hundred pounds than two hundred and can undoubtedly reel off injurious blows.

"What made you do that?"

"Kid came out of his room, sat his ass on a table, and fired up a cigarette."

Instantly, I wonder how he snared the cigarette and something to light it with and where he concealed it all before puffing.

"Could you've written him up and called a caseworker?" This is what Attendant Walton trained me to do when a juvenile commits a major infraction.

"I had to put him in his place," the man says, staring straight over the hallway linoleum. He is at least fifty and has worked here twenty-some years. The rules are no mystery to him.

"So did the other kids see it?"

"Oh yeah! And I didn't have any problems after that." He faces me and adds that letting the young man smoke away with the entire cellblock gawking on while he retreated to the console to pen a rule violation report would ramp up brazenness in every other defiant inmate. This massive attendant is black and assigned to the fourth floor—the floor Attendant Walton warns me to never volunteer to work because of its older, brawnier juveniles and maverick staff. He's right. I could be black and wide as a Coke machine like this giant, and juveniles would still endeavor to chump me out unless I first beat one of them into his rightful place. I absolutely should have quit after that first day in orientation. Damn my work résumé. In a few months, I'll see this huge man camped behind the front desk after being promoted to supervisor.

Attendant Walton introduces me to staff from all floors and all cellblocks during school area duty. Some impress—a six foot five inch guy with a waist and shoulders framed like a kite. He played pro basketball in Europe before a wrecked knee wrecked his NBA plan. A protective aura envelops me when he happens by, even if inmates are in class. Others depress—the much shorter waddler whose face is always coated with a sheen of sweat. I've heard he is "four bills," that is four hundred pounds. Brawling inmates could kill each other or me before he labored across a cellblock to assist. The facility's Children Attendants—the lean and angular, the obese and sluggish—number about three hundred and thirty. Some are barely old enough to buy an Old Style lager at Wrigley Field. Social Security will send checks to others like "Old Man Jefferson" with poufy, graying hair and two missing front teeth in mere years not decades. Attendant Jefferson does Medical Movement runs between cellblocks and the infirmary with dozens of inmates scheduled for pill swallows. Two thirds of us are black men, the rest of Hispanic heritage, and four or five "white guys," those of us who show up again after our first day. I will be told though about men of every skin color who resign after figuring out that we don't cage the boys in their cells all day. Ten years ago, one story goes, an attendant cracked up mid-shift from wife or girlfriend problems and payroll goofing on his paycheck. The man bashed out the hallway window adjacent his fourth-floor cellblock and leaped a story and a half down to the courtyard. A soft all-weather surface covered the Recreation Area, instead of the current ankle- or likely leg-breaking cement. The man scaled a divider wall before supervisors coaxed him down and into the building and then into an ambulance. Even this shocks me. This place is that bad. Will the stress freak me out too? Some shift I'll abandon my block and the facility and become another Audy Home story passed on to future rookie attendants?

I'm assigned to shadow Attendant Walton again my second week. On Wednesday we return to 3G early from our school post, before lunch and alone. Walton hands me his electronic elevator key, "You're gonna go get the boys."

This test, I knew was coming.

Downstairs, I locate the blank wall section where they meet him. Attendant Coleman hollers his "Third Floor Boys!" and out of the blaring rush of two hundred inmates, 3G struts up.

Feet dance, heads bob, shoulders shake, mouths chirp—unlike any formation under Walton's control. They barely resemble two lines, but I start roll anyway with the paper roster Attendant Walton provided me.

Noise and gyration.

"Let's go," I try to sound authoritative, having finished the name check.

They snake toward the elevator shaft. I follow. In front of the doors, the boys laugh and chatter—no longer the somber funeral-attenders they are around Attendant Walton. I call the elevator, praying for it to arrive soon. The longer we wait, the longer the inmates can *act a fool*. Too worried about the elevator, I don't reprimand the noise.

"Step in," I say after thirty seconds when the doors open.

They herd inside with stomps and scuffs. I enter last and fiddle Attendant Walton's key against the panel to engage the elevator. I have no knack for the exact angle needed to trigger the little red light. This too is a first task. The light comes on after four or five turns and taps. I swivel to the group, touching shoulders and backs but can't see everyone. We rise. More giggles worm up from the gaggle of heads. Individual laughers are beyond my detection. Several complain unintelligibly of something. On Attendant Walton's elevator rides, I heard only humming pulleys and cables.

My response is, "Let's get quiet." They don't. I don't know what to do next.

The doors jerk apart and for a few seconds, drown out the chortles and grunts. Ten feet from the open elevator is a brick wall. For Attendant Walton, the inmates organized like automatons in two lines along this wall, every left shoulder kissing the bricks. Not for me. Unloaded, yakking is audible again in this cul-de-sac off the hallway. Milling about, they're giving the Newjack hell, hiding from any supervisor patrolling the outer corridor.

"Line up! Two single-file lines!"

The inmates cackle and sigh. I bark more impotent orders until a sudden, eerie silence sucks my eyes deeper into the muddle—two boys square shoulders and squeeze fists, their noses edging closer. One kid is Hispanic—tubby with dark hair shaved tight along the sides of his head but long against his neck. Taller and thinner, the other boy is black and will have many allies if others pour in according to skin or hair color. I'm the only one with no matching skin and hair. Those twenty press in on the gladiators like flower petals sucking closed around a plant's center. I lose sight of the adversaries but hear one hiss, "Let's go."

I bump spectators' shoulders and hips forcing myself into

the arena. "Back up, back up," I croak out between the scowlers. "Let's go! Back to the unit!" Forget lines.

Nothing more than the two boys' breath mingle, and they disappear into the blob that I prod around the corner and toward the cellblock. Several inmates groan how they want to see the two "box." I'm too flustered for a reproach and just keep moving and herding until I can open 3G's door and say, "Backs on the wall!" I can be tougher now with Attendant Walton at the console. We do the shirts and pants' legs routine—smooth with Walton upright and staring at them from behind me.

I turn and report the almost-rumble to him, the only consequence I can devise in my panicked state. Pansy of me to tattle on the boys, but skirting the brawl was moral victory.

"Turn around and face the wall," Attendant Walton orders, not sounding mad, more bored with the juveniles' unoriginal misbehavior. By facility rules, he can restrict them there for as many as forty minutes. Three hours was maximum count-the-bricks punishment at the original Audy Home. Rotating to begin wall time, the two glare over their shoulders at me. *Correct. You are a pansy, running to Mr. Walton. You don't know how to punish us yourself.*

An imagined scene of even nastier juveniles shoulders-high with me, like those I witnessed in the gym itching for battle with Attendant Pruitt, shoots into my head. Pruitt isn't around, and neither my words in the air nor my palms on their chests halt their advance. A dozen others align themselves by race or gang and zip into the fray. Those with no care who wins slug the back of my skull while I'm clawing the actual fighters apart.

The next day I wait until after lunch when Attendant Walton and I are alone standing near the console. In his hand is the logbook, ready to record something—probably the fact that lunch is complete and there were no missing eating utensils, so there is no need for strip searches or TV area seat cushion inspections to ferret out potential shanks. I turn to him. "This really isn't what I want to do after all. I'm gonna resign. Who you think I should tell?"

Attendant Walton shifts his upper body like a wince. He lays down the logbook. "Why don't we go talk to Martha." We can leave 3G unmanned because the inmates are at school with the 8–4 attendant and we have no confinements. A judge just released Calvin. I wonder if Attendant Walton is deferring to Martha because he doubts his own ability to convince me that I will endure and adapt, that I can be a good children's attendant. If he can't, how can Martha? She lives in Hobart, Indiana, and by her own admission is "a hundred pounds overweight." Working here two weeks now, I can affirm her presence asinine—an obese white Indiana woman, despite the PhD in psychology, coordinating guard training at a Chicago jail whose majority of guards and inmates are black.

"It just really seems impossible," I tell Martha in her office.

"Yeah, I know. It is overwhelming at first."

"I really didn't know I'd have to do all this." By "this," I mean—recording how many juveniles are going to and returning from court, the infirmary, and appointments with public defenders. By "this," I mean—scouting for gang hand signs, drill sergeant driving them through the hallways, fretting about bono fide brawls erupting. By "this," I mean—inspecting the juveniles every time we leave and reenter the cellblock, stressed about missing lethal contraband. And while doing all this, I feel I must prove myself because I'm white, because the inmates will indeed try to "make it hard on me" unless I "snap" and make an example of someone, which other attendants have urged me to do. "This" is not like being a Chaplain Rick volunteer. The cynic in orientation was right.

"But the place works," Martha replies. *You're wrong. The job really isn't that hard. You can do it.*

I murmur something but want to shout: *What do you know? How do you know that I can hack this? You're not assigned to a cellblock!* Martha has been employed here all of a year, and I have yet to see her upstairs patrolling corridors with supervisors and caseworkers, much less stepping inside a cellblock.

She assures me that I won't soon be going solo. I'll remain a third (extra) attendant, and in another two weeks, my new-hire group is slated for classroom training. All new children's attendants are required 160 training hours in their first year. "That'll help," she adds.

Martha isn't helping, but if I shadow two more weeks, I'll receive full salary for five workdays in the dead quiet basement. Then I will quit and move back to my parents' leafy street in Texas where no kids will snicker "Newjack" and file plastic fork handles into blades against cell walls and egg each other on to fist away their discord, encroaching mobs rooting for blood. This seems xenophobic and bigoted, but better a happy racist than an inept humanitarian. For these final two weeks of shadowing, my goal is to save myself. I won't feel guilty about quitting. Assistant Superintendent Davis should have explained *children's attendant* more genuinely. Cook County deserves my resignation. I feel that I deserve an apology—a departing week of easy money.

5

For week three, Martha or a supervisor extends me on 3G, but switches my shift from 8–4 to 2–10. On Monday, another 2–10 attendant shows up to be Attendant Walton's actual relief. With the 8–4 attendant, there are indeed three of us, so Martha wasn't lying—I'm still a shadow. When Edison, the 4–12 attendant, arrives, I explain at the console that I've been training during the day shift. Through black-rimmed glasses, he frowns at the TV area and our boys. "I hate that damn school area. Anything could happen down there. You won't catch me working days."

To avoid school duty and its three floors worth of juveniles crammed onto one floor for five hours, Attendant Edison requested 4–12. He is shorter than me, but his forearms bulge like the middle of a python digesting a wild pig. His head is shaved shiny and dark like his spectacle frames. One attendant has deemed him "a tar baby." Later Edison will point that shiny black head at overzealous spades players and say, "Bring that shit down!" Their voices plunge to whispers. Any inmate on 3G or even 4G scaring Attendant Edison seems fanciful. His fear of the school area troubles me. If he avoids the day shift, I should too.

Attendant Edison's coworker three nights a week is 3G's regular 2–10 attendant, a woman named McAdams, "Ms. Mac." Despite remaining on the same block for my third training week, between 3G itself and the school area, I've met lots of staff. Each can have his own interpretation of policy and procedure, which I must then interpret and apply. Now it's not just a boy's club. I noticed no women at any point in my testing/interview process. A woman though can staff a male cellblock if her coworker is male. Wide, sassy, and front-heavy, Ms. Mac's voice is deep and I'd guess she's forty. "Boy, I will whup yo' ass!" she facetiously threatens Ernest, burr-headed with consistently slurred speech. He'd pretended to walk away when she told him to sit down. Ernest and her other two pets are all my stature and ATs charged with first-degree murder. The four of them fill a table and run games of Spades all evening. Ms. Mac goes loud like her playmates, but Attendant Edison never curses at any of them.

Several attendants have advised me against cards or chess or basketball with the inmates. "Don't get that close to them," one warned. Interacting with the inmates complicates the jailer's relationship with the jailed, but these three accused felons adhere to Ms. Mac's every directive.

Jealousy is tempting because I worry they wouldn't do the same for me without her or Edison nearby. None of Ms. Mac's three pets were my almost-fighters in the elevator lobby, but none forced their capable physiques between the smaller boys to help me tamp down the skirmish. Working with one of the "lame ass" attendants I've already heard about worries me, worrying as well that I might be one of the lame asses myself whom no one wants to team with. Still I'm taking pleasure in the evening shift because at 3:00 P.M., not I, but the 8–4 returns the boys to cellblock from class. What I covet as well about 2–10 is fewer rules to enforce because there are fewer settings for rules. No school area duty during 2–10 means that the only guaranteed work location for 2–10 on 3G is 3G. Should Recreation summon us to the rec yard for softball, the door is twenty yards down the hall—a non-elevator trip. Basketball in the basement gymnasium requires the elevator, but such rec calls only happen once or twice a week.

Few inmates can pronounce "Dostert," so to them, I'm "Mr. D." Attendant Edison's "Dostert" comes out something like "Dystra," so to him I'm just "D." Around him, I feel welcome even though Edison isn't resolving my other frustration—ignorance of what the juveniles are to be doing or not doing at every second regardless of setting. *The Policy and Procedure Guide for Group Services* gives me no help for the moment-to-moment. I want Attendant Edison to say, *Right now they can play cards or watch television, but make sure they don't do X, Y, Z.* My ignorance involves not merely how best to execute major procedures like meals and showers and travel off the cellblock. Other queries plague me too. May a kid leave the TV area without permission? Slop water from the bathroom area faucet over his head and meander dripping back to the TV area? Smirk "Three-and-a-P" while other juveniles grin, and I suspect they're playing me with coded gangspeak? May one idle standing (not sitting) next to a full table of spades players and ponder falling aces and kings? Can they roll pants' legs up flood-style over sneakers? What if one sweet-talks me to opening his cell between dinner and showers so he can retrieve his hairbrush that resembles the kind used to rake grass burrs from a horse's mane? No one is answering these questions.

By 8:00 P.M. dinner, showers, Spades, television, basketball, softball, and ping-pong, or only dinner, showers, and television, are over. It's lights-out, so we lock the boys in their cells for the night, which I have no questions about. Call out a cell number and the inmate walks over, unties his shoes and places them against the brick wall, and enters the chamber. It's lights-out for everyone but the kitchen help who swab the bathroom area, sweep the entire block, and sort and count dirty laundry. These are painless orders to implement because rewards await their completion, namely task points toward earning a higher of the four behavior management levels, a later bedtime while finishing the chores, and any leftover food from dinner to eat with us in front of the television before we lock them in. Earning Level 4 also gives a kid a gold shirt with no bird logo. The kitchen help boys wad the towels, pants, shirts, blankets, and sheets together and wrap with another sheet into a beanbag-sized bundle and dump it outside the door. Laundry workers will retrieve the bundle during the night, heave it into a huge brown bin with wheels, and return the linens and clothes folded tomorrow. Two or three lucky units have their own washer and dryer where attendants label personal items with a black marker to prevent kids from falsely claiming each other's drawers and socks. That's what I'm hearing—boys will steal underwear. Those residing on less fortunate cellblocks hand-wash their own underwear and socks, either in the bathroom area sinks, or in their cell sinks if operable. The Audy Home provides its residents no undergarments, nor do we even launder the single undergarment stuck to their bodies when arrested. On this new evening shift with Attendant Edison, I watch kids lathering up socks and briefs and boxers in the common sinks, pitying fellow overflows likewise with no cell sinks coming next in line to brush their teeth.

"Can I get some water?" Arthur, fifteen and confined all day, calls out. He stands behind his Plexiglas. This is my second evening shift. Arthur wants to drink from 3G's "kitchen" sink.

An obvious evening shift rule, obvious even to a Newjack like me, is not releasing an inmate from his locked cell after 8:30 P.M. lights-out. And come 10:00 P.M., there may only be one children's attendant on the block. If I let a young man out with no coworker present, I could hurt him, or he could hurt me—without witness. I've just yanked Arthur's door handle and those down the row leading up to Arthur's to be confident they are secured before my shift soon ends. Attendant Edison has relegated me this baby-task.

I strain my eyes to see through Arthur's door window. He is less than an inch from the Plexiglas. The cellblock is half-dimmed. "You've got a faucet right there next to you."

"That water's nasty," Arthur says, being no fool about Chicago's public drinking water supply. As a college student I'd cringed standing on Lake Michigan's shore when a dorm mate pointed to a pumping station hazily visible from the sand. I then began hiking a block to Jewel-Osco for jugs of Buffalo Don's Wisconsin spring water to stash in our floor lounge's fridge. The oval outline of Arthur's dark face is visible through the Plexiglas, suggesting that I break another rule—juveniles are not to touch our sink unless working kitchen duty. Many veteran staff members urge me to be extra stringent, given my skin color, so the juveniles can't play me for a bleeding heart and milk me to lax the rules for them.

"Sorry, it's after 8:30, and you're in Confinement anyway. I can't let you out."

"C'mon Mr. D., you owe me one."

During my first week here, Arthur called me "Opie." His disrespect stymied me, but Attendant Walton overheard Arthur and put him on the wall for a full forty minutes. The surprising slur using Ron Howard's redheaded *Andy Griffith Show* character depressed me. I really am ignorant about Arthur's world. Despite his antagonism, Arthur still intrigues me because I've yet to see him smile under his space helmet of Afro. I've heard that a month ago, Arthur slammed a fiberglass chair into his cell door window, one of few that is actual glass. Cracks still spider-web the pane and Arthur did two days of Confinement inside his current cell. Now he is confined for something else.

If Arthur wants to talk, I'd rather listen than continuing down the block to inspect more door handles.

"So why do I owe you one, Arthur?"

"For four hundred years of slavery," Arthur explains matter-of-factly, as if he is the most sensible being on the planet.

Because my ancestors may have enslaved his ancestors, I should violate three protocols so Arthur can savor a "better" sip of jail water. The proposition tickles me—a kid simplifying an adult argument in order to drink from a different spigot. In these two-plus weeks at Chicago's juvenile lockup, I haven't laughed, but now I am, thanks to Arthur. I forget about "Opie." I forget about other juveniles who, when Attendant Edison and Ms. Mac are far enough away, buck and moan at the few rules I am aware enough of to enforce.

I wish that a rogue drink of water could erase four hundred years of slavery, so I smile for all the times Arthur and I have looked at each other and not smiled. I ram my key into his door and let sock-footed Arthur scoot to our kitchen sink. He can suck down however much less nasty Lake Michigan tap water that he wants.

"D, just relax!" Attendant Edison urges from where we are standing near several occupied card tables. I've just inched up next to him to ask whether to allow a juvenile to play ping-pong before he earns level-two in the behavior management system. Inmates earn regular points every day if they cooperate with us and respect each other. More cooperation and more respect yield a higher level and more rewards. I take Edison's advice to mean that he interprets my questions as fear of the inmates, fear that without constant directions and suffocating rules, they will harm me—why I can't relax.

Then he swipes an index finger along my forearm and elevates his fingertip for me to inspect. Then he gestures at my arm, "See D, the black don't rub off!" He smiles wide and toothy. "You can get close to 'em!"

Attendant Edison is joking, and I appreciate his effort to loosen me up, but his implication that I'm scared of the juveniles because of their dark skin stings. It is tempting to recount for him my Audy Home volunteer history and how I shook hands with dozens of black kids and touched my palms to their shoulders for goodbyes until our next Monday night rendezvous. And how one boy, Jerome, had invited me to his house. If black skin frightens me, why did I apply to be a children's attendant at the Audy Home? But I swallow the petty resentment. With Edison and Ms. Mac in earshot, no inmates threaten to fight or contest my instructions. I hope to shadow them again next week before my classroom training. "They need to keep you right here with us, D," Attendant Edison continues. I agree.

Our inmates are locked in for the night. I'm off in sixty minutes. From the TV area's last row, I'm watching WGN news, volume whispering. Camped behind a small rectangular table adjacent the back row, Edison flips through the *Chicago Sun-Times* spread flat. Suddenly, I hear: "D, what do you think a nigger is?" I turn. He is looking at me. Next to the television, a steel fan with blades enclosed in a protective cage whirs, dispersing the collective odor emanating from a pair of shoes positioned outside each of our eighteen cells. The fan though can't blow away Attendant Edison's question: "Come on D, tell me what you think a nigger is."

Until working here, I knew few black people and never knew

anyone who grew up in black inner-city Chicago or black inner-city anywhere. No white person has ever asked me this question, much less anyone black. "Well, I've never used that word, so it's kinda hard for me to answer." I add something about *nigger* being a racist word.

"Why do you think racism started?"

"Possibly because there's something in human nature that tends to fear and dislike what's different or what we don't understand."

I do suspect that more than mere aversion to dissimilarity initiated the trans-Atlantic slave trade, Jim Crow, and segregation. Europeans exploited weak, divided tribes along Africa's west coast, utilizing their forced labor to fuel colonial investments across the Atlantic. Economic opportunists first, I figure. Racial supremacists second.

"I think it's a spiritual reason, D. I think racism has a spiritual origin."

"How so?" He has yet to bring up God or the supernatural.

"What if I could show you that the Garden of Eden was in Africa? What if I could show you from the Word of God that the first human beings lived in Africa?" Attendant Edison hurries out of his seat even though I haven't said anything, unlocks a cell behind us, pokes his head in, and reemerges with the drowsy inmate's Bible. I've yet to witness Edison inspect a cell, but he knows which ones contain Bibles. "Check this out," he drops back into his chair beside me and turns the scriptures to Genesis chapter 2 and verses 10 through 15—verses following two creation accounts where God begets the heavens and the earth and the first humans. "Read this." He hands me the Bible and points down the page at the little numeral ten. On the thin, smoothed pages, I see:

> A river flowed out of Eden and watered the garden. That river then separated and became four smaller rivers. The name of the first was Pishon. This river flowed around the entire country of Havilah. There is gold in that country, and

> that gold is good. There are also Bdellium and Onyx in that country. The name of the second river is Gihon. This river flowed around the entire country of Ethiopia.[1]

When I look up, Attendant Edison says, "So what does that tell you, D? What does that tell you about the Garden of Eden?"

During my Sunday-schooled youth, I hustled through that passage, bored by names I couldn't pronounce and encountered nowhere else. The mention of an existing African country now though rings new and curious. Until now, I didn't recall any biblical appearances by Ethiopia. "Well, if the river flowing out of the Garden of Eden divided into a tributary that surrounded the land of Ethiopia, then Ethiopia must be fairly close to the Garden of Eden."

"Right, and where is Ethiopia?"

"In Africa."

"So that whole area was all Africa! And if the Garden of Eden was so close to Ethiopia, then *it* was in Africa! Mesopotamia, the ancient Near East, it was all Africa!" Attendant Edison leans into his chair back as if having earned the relaxed position for hammering home his point. "Now tell me what it says about this area?"

I stare back at the pages. The black letters and white space transmit no revelation, so I resort to common sense: "It must have been very rich in natural resources, with the mention of a garden, four rivers, gold, bdellium, and onyx."

"Exactly, so the first human beings lived in Africa—a very rich and beautiful land. And we know that white people can't survive in the harsh African climate. So that means the first human beings were black." Adam and Eve more resembled "tar baby" Edison than fair-haired me. "Now lemme show you something else," he pressed but stopped. "I don't know D, you may not want to hear this. You probably won't wanna work on my unit any more. You'll think I'm too militant. But really, I'm a normal guy. I gotta wife. I got kids."

Attendant Edison's previous job was at Maryville Academy, a shelter in suburban Des Plaines for child wards of the state.

Before working at Maryville, Edison grunted for paychecks in a steel mill across the Indiana line. After most shifts, he admits, he slammed a six-pack and smoked pot. Now Salem 100s are his primary vice.

I promise that whatever he says about God and black people won't offend me.

"Look back at Genesis 1:26," Attendant Edison motions at the Bible. "God says: 'Let us make man in our own image.' So if God created the first man in his own image and in Africa, and we know what kind of people live in Africa, what does that tell you about God?"

"I'm not sure. What do you think?" I have an idea, but the longer we talk, the more I want Attendant Edison's opinion unfiltered—not a reaction to my beliefs. I have heard of a black Jesus but never a black Adam and Eve.

"God is a black being!"

Nothing from me. I can't confirm or debunk God's blackness.

Attendant Edison moves his lips without sound as if more pronouncements simmer inside him, but he suspects an insistence that God is black might enrage me. It won't, and I want to hear why he believes in a black God, particularly if it explains the N-word. Most 4–12 children's attendants keep our talk to sports, weather, and policy and procedure.

"This is a black book, right out of Africa," Edison holds up the now closed imitation leather Bible at shoulder-level between us. With each fan oscillation, newspaper pages on the fiberglass desk in front of him flutter up underneath his hands squeezing the Bible.

I sit still and mute, shocked at his schemata's unfamiliarity to me, given my Bible reading childhood and college degrees in theology and history.

"Okay, so we know that Adam and Eve were black and that human civilization started in Africa, a very fertile land," he breaks our hush. "Later on, the book of Genesis talks about Abraham, the father of the Hebrew nation, going back to Adam. So the Hebrews are God's chosen people, through which to bring the Messiah—Jesus. So what does that tell you, D?"

Attendant Edison responds before I do. “It tells me that not only is God black, and Adam and Eve were black, but so were the Hebrew people who became the nation of Israel. Check this out. Read Amos 9:7.” This scriptural dot-to-dot seems oft traveled for him, his fervor mounting toward a climax despite familiarity with each plot point along the way. Edison pushes the Bible back into my hands. I strain again to read in the dim light: “The Lord says this: ‘Israel you are like the Ethiopians to me. I brought Israel out of the land of Egypt.’[2] Now what does that say?”

I have no suggestion. But Attendant Edison does: “It tells me that the Ethiopians are Israel, the Hebrew nation. And because Jesus came from this seed, he too was black.”

I don’t remember this Ethiopia reference either. “Well, then who are the people living in Israel now and the other ethnically similar peoples living elsewhere who call themselves Jews?”

“They’re people of European ancestry who took on the Hebrew religion from the true Israelites—black Africans. So D, now tell me why black people are so persecuted in this country?”

To me prejudicial motivation still equals our unease with variation. We want everyone to be like us and look like us and act like us. If they don’t, they’re inferior.

“It’s not because we’re different,” Attendant Edison continues. “We’re hated because we’re God’s chosen. See D, the white man took more than our gold and diamonds. He took our identity. We don’t know who we are. If we did, there wouldn’t be so many black kids locked up inside this building. This place wouldn’t be so overcrowded. If we knew who we were, we wouldn’t fall for all the bullshit that drags us down. Instead, we’d live like God’s children. That’s what a nigger is, D. A black person who’s been robbed of their identity, a black person who doesn’t know they’re God’s chosen people—the true Israelites.”

We watch each other without speaking. In all my Sunday school and Bible college class discussions of the Bible, the word *bullshit* never emerged, enhancing Attendant Edison’s mystique in the otherwise quiet musty air cycling around us in the TV area.

“Not to say that we’re better than everyone else, because plenty of us are gonna be thrown in the lake of fire and brimstone if we don't repent. But we are God's chosen people—the true Israelites. But some of our sin, even in biblical times, still haunts us today."

Attendant Edison pages backward to Deuteronomy's twenty-eighth chapter and points me to its last verse: "The Lord will send you back to Egypt in ships. I said you would never have to go to that place again, but, the Lord will send you there. In Egypt, you will try to sell yourselves as slaves to your enemies. But no person will buy you."[3]

I raise my eyes up from the silent reading as Edison asks, "Who are the only people in history that we know were carried off to slavery in ships?"

Ocean vessels indeed hauled Attendant Edison's ancestors to the western hemisphere to be slaves in European colonies. I still conjure no way to connect this fact to Egypt—the millions of African captives had purchasers once in the New World.

Again Edison won't wait for an answer, "The *you* is us—black Africans!"

"But it says 'to Egypt.'"

"Right, and what kind of religions did they have in ancient Egypt?"

"Mythology and mystery religions were prevalent during that period." I am somewhat familiar with Near Eastern culture in antiquity.

"And what was the religion of our forefathers?"

I stall, wanting Attendant Edison to fill in the blanks once more. He does.

"George Washington, Thomas Jefferson, all those guys were Free Masons." Not everyone is cocksure about our founding fathers being Jerry Falwell fundamentalists like I once believed. "And Masonry is a mystery religion that started in ancient Egypt, along with Cabalism and pagan mythology. So the United States is the new Egypt. See, D, we were disobedient to God after being freed from the Egyptians the first time. So now we're being punished for that disobedience by being enslaved again, this time in another Egypt—America."

I know about allegorical understandings of the Bible, such

as the Prodigal Son symbolizing the entire Jewish nation, not just any pilgrim, and Hades standing for spiritual estrangement from the Almighty instead of an actual inferno of weeping and gnashing of teeth. Attendant Edison's theory—the God of Abraham, Isaac, and Jacob punishing Israel by means of the Middle Passage—still comes off as bizarre.

"Do you know what the Illuminati is, D?"

"No. What is it?"

A Satanic conspiracy involving the Masons spawned this Illuminati—a secret world government conspiring to exterminate blacks. "It's something way bigger than Clinton, Bush, or Reagan. It controls the media, Hollywood, Wall Street, government, healthcare, technology—everything. It's Satan's tool to destroy us. You wanna know how the Illuminati is working to annihilate black people in this country?"

"Sure," I nod despite the idea sounding fanciful and uninformed, his words hypnotizing like a documentary of some strange, far off land whose soil I have no desire to sink my footprints into, but still tickles me to eavesdrop on from the comfort of a movie house.

"Look at our communities. They're full of guns and drugs. Who's putting the guns and drugs there? The American government," his tone ebbs louder. "They could stop drugs from coming in if they wanted to, but they don't. That's why they pulled all the jobs out of our communities, so there'd be nothing else for us to do but sell drugs, join gangs, and kill each other. They put the drugs and guns in our neighborhoods. They put us in the ghettos and housing projects. They put us on welfare and left us to die. That's what they want."

At home, I find my Bible—the one I've had since third grade. Amos 9:7 does contain Ethiopians, but my translation uses "Cush" in Genesis 2, not "Ethiopia," hence my surprise pondering the Ethiopian Garden of Eden and river Gihon with Attendant Edison. Cush has never made me think of Africa, but in the coming days, I do some research. Many scholars indeed do position Cush in ancient Nubia, the region south of Egypt in modern

Sudan. Tonight's conversation is as interesting a conversation as I can conceive—seemingly possible for me only at the Audy Home and only on 3G with Attendant Edison.

I definitely want to remain on 3G. Attendant Edison controls the inmates so I can slowly learn how to, while prompting me to think thoughts that I never imagined would have anything to do with juvenile detention.

6

On Monday, supervisors place me on 3F instead. So no more discussions about the meaning of *nigger* and God and Israel being Africa. Now I must meet new Children Attendants on a new cellblock and decide on their methods. Juveniles here are only twelve and thirteen. My new mentor, Tucker, the 2–10 attendant, has done a decade on 3F. Wiry, shorter than me, and bubblier than Edison, Attendant Tucker still manages 3F seamlessly. Only a couple 3F boys are ATs. None rave about G-shots or menace each other when Tucker isn't looking. None are close to my size or sprout mustaches and tattoos. None act any differently when Attendant Tucker isn't right next to me. I man our three-at-time bathroom line, and no one argues back when I tell him to be quiet. I train one eye into the bathroom area and the other on those waiting. Attendant Tucker relaxes in the TV area not even watching us. Something I never heard on 3G is his "Goodnight, sir" bedtime greeting to these younger and smaller inmates locking their doors at shift's end, a roll of toilet tissue in his hand, in case anyone might need more between 8:30 P.M. lock-in and 7:00 A.M. wake up. I also have never heard anything bad about Attendant Tucker. When Tucker criticizes a coworker, he does so under his breath. He doesn't call anyone lame or weak or "a stupid motherfucker."

"Take care, sir," he says to me later, pushing through the building's revolving glass door exit. Some attendants consider Tucker odd, doing 2–10 with Tuesday and Wednesday off, despite decades of seniority. He claims no craving for 6–2 with weekends off—too much traffic in Chicago because everyone else is off and zooming about town. Attendant Tucker and 3F hearten me about attending children at the Audy Home. If I can land permanently on 3F, maybe I won't quit after training week's easy money. Block 3F seems easier money too.

In the middle of the week, Attendant Tucker invites me to accompany him to escort our kids without cells to 3K where they will overnight on cots. Inmates there are sized and aged halfway between 3G and 3F. We arrive. One 3K attendant sits behind the console. The other poses between it and the cell fronts. His overflows and ours perch like statues in front of him.

"Fuck with me here, and I'll fuck you when you come to the Ghetto!" *Cause any trouble after I dim the lights and say, "No Talking," then God help you when you get arrested again in a couple years and land on the fourth floor where I work my regular shift!*

"Isn't that a little extreme?" I ask Tucker in the hallway after our boys stand through the shouting man's speech, lie down on their cots, and cover up with their single sheets.

"Yeah, he's from the fourth floor." Attendant Tucker explains that the guy has snagged overtime down here.

More staff than I can name dub floor four "the Ghetto" for the same reason Attendant Walton instructed me to resist being assigned there—it houses the oldest boys in the building and attendants who resort to renegade methods to control them like the huge man slapping the cigarette-puffing kid. In one fourth-floor tale, supervisors mobilized baseball bats from a cabinet near the front desk and raced up a stairwell in riot-quell mode. No time for the elevator. What I heard was: "Things were out of control and they had to get them back under control." Farming the nastier kids, "the real assholes," to one floor does make sense. Attendant Walton alleges that attendants impotent to affect these most ornery inmates (most of them Automatic Transfers) with policy and procedure or their sheer physical presence, smuggle in pot, booze, and skin mags to appease them. Otherwise, such juveniles have nothing to chance by swinging a chair at our heads with forty years at a prison downstate imminent. Maybe the man who busted the hallway window and jumped down to the rec yard hadn't tried any of these stress reducers. One fourth-floor attendant was just canned for running a cigarette racket.

In the version of the story I have, he accepted cash and smokes from parents during visitation to then slip "the squares" into cells after lights-out. How administration nailed the Marlboro salesman, I never find out. Maybe other juveniles snitched, jealous without such benevolent moms and dads.

Like Martha promised, training begins in a few days. Despite the fourth-floor war stories, the near 3G rumble by the elevator, and Arthur's dubbing me "Opie," I feel as good about the Audy Home as I've felt since volunteering with Chaplain Rick. I no longer deliberate each night whether to inform the front desk supervisor that I won't be here tomorrow and apologize for wasting everyone's time. My new vision is to be another Attendant Tucker—mild-mannered, non-violent, and non-cursing, hopefully on 3F or a cellblock like 3F.

On Friday 3F's 4–12 attendant arrives and takes the console. I stroll up from the TV area to introduce myself. A few sentences into our conversation he says, "Don't make this your career. That's what I tell all the new guys."

I just moved from Texas, aspiring for "this"—incarcerated black kids in Chicago—to be my career. And now a black man from Chicago announces that it's pointless to make incarcerated black kids in Chicago my career. Other attendants have already suggested: "You've got the paperwork. You should be a caseworker. You won't have to work the units," as if disclosing winning lottery numbers the night before balls tumble from the hopper. While no college is needed to be a children's attendant, holding a college degree qualifies me to be a caseworker, even though my degree isn't in psychology, social work, or criminal justice. My diplomas read Christian theology and early modern European history. How do these sheets of card stock render me competent to be a caseworker when I still have little clue as to how cellblocks should run? I spent eight months and hundreds of dollars to work the boys' cellblocks. Now the very adults whom I most expected to approve my mission here are urging me to abandon it so I will have my own office and inhale cellblock odor only in emergencies and when checking on confinements or distributing the juveniles' mail, if any. Those staff closest to the inmates, staff like Supervisor Hilliard and various children's attendants, as opposed to administration, seem wary about the viability of my mission. Back in the Texas suburbs, I expected them to believe as much as I did.

I show up for class on Monday, an emotional stew once again, but, as expected, love training—a reprieve from the buzz saw of cellblock responsibility upstairs. Our shift is 8–4 and we have an hour lunch. "Like a week of vacation," one guy says. Supervisors and administrators lecture about first aid, the behavior management point system, and physical restraint techniques from the Crisis Prevention Institute, as well as keeping in your head at all times *the count*—the number of juveniles assigned to your block separated into how many are physically present when the supervisor calls and asks, and how many are off unit at court, Medical, and appointments with public defenders.

"The count is the only thing keeping the kids in this building," one supervisor explains. If you think you are in charge of twenty juveniles, but really have twenty-one juveniles, it is much easier for that twenty-first to slither out the cellblock door and not be missed. Attendant Tucker recounted a 3F boy who whipped on a non-bird-shirt T-shirt his mother extracted from her purse during visitation. On the elevator his civilian duds rendered him like a juvenile's sibling granted special visitation privileges. But an attendant in the elevator recognized the boy and hustled him back to 3F.

Dr. Jacobs tutors us how to identify juveniles contemplating suicide. They cry all the time, sleep all day, never want to play cards. They won't eat. The jail opened twenty-five years ago but still no resident has taken his or her life. Dr. Jacobs provides no details on the ones who have tried. He does inform us that correctional officers at the Cook County Jail, where he previously worked, demonstrated for inmates how to tie their bed sheets into knots and nooses with which to hang themselves. Even Martha teaches a session—juvenile rights: how to treat children in custody legally and humanely and that thanks to an accused prank-calling Arizona kid named Gerald Gault in 1967, American juveniles enjoy *due process*. A sheet of white butcher paper with "Overall Score=96.9%" written in blacker marker hangs on the classroom's back wall. Next to it, a posted letter from the American Correctional Association certifies that our facility satisfies its standards.

"The ACA came looking for monsters," Martha says of the recent audit. By monsters she means children's attendants harming the juveniles. "They didn't find any. So now we have to convince the community that we treat the children well."

She is correct, partially. Attendant Tucker certainly treats the inmates well, but I now wonder if his civility is as much the 3F's inmates' youth as his good heart. Maybe even he would grow hard working different blocks. Recently, Superintendent Doyle fired several attendants whom he claimed lied on job applications regarding their criminal histories. I've heard those released workers had been "on administration's hit list." One terminated man did confess an apprehension two decades ago riding in a stolen car he didn't know was stolen. Another clarified his arrest as a much younger man down south protesting Jim Crow. "Hey, we're the smallest gang in here. We gotta stick together," I hear in the same conversation, protesting Doyle's firings, similar to Attendant Pruitt's comments about Doyle and Davis. According to the *Chicago Sun-Times*, Doyle also removed workers for "acting too roughly with the youth." Current American Civil Liberties Union litigation alleges that attendants have abused the juveniles and ignored sexual molestation between them.

After class, I ask Martha for a copy of the ACA report. I want to know if they see and hear what I see and hear. She provides me one, yet I read nothing about kids raping each other although the audit team couldn't ignore the "considerable amount of graffiti," etched into many of the Plexiglas cell door windows and how "some of the living units need a major face-lift."[1] Seems pretty minor compared to what I'm actually dealing with. Doyle and staff must have put on a good show for the auditors.

The ACA observations do credit the Nancy B. Jefferson Alternative School with "a full academic program."[2] The West Side's

Joan of Arc might be proud, but for kids in jail, a "full" academic program excludes a science lab with Bunsen burners and the test tubes that our students could smash into shards and brandish. No field trips to the zoo or planetarium either—students would have to be chain-gang shackled. In my two school area weeks with Attendant Walton, 3G juveniles attempted to cart back far more Snicker's, mini-packages of Oreos, and bags of Jay's potato chips than spirals or textbooks. A couple worksheets was the sum total. Walton hawk-eyed the inmates who entered our line after school to thwart food smuggling onto the elevator. No cookies or crackers or candy in the boys' pockets means less to punch over, gamble with, or extort one another for. Smart students devour teacher bribes before class ends.

I want to question Martha why she isn't enrolling me in an impromptu session of the gang awareness workshop that also is part of training. I need it, but it isn't scheduled anytime soon. While I don't learn about gangs, I do learn how two attendants can subdue a hostile gangster by sandwiching him between our hips and wrapping each of his arms around our waists—the Crisis Prevention Institute strategy. "That shit ain't gonna work," one attendant says where only I can hear.

He raises his hand and clarifies that sometimes the only option is to "break a kid down." The instructor's response is nondescript. Policy and procedure still reassures me. At least in theory, I know how to restrain an inmate.

On Friday, I'm hardly Attendant Walton or Attendant Pruitt but am more at ease about no longer shadowing. Next week I'm doing B-Relief—Tuesday through Sunday with only one dayshift. I requested to be 2–10 permanently, but can cope for now with a lone school area duty tour, especially if I draw 3F, whose inmates I can yank apart by myself even if, while piling out of the elevator, they rumble all at once. I never witnessed two of them disagreeing about who was first in line for the bathroom much less flinching to slug each other. They recreated the friendly inmates from my volunteer days. No strutting. No tattoos. I heard no G-shots fantasizing. No threats. All spoke in normal tones of voice. The idea of any 3F kid being arrested baffles me.

7

"Dostert, 4K," Supervisor Maywood says at the time clock on Tuesday, my week's lone day shift, my first day as a real children's attendant. Supervisors should start me on the third floor, not in the Ghetto. Supervisor Maywood adds something about wondering how I will fare on a tough block. Many attendants complain that this guy "loves to fuck with us" and considers any suspensions he elicits to be trophies. I've already wondered if, as the only Caucasian in my new-hire group, some Affirmative Action initiative gave me the position. Supervisor Maywood may hate that policy and is aiming to weed out the token white guy. I drag my timecard through the scanner to visions of fourth-floor supervisors wielding baseball bats, attendants smuggling in porn and pot, and one freaking out on the job and flying out a window.

I walk into 4K. The midnight to eight attendant hands me a key ring. The 6–2 man also has one. Because fourth-floor inmates are older and bigger, both attendants have keys—in case one is overpowered. Two dozen residents sitting at the breakfast tables peeling bananas and spreading jelly onto white bread glance up. The biggest 3G kid would be average here. None sneer or whisper, "Newjack." I'm thankful.

Much younger than Walton, the 6–2 attendant is round with little neck and plants himself like a boulder near the food cart. As if something bad might happen if he doesn't, he scans the seven tables, his eyes moving in his huge stationary head. The boys chew and swallow and nothing bad happens. Eventually, my coworker creases his face and calls them to the cart a few at a time to scrape and report to the TV area—just like on 3G. The most imposing inmate stands up. He has an inch of height on me, his shoulders equally broad. Later I'll learn that he is charged with first-degree murder. On 4K, I'm a man among men.

I sign the logbook at the console. Today's page isn't filled with the entries of inmate classifications and whereabouts that Attendant Walton no doubt has created by now downstairs on 3G. Maybe warding off potentially life-endangering group disturbances preoccupies attendants in the Ghetto too much to burn time scripting up the logbook. I look at the roll board. At least half of 4K are Automatic Transfers—more accused murderers and carjackers.

After cleanup, the 6–2 man calls the juveniles from the TV area, assembles them into two neat quiet lines. He hands me the key ring and escorts the boys to school. As the 8–4, my job is to remain on unit with any confined inmates. There are a couple, so like Walton trained me with Calvin, I find the mini-clipboard on the console and pass by those two doors for the 9:00 A.M. inspection. Every fifteen minutes, my initials on the Confinement log will testify that at this moment, neither inmate has hung himself or is smashing his head into cell wall bricks. Both are dead asleep. No need to use the cell door key, to open any cells.

I return to the console. The 6–2 left one other boy, but he isn't locked inside his cell. Cecil idles at a table to my right, his hands resting in front of him. He is slim and short, certainly for 4K. Physically speaking, Cecil is one I'd prefer most to be alone with if unavoidable. I could take him no problem. A Movement and Control attendant will soon escort him to the infirmary on the third-floor—Medical—and he will miss the start of the school day.

Cecil waits without writhing in pain. Instead of looking at me, like I'm looking at him, Cecil beats his eyes about the cellblock and through the glass wall behind me into the hall.

"How come you have to go to Medical?"

"They gotta take a bullet out of my back."

I try not to let on that I'm surprised. "So where's this bullet?"

Cecil stands, turns around, and draws up his shirt. Below one shoulder blade a purple welt oozes shiny pus.

"When did that happen?"

"A few years ago," he drops into the chair.

I don't probe about how or why he was shot. The bullet must be surfacing, completing its trajectory to exit his body, fulfilling its shooter's intention. I doubt our nurses can extract lead. Medical has no operating table. Cecil will be shackled and driven to a hospital instead.

"Can I have a pencil and paper?"

"Yeah. Who you writing?" I lift the console top and rummage his request out of the drawer. Potential weapons like pens and pencils are stored safe from juvenile access.

"My baby's mama."

Cecil says he is sixteen, and his girlfriend is nineteen, and their son is three. He moved into an apartment with them and his older brother after his mom kicked him out. I want to ask if the apartment was an unoccupied and unlocked unit in a high-rise housing project, but don't. Then came his arrest. Again I don't question why. I don't question why Cecil was having sex at age thirteen or if he felt guilty about it, nor do I challenge his story. I feel guilty about simply wanting a peaceful shift. Cecil is quiet, and I can't chance this changing. I'm a long way from 3F.

After Cecil is picked up, I thumb the logbook pages and their scant entries again. The 6–2 never touched it during or after breakfast. Whichever entries are missing, the next should be the 8–4 documenting his inspecting all the cells, "systematic and thorough," like Supervisor Hilliard had instructed. Attendant Walton never led me through one cell search, much less the entire row's worth. No one else has trained me either. Always with Walton in the school area, I never directly shadowed an 8–4 children's attendant. Twenty feet of dull brownish floor tiles separates me from the line of steel-framed cell doors, six or eight brick lengths between each of them. Even though Supervisor Hilliard has sanctioned me to, trolling through the 4K living quarters for evidence of what additional sins these inmates may have committed seems like a punishment I'm not authorized to mete out. These young men have committed too much vice and had too much vice committed against them for me to excavate for more. Cell inspections feel like a violation that would inhibit me from ever greeting a kid the same way again, knowing that I've fingered his bed sheets and turned over his furniture. Official guards with uniforms and badges should do it. Other than initialing the Confinement log in fifteen-minute intervals, I idle at the console the entire morning.

The 6–2 man returns the boys to unit at noon. Like breakfast, lunch happens rhythmically with the juveniles acting roles they know well. I've already shunned one of my 8–4 roles: cell searches. But my coworker won't let me shirk another. I must march the juveniles back to school and return them to 4K after class.

"Okay, line up!" he barks out to the boys in the TV area.

They relocate to the cellblock front and configure into two lines. No one argues, pushes, or laughs. These are the most physically intimidating Audy Home inmates I've seen. Three are my size, one even taller. I'm about to be alone with the entire twenty-odd of them.

"Gentlemen, this is no different than any other time," the 6–2 attendant says. He knows the boys may act up. He knows they know that I'm a Newjack.

"Go ahead," I direct in my mean tough voice, doubting that I am tough or mean.

They step out, and I follow. None look back at me or jabber, and the human columns march straight for a hundred feet until the glass wall turns to brick, and the 6–2 man can no longer see us. Then my two lines fragment into islands of gyrating motion, the mostly dark heads mostly at my eye-level pinging out in various directions away from the hallway's middle.

"Come on, let's go," I say. We're at the elevator corner.

"No man, you go!" several inmates yelp at each other when I command them into the carriage. At least no one is squaring off to fight.

I step toward the bunch. They lunge away as if I breed a contagious disease, but do funnel into the elevator, their complaints morphing into smirks and light shoves.

"Let's get quiet!" I fumble my key against the security panel. I have my own little magic rectangle of plastic now. Without much practice surrounded by panting inmates though, I've yet to perfect the exact angle which will trigger the red light and plunge us downstairs.

The boys blab on and I don't know what to do. Attendant Walton never instructed, *If your residents get rowdy on the elevator, then*—because his residents never exhibited rowdiness on his elevators. Without Cecil here, I know zero names. I can't detect who is yakking and who isn't, even if I did know names. The elevator drive mechanism finally engages and we drop two floors. The door parts. Boys burst into the hallway and blaze off to class. I only follow but don't yell for them to stop and assemble into lines because if they ignore me, my inability to control 4K will be obvious for dozens of attendants and hundreds of juveniles.

I locate the 4K attendant school post and sink into its chair, any 3F-engendered warm fuzzies now obliterated. I stare around the hallway at other attendants posted in chairs outside various classrooms. No one stops by to talk like when I was shadowing Attendant Walton.

At 2:00 P.M. I use the wall phone to ring up 4K. The 2–10 attendant listens to me recount the humiliating elevator ride and classroom delivery. "Okay, if any of 'em talk again, let me know and I'll put 'em on the wall," the soft-voiced man responds, sounding timid, not gruff like the 6–2, but at least he is proposing a consequence for the juveniles' defiance. I'd issued zero warnings or threats.

"Fourth-Floor Boys!" Attendant Coleman hollers ninety minutes later. A couple hundred approaching inmates and their voices ricochet floor to wall, wall to floor, floor to ceiling. They press right or left like swinging gates into lines in front of their blocks' attendants. Not 4K. My boys amble up yapping in fits and starts. The 3G boys were angels compared to this. I call roll and most "Here!" answers seem mocks that really mean, *Yeah, fuck you, I'm HERE and gonna be a bastard until you can debastardize me!*

I spot Cecil. The nurses didn't poke and jab very long. No bullet removals at the Audy Home, indeed. If I can catch Cecil's eyes, hopefully he will recall our amiable conversation about his baby's mama and go along with my instructions to stand quietly in position. We see each other, but Cecil jaws away like the rest.

"Let's go," I say, trying to end this public humiliation. A third of the jail is looking on. Inside the elevator no one else will see us.

We jut through the crowded hallway in swaggers, with my inmates marking out their own path and brushing boys in other lines. I know nothing to say that will change this. Attendants gape at me, pitying the Newjack and, I'm certain, wondering what reasons the geniuses in suits like Assistant Superintendent Davis harbor for hiring white attendants.

On the elevator, the boys cackle and jostle and bitch again. Off the elevator, I belt out, "Line-up! Two single-file lines!" Nothing. I yell it again, and their disorganization swallows more floor space, as if the simplest routine in their Audy Home lives, one the boys have performed hundreds of times, is suddenly terrible and excruciating, and they're endeavoring their damnedest to escape it and torment me for attempting to require its adherence, or because they can, they're making me pay for their displeasure with the 6–2 man's ironclad reign.

"Back to the unit, let's go!" I decide, dreading for other attendants to pass us with their perfect and orderly inmate formations. None do. I'm lucky that 4K lies thirty yards from the elevator. We straggle over the linoleum, a mob instead of an infantry regiment with the 6–2 attendant at the helm mere hours ago.

A hulking murder suspect, his nose arched and his head shaved, stops.

I stop too and say in a normal tone, "Come on, let's go." Raising my voice hasn't worked. The rest of the block is trickling down the hall, leaving me with Riles. Riles Davis.

Widespread a name as Davis, I still suspect rumors that Riles is related to Assistant Superintendent Davis, a grandson or nephew, are true. I've already heard of other inmates blood-connected to employees and the awkwardness this creates for us. The elder Davis could be lingering on here when he could have already retired. But he's doing the family a favor by staying on to monitor and maybe do favors for young jailed Riles. Or there is no relation, and Riles's mother simply rhymed her son with the famed jazzman, wishing for him a more promising life than what surrounded her and him at birth. But the shape of his face and his size and height, he more resembles Fred Davis than Miles Davis.

"Let's go," I say again. I don't want to appear hostile. He's close enough to touch.

The corridor is empty but for 4K and me. I don't know how I'll react if Riles attacks. His expression is serious. "We don't gotta walk in lines," he announces as if I've just asked him a deeply philosophical question, and he is serving me great favor by answering it thoughtfully. I see no lines here, so why he is complaining? The other boys are creeping farther and farther away, and I would love to scream at Riles that he has to do what I say because I'm not asking him to do anything he hasn't already done for the 6–2 attendant.

So my black coworkers are indeed telling the truth. It's dawning on naive me that many black juveniles think I took this job because I hate black people and take jollies off involving myself in their incarceration. They really are trying to render my children's attendant life hell.

We tromp into 4K. The 2–10, a black man wearing glasses, pops up from the console. The boys chatter on and meander in every direction, radiating outward like ripples in a pond. What a difference between the 6–2 and the 8–4 attendant. The boys should be proceeding dead silent to the cell row wall and turning around.

"Line up! Backs on the wall! Let's go!" I call out.

The 2–10 attendant hedges out from behind the console beside me to facilitate the spot-search. The boys gab and cackle. They were silent in line for the 6–2 man. Their feet stomp. Only a few shirt backs touch the bricks.

As if he lacks confidence in his own commands, the 2–10's voice peters out at the end of each directive to lift the next clothing article or remove their shoes and slam them together.

My new coworker dismisses them to the tables for cards and to the TV area but fails to ask me which ones deserve wall time for elevator defiance. I retreat with him to the console, our eyes on each other. Is he a Newjack too? Why has Supervisor Maywood put me with him? Maybe he really does fuck with people.

The boys shout and slap the tables when laying down a card. Yakking in the TV area mutes an afternoon sitcom. Attendant Edison's "Bring that shit down!" comes to mind, but these boys will howl at it from me and roar and thump even louder. I've never in my life said "shit" out loud, and it would be useless here, uttered from stress and failure. The 2–10 lurches up and inches toward the tables, as if physical advancement reinforces his seriousness and a potential further consequence for not complying. "Step to your rooms! Take off your shoes! Overflows, go to the TV area!"

Inmates stand up from the tables and TV area and amble toward their cell doors. Collectively unruly residents can indeed temporarily be sequestered in their cells. An example is a group disturbance when everyone is fighting everyone. The 2–10 and I don't have that. We have everyone fighting us.

Darting back behind the console, my coworker hits a switch to simultaneously unlock every cell door. He hurries to cell one and tells its occupant to enter. The boy complies, but with a slow, measured aloofness: *I'll go, but you can't make me, and I know what to do next!*

Inmates are not to be locked in cells with their shoes on—socked feet can't kick out a Plexiglas window as easily as those protected by Pumas and Nikes. Such policy also prevents a depressed juvenile from hanging himself with his shoelaces. But these 4K assholes aren't depressed. They're savoring a riotous time with the 2–10 and me in charge.

Master key in his hand, my coworker hustles down the row and locks the doors one at a time. Each snickering inmate moseys in on stocking feet as I watch near the console, my stomach lurching. Before my coworker reaches the last cell, a kid in a lower-numbered cell pounds his Plexiglas door window with the sides of his fists.

"Send it up!" intersperses his strikes against the Plexiglas. In other words: *Start A Riot—We're Being Mistreated!* One joins him and in seconds, others. The ruckus imitates a toddler on a drum set. Then others up and down the cell row catch the beat. Within minutes, what sounds like all the inmates are synchronizing their whacks into one booming thud, batter-ramming their door windows like barbarians assailing a castle door. The entire wall vibrates at the 2–10 attendant and me.

I glance at Cecil in his cell in the row's middle. He bangs too. Our conversation this morning means nothing. My giving him pencil and paper to write his baby's mama never happened. Other staff members pass 4K in the hallway. *Why are your kids going buck wild?*

The cacophony surges on for half an hour until the 4–12 man shows up. No more physically imposing than the 2–10 or me, he isn't flustered. *Get the hell off this cellblock so I can fix this disaster!* I wonder what he thinks of my coworker who has been here for a year. Governing thug black youths with success isn't predicated entirely on size or skin color. More of my ignorance is exposed.

Downstairs at the time clock is Supervisor Mitchell, who teamed with Assistant Superintendent Davis during my individual interview. I've had no contact with Mitchell since then, since he listened to me answer the apple question. What a helpful, relevant-to-managing-4K query that was.

He asks what block I just worked. I tell him.

His eyebrows shoot up, "Wow! Mr. Dostert. You're startin' in the big leagues."

Yeah, wow, Supervisor Mitchell. What a fuckup you are thinking I could be a children's attendant and voting to hire me. Four weeks of shadowing and a week of training lectures have added up to my first cellblock being sent up.

I nod barely and turn my back to Supervisor Mitchell and his gold chains. I head down the stairs and duck myself out of the building.

8

A different supervisor assigns me to 3F on the 4–12 shift for my second day as a real children's attendant. Word about 4K must be fodder for the whole building. But yesterday's meltdown is Supervisor Maywood's fault. No white guy from the suburbs should begin his children's attendant career on the fourth-floor. I'm showing up today in good faith that supervisors will place me on an easier unit. Had I not believed they would, I'd have called in a resignation from my suburban La Grange apartment where I've just moved from my friend's North Side couch. Then I'd mail in my timecard. At least all supervisors aren't incompetent, or like Maywood, devious. Unit 3F's younger inmates are right for me. Stellar Attendant Tucker is off, but 3F's Wednesday 2–10 attendant, exercises a similar command of the inmates. For day three, I'm sent to 3F again, another 4–12. When I walk in, Tucker is at the console while the 8–4 attendant monitors the boys in the TV area.

"Mr. Dostert, how are you?" Attendant Tucker smiles through his salt-and-pepper goatee.

"Okay, glad to be here, look forward to working with you." What I really mean is that I'm ecstatic to escape the Ghetto to a cellblock where no inmate outweighs me. The 8–4 attendant leaves. After signing the logbook, I follow Tucker to the cushioned TV area chairs behind our kids on the five plastic seat rows, interspersed with a couple cushioned seats, each occupied. School has ended. Cartoons are playing until dinnertime.

"I did 8–4 on 4K on Tuesday."

"Oh boy, Mr. Dostert," Tucker winces and adjusts his glasses.

"Yeah, the 2–10 guy I worked with really didn't have control. The 6–2 man was great, but those last two hours weren't good."

I don't tell Attendant Tucker that the juveniles ignored my directives not to talk on the elevator and waylaid their doors while the 8–4 and I stared on dumbfounded. Tucker already feels bad for me. No sense in both of us feeling really bad.

My week's final two shifts are midnight to eight. I draw 3F again, never crossing Supervisor Maywood at the time clock. He does the dayshift.

Everyone is asleep when I arrive and take the console. A boy soon appears in his window, waving his hands and pointing at his cell floor. I stroll over. Water seeps underneath the door from his toilet toward my shoes. "Did you flush it?"

"No, it just started overflowing!"

I open his door, technically a violation because 3F has no overflows on cots and thus no 10–6 attendant. I'm alone. Anything could happen between the kid and me. Forget the rules. The supervisors, one of them at least, had ignored what I'd inferred was an unwritten rule about white Newjacks starting on the Fourth-Floor. With no dim Plexiglas between us, I see the last glistening dribbles of water glistening on the steel bowl's lip, but the toilet is quiet. The boy tiptoes out of the cell alongside the puddle, trousers wadded in his hand. He pulls them on over his boxers, steps into shoes, and zips to the bathroom area to retrieve the mop. The kid's plumbing must malfunction often because he soaks up the water like he's done this before and requests the air freshener canister from the console. Gangly at twelve years old, he sprays his smelly cell, removes his pants and shoes, and crawls back into bed. No bitching about toilet water on his floor. I watch and relock his door, wishing that 4K's residents had flattered me with such flexibility.

On my 2:00 A.M. night log walk-by, as with confinements during daylight, to ensure no inmates, Close Watches or not, have harmed themselves, a different boy is out of bed and hunkered down next to his door window. I stop at his door. Undersized, certainly at fourteen, he'd be no taller than the middle of my biceps, were it not for his willowy half-foot Afro. I remember him from a PE class during school area duty. Right away, I'd noticed this runt among all the huge inmates, hair flopping as he dashed around the basketball court. His slight body and puffy hair made me think of a globe-shaped lollipop on a stick.

One of us says something and then some odd turn of words has him announcing that he "would never work at the Audy Home."

"Why not?"

He looks up at me, as if I, poised on the other side of his Plexiglas, am a crazy person. "And be in here with all these bad kids?"

I definitely prefer 3F to 3G and 4K.

Before the week of classroom training and its subsequent week of split shifts, I advised Supervisor Hilliard that I want 2–10 as my permanent shift. I already wanted to skip the school area as much as possible. Had I waited until after 4K, I vainly would have requested the 12–8 graveyard, so as to avoid the juveniles completely—the strategy of many attendants with high seniority. Administration gives me the 2–10 with Tuesday and Wednesday off. My first 2–10 after training is 3K, where boys range down the age and size scale from 3G inmates but markedly up the scale from 3F's. The 4–12 is a slender woman with dark hair lying on her shoulders. Attendant Valdez is about my age and not half the mass or weight of 3G's Ms. McAdams, who seems right in her element among heftier boys with gang tattoos, shouting and flinging aces and queens onto scratched tables. Nor does Valdez threaten to "whup" anyone's ass. Her cheekbones seem high and defined for a woman who isn't supermodel tall. By my last count, I know of half a dozen female attendants stationed on male blocks, none on the fourth floor. I've met two men who, when asked to, enthusiastically staff 5J and 5K—the only female units. Everyone else warns that the girls will flash us and allege rape. Moreover, their fights are excruciating to stop. One obstinate girl I heard about engaged five staff, two men and three women, to haul her into a cell. The shift with Attendant Valdez comes off without incident. Perhaps directions are more palatable issued from a striking, if gentle, woman. Valdez is a part-time college student who will disclose to a few inmates and me that she once "beat up some people."

I do 3K again. Before dinner I notice Nathan, stocky, in the condition of a soccer player with prominent thighs and a narrow waist, an AT and fifteen, camping out in a chair next to the console. Attendant Valdez is reading from a Bible to him and a couple other boys arranged in a half-circle. They sit close, I suspect, for the same reason that my eyes linger when she leans forward and her snug shirt teases up to expose the rays of an Aztec sun tattooed on the small of her back, the lower rays extending below her jeans. I wonder if Jerome and Terry and their peers had similarly duped me, their interest in my biblical lessons a mere ploy to escape cellblock monotony. I want to clue in Attendant Valdez how Nathan doesn't care for any of the stories she reads him from her Bible. He is far more into reading her curves and, with them, telling himself his own story. I don't tell her. She must be new like me. She must be naïve, but such innocence breeds a nostalgia for the optimism that carried me as a Bible study volunteer. She can't remain naïve forever though, but saying something might embarrass me. And no man wants to embarrass himself with a beautiful woman. Then I'd be the worst kind of Newjack. Or maybe Valdez endures the ogling to communicate her message and with it, care, thus manipulating them while they think they are manipulating her.

"Armed robbery with a firearm," Nathan admits to me at a chess table. His glance tracks off the table, off me, off the players and game we're watching, as if deliberating something serious inside his domed head. He offers no denial of the charge.

In my own head, I count the months of his incarceration and calculate that the two boys convicted of throwing little Eric Morse off that housing project window ledge were still here when Nathan arrived a year ago. One defendant lived on this cellblock. This makes me feel that my children's attendant days connect with my volunteer days when those two suspects were doing their first detainments. And I'm forever curious about how kids perceive each other's alleged crimes. I must ask, "So the older kid who dropped the boy out the window was on 3K?"

Nathan's answer, "Yeah, he was here. I didn't associate with him. He was evil."

I wonder if Nathan considers himself in any way evil for his gun-backed stickup.

As well as 3K is going, no gym calls have come, so I haven't escorted Nathan and his cellblock mates onto the elevator and downstairs to the basement. But we are summoned outside for softball. Attendant Valdez tells me to march them down the hall and into the rec yard. She will remain on unit to monitor our two or three confinements. I sympathize with the boys now—arguing with a pretty woman is hard. After some chatter while lining up and Valdez threatening to banish them back to the TV area, the minute-march through the corridor is quiet. I pull back the door to the rec yard and inhale. Besides exercise, outdoor rec calls offer a breather from the building's stale air. The cellblocks themselves enjoy no ventilation. Worse are the fourth- and fifth-floors where no hallway doors open to Mother Nature. On days without outdoor recreation, three or four weeks worth in winter's true dead, upper-floor inmates filter nothing through their lungs but our institutional air. Third-floor attendants, when heat vents blast, can prop the rec yard door and supplement our usual sour air with icy but fresh city air.

To our right is one of two steel walls eight feet tall, separating the rectangular recreation space into three sections. Should fifty juveniles brawl at once, we can more easily quash the fracas when the gladiators' concrete arena is smaller. Murals of Frederick Douglass, Malcolm X, and Martin Luther King Jr. peer out from the partitions. There may be scant difference between the bondage that Mr. Douglass left on Colonel Lloyd's plantation and what many Audy Home residents escape when they land here. Hopefully some, one, any of our inmates will regenerate themselves from hoodlum to reformer, like Malcolm X following his incarceration. Bugs Bunny, Yosemite Sam, dinosaurs, and abstract patterns painted by juveniles from a since defunct art program adorn other divider wall space—an odd mix of the somber and jovial. The cement playing surface is unpainted. When the facility opened nearly twenty-five years ago, "water sprinklers—for splashing on hot summer days" equipped this area.[1] I spot zero spigots, only steel mesh benches lining the yard's perimeter. Trash and debris scraps collect in corners, some of it no doubt sucked up off Roosevelt Road by the wind and sent over the roof to settle onto our playground. The rest is smuggled down from the cellblocks and stealthily discarded by inmates committing petty acts of defiance to lash back at much greater freedom deprivations. The undecorated portions of the divider walls remain white like all exterior walls of the residential floors enclosing the roofless courtyard. The fifth-floor roof is high enough that, from the courtyard, inmates can't view any of the surrounding city. Aside from the DCFS building, only the blank sky and three stories of our jail are visible—as if the rest of Chicago doesn't exist. What are visible are entire cellblocks with their attendants trailing silently through the three hallway levels like insects moving about in a giant ant farm.

I order 3K onto the nearest benches. The other cellblock arrives, and we play softball with aluminum bats even though a few years ago an inmate rushed another with bat in hand. A street gang shootout had just slayed the bat-wielding kid's brother. Once arrested, the alleged shooter arrived at the Audy Home and rec unknowingly pitted their cellblocks against each other in softball. An attendant restrained the assailant before he meted out his own justice.[2] No 3K inmates bolt from home plate to bludgeon an opponent, but most won't forgive teammates for strikeouts and muffed pop flies.

We're sent outside the next evening into warm but not beastly August dusk. I line them up. They cooperate without much noise, which is encouraging. Confidence up, I pace in front of the formation like an irked commanding officer.

"Don't scream at each other if someone makes a mistake, okay? It's just a game. Have fun with this!" Then I dispatch them onto the cement diamond.

A line drive rips through our second baseman's hands. "Cooommeee ooonnn!" Derrick, an AT the same age as Nathan, berates from third base. He spews more chastisements, as do others.

"Fellas, relax!" I yell from the metal bench behind home plate. "Just play the game!"

Few but Nathan do. He plays without eruption when his peers screw up. I like Nathan now and can't demonize him any more for what I know is his lust for Attendant Valdez, enabled by her good Bible intentions. He makes my job easier. I will soon learn of his sentence—twelve years—and resent his judge, wishing Nathan fewer than twelve years for that armed robbery because of the way he played softball.

In 3K's TV area, Derrick wants to leave for the bathroom area. I let him. Swaggering back on his return, he play-shoves and pushes with an inmate whom I've also excused from the TV area to discard a piece of paper into the rubber trash can near the console.

Arms and hands on each other, they jar a meal table, which skids against the floor.

"No more!" I bark. Derrick and the boy ignore me, grab, and gyrate all the more. I should have waited for one to return before dismissing the other.

"That's enough!"

More horseplay and clutching.

"Step to the wall!" I leave my seat and stride toward them.

Derrick sets his opponent free and sulks to the wall, faces the bricks, and wraps his hands behind his back. His counterpart does not. He sticks like a fence post in the middle of the cellblock near the table he and Derrick knocked themselves into.

"I didn't do nothin'!"

"Step to the wall!" I repeat louder, a few feet from him.

"I didn't do nothin'!"

"Step to your *room*!" I defer to a greater consequence because he's stonewalling the lesser. I refrain from using "cell" aloud, going along with everyone else—kids, attendants, and supervisors. Either way, at last I've figured out behavior modification, a term and process foreign to me before working at the Audy Home. You start soft, then if ineffective, temper to severe—what was quantum physics to me on 4K about six weeks ago.

The inmate, fifteen and slender but with defined shoulders and a trim mid-section, looks past me to my coworker at the console, a well-regarded attendant whom I hear holds a martial arts belt. He could maintain control in 3K without me. Attendant Valdez is off today.

"You better go," my coworker stands up and says.

The kid does.

"Take your shoes off," I tell him at his door.

He does and I lock him inside. At the console I write up a rule violation report. "There you go. You got you a confinement," my colleague says.

In several minutes I finish writing and glance up. Derrick is serving his wall time without swaying his hips or laughing or scuffing his Nikes. I can punish him there a full forty minutes, but he's modified his behavior. To Derrick, who, like Nathan, I am warming to, I call out, "Go ahead and sit down." He returns to the TV area.

A jury soon convicts Derrick, and his judge gives him sixty-six years, and it is too late to modify any behavior.

Without rules to behaviorally modify Derrick, his wrestling mate, and our six hundred other inmates, anarchy would engulf this facility in a Hobbesian state of nature. Even with rules, attending children still seems "a war of every man against every man" with many lives here resonating "nasty, brutish, and short." Our anarchy-avoiding rules have two classifications. Residents violate a minor one by:

1 Talking in the Television Area
2 Standing up without permission
3 Walking around the unit without permission
4 Cursing

5 Challenging staff instruction, talking back to staff, or making negative comments about staff.[3]

"Turn eighteen or don't get locked up," is how one attendant urges inmates to cope with the no cursing dictum. He curses plenty at the inmates himself though. When a juvenile commits one such minor infraction, we can counsel him, that is walk him through his mistake and give him pointers on how not to mess up again, give him wall time, or banish him to his cell for a cooling off period, not to exceed sixty minutes. If a juvenile really agitates us, we can plant him in a chair along that same wall until bedtime. Worse than an hour in his cell or forty minutes counting bricks, he misses everything then, including television.

To isolate an inmate in his cell for more than an hour, much less confine him there, pending a supervisor or caseworker's verdict after reading our report, he must have done something major:

1 Security Risk, including using false identity, walking off unit, attempting to escape, being out of assigned area, entering another resident's room, refusing to give identity when asked.
2 Physical assault on staff, including, but not limited to, threatening, intimidating, cursing, punching, hitting with something in one's hands, pushing, kicking, and biting.
3 Physical assault on resident, including threatening, intimidating, cursing, punching, hitting with something in one's hands.
4 Contraband, which includes articles that are: a. Readily capable of being used to cause death, serious physical injury or aid in escape, including, but not limited to, money, weapons, explosives, controlled substances, alcohol, inhalants, medications, tools, other sharp objects, cigarettes, lighters, and matches; b. If possessed, are prohibited under any law applicable to the general public (such as illegal substances); and c. Unauthorized

and in the possession of the resident or in the resident's room.

5 Deliberate destruction/defacing of facility property, including of JTDC/school property, including writing on desks, walls, doors, tearing T-shirts, digging into walls and tearing mattresses.

6 Uncooperative, defiant attitude, including not following instructions.

7 Gang activity involvement, including discussions about gangs, representing gangs, writing gang graffiti, possessing gang literature, using gang language, using gang references in conversation, or handshakes or other gang symbolism.

8 Fighting with resident(s), regardless of who starts the fight.

9 Disruption of group activities, including behavior contrary to what is expected of residents, e.g., being loud and noisy, not following routines, horsing around.

10 Theft from resident or staff.

11 Sex-related incidents, including patting, petting, touching. Persistent verbalization about sex with a resident(s).

12 Throwing or shoving furniture in resident room in a destructive manner.

13 Gambling.[4]

All these minor and major prohibitions are to modify the juveniles' behavior—progressively eliminating more and more privileges until misbehaving becomes unpleasant enough that they behave. This worked with Derrick but not with Derrick's pal. One attendant preaches about enforcing the rules in such stringent manner that we don't "let the kids be assholes." It isn't enough to ask them to follow the rules because the rules are the rules, and they are in jail. Cellblock 4K taught me that. Should the infraction be subject to criminal prosecution, like an inmate hiding drugs, we notify administration, which then notifies law enforcement. Whether or not we contact police, we instruct the violator to enter his cell. Some children's attendants use, "Step to your room." Others, "Step to yo' house!" or, "Step to yo' crib!" or even, "Step to yo' shit!" Particular coworkers brand anything "shit" or "my shit," be it their clothes, their food, their personal business, or contents of their duffel bag. Whatever we call it—shit, house, room, or cell—if a kid does something major, he must go there. If he refuses our command, we're not to touch him unless he poses danger to himself, other juveniles, Cook County property, or us. Instead we summon a caseworker or supervisor. If they show up and can't cajole the inmate into a cell, then the group of us must *place* or *put* him there. That way, any injuries will be witnessed. Should an inmate lunge at us, Policy And Procedure does govern the use of force. "Justifiable self-defense, protection of staff and residents, protection of property, and prevention of escapes" are the only instances when force can be applied—"only as last resort." It can't be punishment, and "only the least force necessary under the circumstances shall be employed."[5] So there are rules to govern our application of the rules.

Juveniles like Derrick's cohort who jeered my wall-time command aren't the only persons at the Audy Home subject to reports. Should an inmate believe that a children's attendant has not applied "the least force necessary," or abused him another way, he can write a grievance. Worthy offenses include "action or inaction which results in death, brain damage, skull fractures, internal injuries, wounds, sexually transmitted diseases, sexual penetration, sexual exploitation, sexual molestation, burns, scalding, poisoning, bone fractures, cuts, bruises, welts, human bites, sprains, dislocations, tying, close confinement, substance misuse and mental injury."[6] The 4K boys caused me "mental injury," that is for damn sure, but I can't file a grievance against them. If a juvenile complains about us though, we must provide him a grievance form and a pen or pencil. The appropriate floor manager then has fifteen days to investigate. If the allegation is serious, the caseworker contacts the Illinois DCFS Hot Line (1-800-25ABUSE) and completes a Child Abuse Hot Line Report. DCFS then decides whether the complaint is "indicated—guilty, or unfounded—innocent."[7] Superintendent Doyle implemented this procedure. So now DCFS has a much greater presence inside the building, according to veteran staffers who complain that prior to Doyle, DCFS rarely interviewed us. Doyle's predecessor "handled everything in house." Attendant Edison has told me that Doyle warned his new-hire group in orientation that if they mistreated any juvenile, he would "personally ensure" that they would "never hold another job working with children." To the *Chicago Tribune* two years ago, he said, "If you treat them hard, they will come out harder."[8] I agree with Doyle. Treat a kid like shit, odds are, first chance he has, he treats the world like shit. But with no effective alternatives, a boy staring at three walls for a couple of nights and days, still emerging to mingle for an hour in the rec yard with other confinees after screaming vulgarities at a grown man or breaking another inmate's nose, I believe, is not treating a kid hard.

When grievance accusations are valid though, some children's attendants devise ways to discredit what inmates allege on these forms. Attendant Tucker from 3F often shuttles me to Union Station after work for my commuter train ride home to La Grange. But tonight Tucker is off, a younger guy in a cap and track pants offers. He just signed his first mortgage and the house is near Metra's first stop after Union Station. Colleagues tooling around in newer cars jab fun at his jalopy. He counters that he simply devotes his money to "a crib" instead of a car.

"There's been times when I know I should've gotten twenty-nine days. But it's all in the way you write your report," he says to me, steering his battered Oldsmobile down to the parking garage's exit.

"What do you mean?" I'm curious why this husky but short attendant about my age once merited the maximum suspension—"twenty-nine and pending"—twenty-nine unpaid days off and no guarantee of reinstatement.

"By writing a good report, you cover your ass. One time, a kid told me he didn't want a room because it was too hot and that he wanted to be an overflow so he could sleep on a cot."

Audy Home cell windows don't open. Cell temperatures match what can be the building's seasonal temperatures—sticky or chilly.

"I told him: 'Tough shit. It's not about what you want, it's about what we want. And we assigned you to that room.' He said he still wasn't gonna go to sleep in the room. So I started pushing him in the room and the motherfucker swung on me. Dude, I dropped the keys, threw my chain inside my shirt, and started kickin' his ass."

"So you hit the kid?"

"Hell yeah I hit him! I grabbed him and gave him a bunch of rib shots, then hit him in the face a bunch a times. Busted his lip and slammed him down and pushed his face in the floor. By that time he was cryin' like a little baby, 'I'm sorry! I'm sorry!'"

"What happened after that?"

"He slept in that room like I told him to."

"You never took any heat for it?" I ask as we motor onto Western Avenue from Ogden.

"Oh, yeah, he wrote a grievance and told a caseworker that I fucked his lip up."

"So how did you not get twenty-nine days if the kid's lip was actually cut?"

"Again, it's all in how you phrase your report. I just wrote that the resident became hostile and had to be restrained. In the process of restraining him, his face accidentally bumped the wall and his lip was injured."

"So then did you get any time off at all?"

"Hell no, 'cause I covered myself with that report. As long as I turned it in, there wasn't shit the kid could say."

Other coping strategies exist as well when juveniles incite us to crave a world without rules, a world of freely exacted revenge—Hobbes's state of nature. "Dostert, I'll never forget the night I got sucker-punched right in the jaw," an attendant who grew up a block from the Audy Home recounts. Attendant Simons, too, often runs me to Union Station after our 2–10. He's my age too and started here my final months as a volunteer.

While I studied European religious history at University of North Texas in quiet Denton-on-the-prairie, Simons worked as a Chicago children's attendant and was slugged.

Attendant Simons is detouring tonight, but assures that I'll make my train, maneuvering his sedan into an alley between two blocks of tri-level row houses, the kind where the entire block is one continuous building. Simons stops his car with the engine running and exits to unlock his trunk. He lifts out a plastic grocery bag of clothes and sets it on the pavement next to a garage door. Confused, I wait for him to reverse out of the byway and into the street before I say anything. Simons explains that he was raised in this very residence and homeless Chicagoans rummage the alleyway during the dead of night. "Why throw the clothes away, if someone else can use them?" Never has he discovered his sack there the next day. Now he lives up near O'Hare Airport. But those who need the extra clothing don't know he is gone.

"What happened?" I ask about the blow to his jaw.

Traffic is snaking slower than normal along Jackson Boulevard. Something just ended at Chicago Stadium's replacement, United Center. I always know when the Bulls or Blackhawks play or when a megaband performs by the noticeable contingent of not-so-cheap sedans and suburbans that otherwise don't venture into this ward.

"It was a Sunday night two or three summers ago. I had the overflows lined up at the door. It was so damn hot that night that I only gave out one sheet to each kid. But this one bastard starts complaining and crying for another sheet. I told him one sheet was all he was gettin.' But then I made the mistake of turning my back to him."

To transport overflow inmates to a sleeper block, we line them single-file at the door. The inmates pull out their pockets, hike up their pants cuffs, and lift their shirts above their waistlines to flush out any contraband. Bed sheets are shaken, refolded, and placed under their left arm. Right hand goes into the pants pocket, and the attendant marches them to their assigned unit where cots are set up. Attendant Simons executed all this on that stuffy summer evening, but faced himself away from a particular inmate before uttering his command for all of them to step through the doorway.

"I never saw it coming."

"What'd you do?"

"There was nothing much I could do. By the time I spun back around, the other two staff had swarmed him before I could get my hands on him."

Because its inmate count ran unusually high that night, supervisors had assigned his block a third attendant. The other two forced the kid into a cell, and Simons drove himself to a hospital for X-rays. Cook County didn't reimburse him for the gas he burned traveling there.

"It was out to here," he poises his right palm an inch away from the side of his face to recreate how severely the punch had swelled his jaw.

One of the intervening attendants asserted to Simons before he left, "He'll get a blanket party tomorrow night." Following lights-out when all juveniles would be locked in their cells and the overflows delivered to a sleeper unit, he and Attendant Simons, although neither unusually muscled or imposing figures, planned to open the boy's door and cloak him with blankets. The covers would mitigate their blows. No bruises. The next afternoon Simons reported for work. No fractures, but he pressed an assault charge against the inmate. The court though never contacted Simons about testifying against the juvenile, nor was he ever advised as to his litigation's resolution. Attendant Simons checked his unit's roll board. His attacker was no longer housed there. A caseworker had transferred him to another cellblock.

Simons eases his car to a stop along Jackson in front of the south Union Station entrance just in time for my 10:36 P.M. train. "So I never got a chance to even the score."

Some evenings, Children's Attendant Simons plants care packages for Chicago's most impoverished. Others, he schemes to bludgeon one of its incarcerated kids in the dark in his bed.

Even with our rules to derive order, rules I'm slowly comprehending and applying, the Audy Home induces an otherwise altruistic coworker from my own generation to bloodlust to do something bad, perpetuating that "war of every man against every man." Now I worry that some similar inmate exploit will soon boil over my latent bloodlust, and I too will plot to beat a kid.

9

From my apartment parking lot I turn north onto Brainard Avenue and cruise past well-kept Georgian and Ranch-style homes, bright flowerbeds nestled in their tidy yards. Also close is a forest preserve and picnic-tabled clearing where families barbecue on weekends. Even with new luxury condos overlooking the village center, La Grange is unmistakably suburban and simulates where I grew up—quiet, each household owning more than one motorized vehicle, few dark faces, and a lot of children playing soccer and riding bikes to school. In a way I did grow up here. It's ironic now that my dad's family migrated to La Grange from Chicago's Kelvyn Park precinct fifty years ago. I limited my apartment search to certain suburbs because of the high safety-to-affordability ratio. Residing as well in this protected enclave, I too never fret about gangbangers shooting out my streetlights or not being able to shop for groceries because I can't afford a car and taxi drivers have boycotted my blighted block.

A mile up Brainard, the eastbound Burlington Northern Santa Fe Metra commuter train will stop one street over at Stone Avenue halfway along the train's hour and a half journey from far-flung Aurora to Union Station in Chicago's downtown Loop. From day shift training and the 8–4 disaster on 4K, I remember the weekday morning passengers in their slacks and ties, skirts and jackets, clutching steaming paper cups of joe, many clad in Reeboks for a hike to an office somewhere in the skyscraper labyrinth, stepping onto the train like automatons. But my train today, the 1:00 P.M. pickup, elicits skateboarding teens lured by Lake Michigan's rustic seawall and families bound for Grant Park, the Museum of Science and Industry, and seasonal slews of neighborhood festivals. My jeans and solid T-shirt render me one of these leisurely travelers. Yet once in Chicago, our agendas will diverge. I doubt a single other commuter here is aware that half of Audy Home inmates were born to teen mothers.[1] My fellow suburbanites have never heard of the Four Corner Hustlers either. They know nothing about hypes and TEC-9s.

Most passengers linger outside the station rather than swelter on the pew-like wooden benches inside. Except for the tiny ticket office window, the old arched rock edifice lacks air conditioning. I enter despite the clammy depot air, preferring to sit when antsy, still disturbed by 4K and my 2–10 coworker there, hardly neutralized by my relative successes on 3K.

"Twenty-three-forty," the lone Metra worker, a dumpy man with white hair trimmed almost to his wrinkled scalp, announces in a lilt behind a deep glass window. Someone has requested a ten-ride ticket. Monthly passes are $74.25. If Metra charged according to the diversity of terrain their cars streak through, my budget would force me to drive.

The ticket line finishes and the worker emerges from the office. He stands in front of the benches and chats with travelers about how on weekends he and his wife venture up to Wisconsin to visit their daughter and her family. Idling on one of these benches, I picture my college friend Joe and his wife Beth in their charmed Wisconsin surroundings and crave meandering down those country lanes. It is Friday and I'd love to spend tomorrow or Sunday grilling burgers again and giving ear to Bob Uecker's quirky Brewers baseball radio play-by-play at my friends' wood frame abode nestled in Kenosha County's slight hills of corn and soybean. Instead I'm about to deal with young men birthed by teen moms now adopted by the Gangster Disciples, Vice Lords, Latin Kings, and 2–6 Nation who may, particularly if I land somewhere like 4K again, blurt, "Nah, fuck that!" when I tell them not to talk in the TV area. And how I respond to that one juvenile will determine for the shift's remainder what other inmates do—whether they win and "act a fool," or I win and they speak in even tones and ask permission to stand up.

"Weeell, I think I see a headlight," the ticket worker drawls, lifting his chin to gaze out the station's back window. He moseys outside. The other passengers and I follow him.

The train pulls up and the motorman steps off one of the railcars holding a large envelope marked: Mail—Stone Avenue. I speculate on its contents so as not to think about supervisors returning me to 4K or 4-anything. My dream shift remains 3F every day. I hear one of them say, "Have a good weekend." I must log three more shifts before my weekend—Tuesday and Wednesday.

From La Grange to the Loop, the train slides by the Brookfield Zoo and thirty blocks south of a Queen Anne Victorian where Ernest Hemingway was born in 1899. But the kids I have a date with today are meditating more on their missed "herb" smoking while incarcerated than on an old salt and a feisty fish. Riverside's trackside cafés come next. After Berwyn and Cicero, we penetrate Chicago. My reading material, a book on urban crime and poverty by renowned University of Chicago professor William Julius Wilson, falls to my lap. My stomach tightens. My bladder is filling. Cityscape outside my train seat window won't let me pretend, as I do fleetingly on off days, that inner-city turmoil transplanted into a giant steel and brick box, be it 3G punks revving for a brawl near the elevator, all of 4K attacking their cell doors, or every sad event outside the giant steel and brick box facilitating this turmoil, is someone else's dilemma. For the next eight hours, the turmoil will be mine. The sleek line of silver cars zips north and east by shotgun houses and scrubby parks and factories and wails to a halt on an aging weed-covered viaduct over Western Avenue near 18th Street—the stop closest to the jail. I climb off alone. Next the train will curve northward into cavernous Union Station. Were this my day off, I would exit there, too, and wander blissfully along Oak Street Beach or meet a friend for Thai satay in Roscoe Village and not care if brawls loom on 3H or 4B or 5E because Renegade Vice Lords outnumber Black Disciples there.

Metra once staffed this elevated ticket booth. I peek through the window frames, their glass panes knocked out. On the floor are window shards, other rubbish, and a shattered Olde English

Forty bottle. I turn from the booth and move along the platform toward the stairs. Squiggles of spray paint and magic marker deface the walls, as well as billboards posted above warped wooden benches for waiting passengers—benches warped more from years of wind and rain and melting snow than from riders hunkering down on them. Few people catch the train here anymore. I descend a concrete stairway that smells of urine onto a pockmarked sidewalk littered with gravel underneath the overgrown trestle. Exhaust from dump trucks and eighteen-wheelers rumbling through hangs in the dank air like Chesterfield smoke at a corner bar.

My cross-trainers churn north over more ravaged pavement, cluttered with pebbles, concrete chunks, and glass bits. Wind-blown shreds of truck tire and weather-beaten cardboard plaster against portions of a rusting chain link fence taller than me. This train and foot journey saves thirty-two round trip wear-and-tear miles on my Toyota—worth more than any possession I'm carrying, stiff-legging my way up Western Avenue. Moreover, I'm nervous about inmates who climb onto overturned bed frames and look out their windows. Those housed on the jail's east perimeter can see across Hamilton Avenue to our parking garage and note what vehicles we drive. Some have threatened to blow up our cars or have hit men wait for us. "Yeah, you drive that little green car," a kid quipped one day. My Tercel is teal, but his watching me further motivates my usual train commute to work. I hedge onto Ogden Avenue after several sweaty minutes and now am parallel with the Acme Barrel Company, a factory abutting the sidewalk. On the exterior, it could stand in for a long flat chocolate cake with no decorative tufts of pastel icing. Manufacturing odors blast me from open portals. Oily brown grime crusts the path under my worn-out Nikes. I've stowed newer shoes in my duffel bag. At the factory's corner I pass a dented barrel stuffed with crumpled Budweiser cans and cartons and skirt from Ogden's diagonal swath onto West Roosevelt Road. Jamming my heels into the pavement, I stride east along the south perimeter of my destination's massive rectangular prism.

More vacant lots than storefronts line this six-lane stretch of

Roosevelt. The few structures bordering its south edge across from the Audy Home include the Greater New Friendship Missionary Baptist Church, the Triple-A Grocery, and six or seven gray and beige tenement-styled buildings, most abandoned with empty window spaces. Billboards, some bolted to sides of faded brick buildings, others topping short steel posts, rise from the desolate lots. They advertise KOOL smokes, Heineken lager, and Martell Cognac to passing motorists, bus riders, and the occasional pedestrian—no tourists window-shop their way through this part of town. Neither do I, already coping with stress for my shift. I scarcely detect a figure in the corner of my right eye, a kid, I doubt older than sixteen.

"Eeeeyyyyy, you still up in that mothafucker?" he saunters across Roosevelt, head thrown back, squinting up into the afternoon sun at a silhouette positioned in a fifth-floor cell window on what must be an overturned bed frame. The sidewalk boy's words bounce off the immovable fortress and reverberate through the industrialized late August air.

I keep walking.

"You gotta pen?" he blurts, now behind me on the sidewalk.

I whirl around. Dark jeans and an untucked blank white undershirt outline his taut frame. I extract a black ballpoint from my bag.

"That's aahhhiight, I got one." He yanks a writing utensil of his own from a pants' pocket, as if he had planned to bluff me all along and looks back into the sky, scribbling on his palm as the inmate flashes him finger numbers.

The young man in the window must be new to jail life; he assumes that his friend can ring him up while he is locked down. But signaling his pal our phone number won't land them any closer than they are right now. "Up in here," as the juveniles say, they receive no phone calls. Policy and procedure grants them five minutes a week to dial out. They must settle on calling mom (their "old girl" or "Old G") or calling their favorite actual girl, hoping she hasn't met someone else in their incarcerated absence and is calling every other guy on her block.

At the front desk, supervisors return me to 3K and Attendant

Valdez. I dodge the bullet for yet another shift. Despite the manageable duty and growing sequence of days separating me from 4K, it is evident that juveniles surly over losing verbal touch with kin and companion is hardly the only downside of their being locked up inside the Audy Home, hardly the only obstacle obstructing my philanthropic aspirations left over from my volunteer Monday nights here with Chaplain Rick.

10

"Dostert, 3D," the time clock supervisor says on the Friday before Labor Day. "Two to four there and then four to ten on Medical." Since becoming a 2–10, I've been floating, filling in for attendants taking vacation, personal days, or sick days. I have a regular shift but no regular cellblock like Attendant Walton has 3G or Attendant Tucker has 3F. Feasibly, every new day can mean a new cellblock and a new coworker—a new, more veteran coworker who goes by the book or one who runs his own program. I know little about 3D, so the new assignment sinks my stomach some, but it's only a couple hours. And Medical doesn't scare me. The inmates rarely leave their cells.

School is out today—a four-day holiday weekend for the teachers downstairs. The 3D inmates are on unit and the 6–2 man passes me at the console heading out. The 8–4 nods with no smile, slumped against the back wall of the TV area, monitoring boys there. From this distance, the outline of his head and his stomach are prominent, like the middle and upper contours of a snowman. Physically unexercised as the 8–4 attendant appears, the boys are behaving. The unit is calm. Other juveniles mill around the ping-pong table where a game is in progress. Most inmates match 3G boys in size. Several are fifteen- and sixteen-year-old ATs like G-shots Reginald, but without the overt antagonism of the 4K assholes. Still, these collectively are the biggest inmates on the third floor. As with 3G, skin tones here shade every seemingly possible brown. The lone white kid has the bushy hair of a circus clown. Squat and far from slim at the waist, he ambles with a limp and is an AT too, but his face seems cognizant of everyone around him in a way that, to me, deconstructs a felony suspect's stereotypically sullen, belligerent stare. I feel racially prejudiced again, positing this white kid more innocent than his darker peers based merely on his disposition during my first glance. The older the inmates, the more I worry about race, so to prove I'm no bigot, I'll mix myself in with them right away.

I go to the ping-pong table. In a few volleys, the game ends and the losing player rests his paddle on the table. I pick it up to take on the winner.

Another juvenile darts up. "Hey, I got next!"

"Oh, okay," I feel rude and hand him the paddle.

Backing away toward the cell row, I watch. The inmates start a new game and snicker at each other. I'm not sure why.

To my left, the 8–4's shoulders twitch, and he stands up and storms over, "Boy, what the hell is your problem! You know staff plays whenever we want!"

Nothing from the juvenile. Thirty pounds heavier than me and nearly forty years old, my coworker crowds the kid, a head taller with his open mouth inches from the boy's nose.

"Go to your room, son!"

No chiseled muscle statue, this attendant remains coercive. The boy surrenders the paddle and cowers to his cell. The 8–4 follows and locks him in. An inmate in the TV area must have noticed the gag, leaned over, and tipped him off.

The other inmate and I begin serving and returning. I keep score, but am too embarrassed to look him in the face while calling out numbers. I extended an olive branch to prove I'm not here to make incarceration any more miserable than it already is. One inmate has snapped my olive branch to pieces and stomped it under foot. We finish the game in silence. I want to quit and he doesn't suggest another match. I want to quit because the more I patronize any 3D kid, even one who hasn't directly mocked me, the bigger the chump I am. I should have ignored them, so as to come off seasoned and not "get played" trying to be humane. If an inmate can trick me out of a ping-pong game, he can trick me out of anything.

"Everyone have a seat in the TV area!" the 8–4 barks, never moving from his position in the back row.

My ping-pong opponent and the inmates at card tables drop their aces and jacks and follow instructions. I tag along, suspecting a lecture. I need to sponge off any attendant who controls his cellblock like this 8–4. The kid who weaseled me off the ping-pong table didn't balk at cell banishment. He isn't pounding his door either.

"You're too loud and you forgot the four-to-a-table rule!" my coworker starts before the last inmate is seated.

A few inmates had repositioned extra chairs alongside full tables of card players. The 8–4 says zero about the kid chumping me, I suspect, because he doesn't wish me further humiliated.

"We'll sit our asses right here and think about it for a while. And do *not* forget that if you act a fool, and I tell you to step to your room and you don't step, I'll escort you to your room! And I'll try to break an arm or a leg. It's happened before and nothin' was done to me because I'm authorized to restrain you."

I had no honest idea we should rule this strictly—forbid a kid from moving a chair. But eight or ten chairs ringing a four-chair table would appear sloppy to a supervisor. Any attendant busting limbs is news to me, but I've only been here seven weeks. With a mumbling attendant leaping out a window and supervisors brandishing baseball bats to squash riots for fodder, a fractured arm on an uncooperative kid probably went under-publicized. The boys don't respond, looking like they believe my coworker's every word. They just swivel their heads back around toward the screen.

We supervise until 4:00 P.M. when Attendant Pruitt, who during training in the school area told me about seeing only "seven or eight white guys work here," steps into the cellblock near the console. An attendant from my new-hire group, Jensen, follows him.

I remember Jensen from the one day of orientation when Supervisor Hilliard taught us about cell searches and mystery bonfires. Attendant Jensen is shorter than me and skinny. His hair isn't Afro-long, but its moderate length seems outdated for an adult. A permanent smile expands his gap-toothed face. He's a part-time minister, and I'll overhear him talking about a

"Weekend Healing and Miracles Crusade." He should pray for miracles in this place. How about a Newjack like me running 4K without any screaming inmates pounding their cell doors? Looking across the training room at Jensen, I'd posited myself a more capable children's attendant, the only such rookie about whom I leveled this criticism. Jensen grins too often. *Let's see if we can find you both an apple*, I imagine him responding to Assistant Superintendent Davis's apple question. But after 4K and now being fooled off a 3D ping-pong table, I'm better than no one. Floaters like Jensen and me and overtimers like Pruitt are here today because 3D's regular 2–10 attendant is taking the holiday weekend off, and there is no regular 4–12 attendant. Nothing bad ever happens though with the regular 2–10, sized like a rain barrel from the waist up. Elmer Fudd could do 4–12 here. Passing 3D, I've always noticed juveniles through the glass wall walking, talking, standing, and sitting—controlled and civil. Today Attendant Jensen will play Elmer Fudd while Attendant Pruitt scores six hours of time and a half because a supervisor doesn't trust me with a moonlighting pastor or trust a moonlighting pastor with me.

The 8–4 leaves, but I follow him to the console, where Attendant Pruitt is signing in, and lag there before heading to Medical. I want to see how Pruitt opens a shift. He whacks the TV switch on the console panel. The screen zaps blank and heads whip around to us.

"Line up!" Attendant Pruitt hollers and moves out from behind the huge desk, eyeballs cocked at the TV area. He stops halfway between the console and the cell fronts.

Attendant Jensen and I idle behind him at the console. Many staff and even some juveniles affectionately call Pruitt's 4C unit "Camp C"—as in Boot Camp C. Pruitt is no rogue fourth-floor attendant. Boot Camp permits no drugs or porn or unpunished vice.

The boys upright, file out with no chatter, and form a shoulder to shoulder line in front of the cell doors as if for a spot search after school or recreation. With no one looking at the floor or walls, they face Pruitt, who wears a black and yellow Negro Leagues replica baseball jersey.

"Gentlemen, I'm Mr. Pruitt. I don't expect any problems tonight. If there are, I don't have any problem poppin' these doors and puttin' you to bed early." He pauses. The boys say nothing and move nothing. "Any questions?"

"No sir," they answer together. No way would the slick kid now bolted behind his cell door fathom scheming this man out of a ping-pong game.

"Level fours, take a step forward."

Three inmates donning bird-less gold shirts move up.

"I don't work with anyone but fours. So you guys are my kitchen. Stay right here. Everyone else back to the TV area."

Without cringe or complaint, the twenty other juveniles, all in white bird-shirts because they are level ones, twos, and threes in the behavior management system, relocate to seats facing the screen. No one is back there with them, yet no one talks.

"All right, I can't stand filth. Get the broom and dustpan and sweep the unit down," Attendant Pruitt directs the three level fours.

For this they will earn additional task points and secure their level four shirt for next week. The floor does need cleaning. Paper scraps and balls of lint and hair are gathered along the base of the walls. Given the ping-pong trickery and the 8–4's menacing speech, I missed the "filth." The 8–4 has worked 3D for years, so even had the clutter caught my eye, I wouldn't have suggested tidying up. But 3D is Attendant Pruitt's block now.

A supervisor returns me to 3D and Medical on Saturday. Pruitt and Jensen arrive at 4:00 P.M., and I work the infirmary for another six hours. In addition to the nurses' exam room, the medical block has nearly thirty cells in which we *medically isolate* the juveniles for much of the day while they convalesce after surgery. Others are assigned here should their initial medical screening determine that they need twenty-four-hour medical or psychiatric supervision—anything from the flu to schizophrenia to bipolar disorder. An investigative panel of juvenile corrections consultants will soon declare that Dr. Jacobs and his part-time psychiatrist are "inadequate to treat depression and other mental health issues suffered by many of the youths." Additionally, our facility exhibits "a woeful lack of programming and counseling."[1] A teenage girl isolated here recently swallowed the batteries from her transistor radio. One chunky kid pacing his cell, rubbing his hands over his round shaved head, insists that he is nineteen, not sixteen, and should be held at the county jail, not the Audy Home. When an inmate in a neighboring cell squawks an insult, I catch the finale of the stout kid's booming omen of a reply: "—when I shove my dick up your ass!" Judges also designate certain defendants for *court-order isolation* in Medical because they are charged with molesting another child or sport such notoriety that administrators fear other juveniles planting a hit on them if housed with the general population. Dr. Jacobs isolates some here for protection if they're overtly homosexual. One current Medical boy, tall and with loose seemingly permed Afro curls, allegedly offered food to cellblock mates for the promise of "letting him give them a blowjob" during shower time, should the attendant on shower-duty step away. On Medical we shower the inmates individually in one of two separate bathrooms. We only let inmates out a couple at a time to the TV room—formerly two cells with the adjoining wall knocked out. Recreation staff picks them up a few at a time, those who are physically and socially able, for trips to the rec yard. So medical duty is the facility's easiest assignment, amounting to eight hours of fifteen-minute walk-bys to initial the Medical log. The supervisor arranging this must know what the supervisor who put me on 3F the day after 4K knew. As importantly, he isn't like Maywood. He has no wish to "fuck with" me. I'm glad for at least two compassionate supervisors.

Cellblock 3D is my only assignment on Sunday. Supervisor Taftmont, not the supervisor who anchored 3D with Pruitt the previous two days, says nothing about Medical. I'm tempted to ask if I'll be doing the entire shift on 3D, but don't. Of all the supervisors, Taftmont seems the most misplaced. He doesn't resemble a stereotype—the pimp, the drill sergeant, the boxer's aging trainer, the potbellied mechanic with tiny holes in his thin shirt. He doesn't seem one to "fuck with" people. Standing behind the small desk near the time clock, Taftmont is tall but average in physique. His mellow voice reminds me of being anywhere but inside the Audy Home. Some attendants grumble about his promotion to supervisor, alleging, "He knows someone." Taftmont likes collared shirts and is proper enough that I'm hesitant to challenge his direction, as if doing so would be doubly rude of me.

The same 8–4 is here again. A few of the inmates smirk, and I look away. As preparation for Sunday visitation, my coworker orders every juvenile into the TV area at 2:15 P.M. where they will remain until 4:30 unless a parent or grandparent or legal guardian shows up. The 8–4 plants himself there too and tells me to man the console to sign in visitors. We eventually trade locations at ten minutes to the hour so when the 4–12 arrives, he can sign out in the logbook and depart from the console, which is much closer to the cellblock door.

I twist in my TV area seat from a nervous urge to urinate. The nearer the clock ticks to 4:00 and the 8–4's departure, my head swings right in quicker clips toward the unit door. The National Football League season opened at noon, but I can't enjoy any of the Cowboys-Steelers game the 8–4 tuned in before taking the console.

Elmer Fudd enters 3D. The 8–4 hands Attendant Jensen the cellblock keys and walks out. Jensen sits down at the console.

I hope Attendant Pruitt's 4C relief is late and that he is heading down here for more easy overtime and the phone is about to ring and wise Supervisor Taftmont will instruct Jensen, "Tell Dostert that I need him on Medical for the rest of the day."

4:15: still no Attendant Pruitt.

A random supervisor speaks on the intercom for all visitors to exit the cellblocks. I want them to stay. The five or six tabled inmates have been civilized with their moms and grandmoms and an uncle or two in front of them, as are the eighteen others with me in the TV area. But visitors can't stay. Now it is my turn to render the inmates civilized. The half-dozen boys remain at the tables as their visitors stand up. Once they are gone, I'm going to do what Pruitt did—kill the TV and in my sternest tone enunciate, "Line Up!"

Our last parent moves through the door into the hallway, and as if on cue, Attendant Jensen bolts away from the console. On Pruitt's spot from yesterday, he yells, "Okay, who wants one of these!" and waves a blank rule violation form above his head like he's enraged. "Now everyone line up right here!"

Inmates in front of him cackle and hoot and slap their tables.

"Let's go. Line up, gentlemen," I say, deflated, to those in the TV area.

I've all but apologized for my coworker egging them on to misbehave, as if his doing so will induce good behavior. I call the inmates "gentlemen," borrowing from Attendant Pruitt in a grasp to set into motion a counter self-fulfilling prophecy to Jensen's masquerading as some badass taunting inmates to stamp out potential misbehavior. Jensen can't be himself and be a children's attendant on 3D, not working with me instead of Pruitt. He did nothing like this yesterday. Attendant Jensen was his usual God-loves-you-and-so-do-I self.

I straggle toward Jensen in front of the other boys who are milling about underneath the clock in front of the cell doors as if Pruitt and the 8–4's absence has ripped the veil of civility, never to be mended. Over scoffing interruptions whose individual words aren't registering, we try to warn them in their semblance of a line about acting up. Neither of us knows what to say now. Two Elmer Fudds are working 3D today.

Then I remember that we must strip-search any inmate with visitor contact. "If you had a visitor, sit back down at a table! If not, go back to the TV area!"

Some do. Most do not. They act like being ordered to the TV area is a brand new concept, reminiscent of 4K and my attempted marching lines after school. Should anyone have pocketed contraband from mom or grandma or guardian, they already could have slipped it to someone who had remained in the TV area, visit-less. Instead of flailing his arms and ranting,

Jensen should have beelined from the console to the bathroom area and individually summoned the visited inmates to execute the searches while I continued to isolate everyone else in the TV area.

Behind the console, I dig into my duffel bag for a pair of rubber gloves. I stretch them on and stride past the tables for the bathroom area. Noticing other attendants gloving their hands for strip inspections gave me this idea. Up to now, veteran attendants have facilitated the post-visitation disrobings. And I never worked 3K with Attendant Valdez on a Sunday when strip-down duty would have fallen exclusively to me.

"You gonna stick your finger up our asses?" A juvenile still meandering around the tables choreographs his extended index finger in an upward spiral.

My head twitches in his vicinity, but I jerk it still without seeing his eyes.

Eye contact would maximize his disrespect and gratification. I associate prostate exams with middle-aged white men working coveted jobs with coveted health insurance, having learned of rectal probes from my dad when he admitted to enduring one. This poor black inner-city kid being hip to such a procedure depresses me. Like Arthur during training weeks on 3G stunning me with "Opie," I know much less about dysfunctional urban youth than I think I do. I should send this particular dysfunctional urban youth to the bricks for wall time, yet I'm too discombobulated to hit him with a directive and doubt I could enforce it while doing the strip searches. I'm desperate to finish and herd these half-dozen boys to the TV area—the best location for Attendant Jensen and me to reconstruct order.

After Jensen's taunt and the kid whipping his finger through the air, the finger that he mocked as mine up his rectum, the next four and a half hours become a Rorschach blotch. I miss steps in the strip searches. I don't make each kid turn his socks inside out. I don't run my gloved fingers along the seam in their trouser waistbands for tears where cigarettes or rolled-up dollar bills might be stashed. I miss things all shift, and I miss things that I don't know I miss. Jensen and I waste our voices in the TV area because the boys won't shut the hell up. We put some on the wall, but this many jabbering at once vexes us to single out each offender. Our imprecise rule enforcement elicits: "He was talkin' too!"

We don't know what to do. I've yet to see competent attendants deal with an entire TV area blabbing simultaneously. Entire TV areas never blab simultaneously with competent attendants in charge. Attendant Jensen's challenging the boys to misbehave is being met.

Before dinner, Attendant Chambers from Medical stops in. He's burly with a wispy mustache. I met him yesterday during my 2–4 there, and we discussed his Cubs' fading playoff odds. He has noticed disarray through the glass wall. Eyes wide, Chambers joins us in the TV area.

"Why you guys actin' like this?" he calls at the boys from next to me on the back row. He reminds the inmates of when he filled in on 3D and they had behaved. Like Attendant Pruitt, Chambers never looks ruffled or disrespected.

No discernible answers. There is quiet, but even Attendant Chambers can't render them dead silent long enough. An hour of relative freedom has intoxicated the inmates with doing what they want when they want. None smart off to Chambers though, so I want him with us. "I'm about to just shut it down," he turns to me, snapping.

Boys on the closest rows hear him and go mute.

"Yeah, I think you should," I add. He doesn't stay. He leaves. As a Medical Movement attendant, Chambers must soon pick up juveniles for scheduled dosages. If he commands 3D into their cells for an hour cool-off period and departs, they'll go buck-wild once Attendant Jensen and I release them. We must assume control ourselves.

Thirty minutes later, the food cart arrives, and we assemble the inmates around the tables. A big-lipped kid standing near me snatches a twin pack of butter pecan cookies from another kid's dinner plate. His arms are as thick as mine. I glance across my shoulder at him. Our eyes are level and the look in his says that he doesn't care that I feel a worthless humiliated failure. Only he and his desires exist.

"Gimme my cookies!" an inmate close by yells through a haze of defiant voices, lunging back and brushing me.

I should plant this entire asshole bunch on the wall until every damn last one of them complies, sadly even the few who aren't being assholes like the pleasant level four circus clown looking kid and the pleasant black and brown inmates. Then I should burn holes into the backs of their heads with my eyes for fifteen or fifty long minutes before directing them one at a time back to a table to eat. If they speak, I point them right back to the bricks. Walton would. Edison would. Pruitt would. 3D's 8–4 would. But I don't. I've never been the heavy on a cellblock.

We let the kitchen helpers Attendant Pruitt picked yesterday do the dinner cleanup and then allow cards at the tables, but the cackling and table-slapping is too much. Jensen and I send them all to the TV area. He follows them there, and I remain at the console hoping to look in control. A kid lopes out of the TV area toward me. "Do we have a gym call?" he asks.

"No. No call yet." Enough light still hangs outside for a softball summons out to the courtyard. We have even more time for a hoops session in the gymnasium.

"Can you call 'em and see?"

"Yeah, I'll do it in a minute," I say. The kid wanders back to the TV area.

A lie. I never call Rec for permission to visit the basement gym or courtyard outside. Attendant Jensen and I would lose this group in the hallway and on the elevator. By staying on unit, we only chance direct passersby noticing our impotence.

Following dinner, the shift yields more TV area cacophony without Attendant Chambers until a caseworker stalks in and they go mute.

Chambers must have informed her, or navigating the hallways, she too discerned through the bay window how messed up 3D is—inmates sauntering about as they please, inmates laughing and talking in the TV area, chairs not pushed under tables, and forlornness framing two Newjack faces. A stocky woman with curls of dark hair bunched on her head, the caseworker assembles the inmates into a line in front of the cell doors. Jensen and I follow them into the common area as if we also are in trouble. We stand behind the console.

"I can't believe you actin' this way! This ain't no 3J! This is 3D! You supposed to be the most grown up boys on the whole third floor! What is you all problem?"

Block 3J houses the facility's second youngest residents. The 3D boys offer the caseworker in tight pants and a baggy blouse no reply. Their attention is hers. In my head I know I'm galaxies more physically able to yank them apart if they brawl or pin an unusually defiant one to the floor or wall. Her hips are wide as an easy chair and her face puffs out like a drunken hobo's. What she is doing now though requires zero muscle from my nearly six-foot 175-pound frame. And for that I'm further disgraced. I should sneak off this cellblock, shout at Supervisor Taftmont that he is a damn fool idiot and sprint out of the building. This way out-of-shape woman caseworker can finish my shift. She'd be more competent.

"For the rest of this night, if either of these attendants write you up, I'm confinin' you for five days! Did you hear me! Five days!"

Per facility rules, Confinement sentences can run this long but only to address severe offenses, like fighting, smoking, or assaulting staff. The caseworker is bluffing to help us. But Attendant Jensen and I share more blame than the inmates. We can't checkmate them into behaving like the regular staff, and Pruitt and Chambers can. Now 4K is nothing. I wince at supervisors and other attendants hearing about this.

The caseworker woman sashays out. Discord returns. I write up a handful of inmates. Jensen writes up a handful of inmates, one for throwing a paper wad at him. *You're so pathetic that a ball of paper is a threat.*

At 10:00 P.M. I exit the facility and remember the civilian kid prowling the sidewalk along Roosevelt. Now I agree with him. The Audy Home is a "motherfucker." I just needed six hours of motherfucker on 3D with Attendant Jensen to figure it out.

11

It's Labor Day. Supervisor Taftmont directs me back to 3D as if I've been running this beast of a cellblock like General Patton for years. This guy isn't smarmy like Supervisor Maywood, who put me on 4K, but like I did after 4K, I stewed on my couch this morning until the last moment to go outside, unlock my car, and drive to the train stop—debating whether to call in a resignation. In the end, I forgave myself, rationalizing that I'm too inexperienced for 3D by myself. As with 4K, 3D is admin's fault. I shouldn't feel this terrible. But what I do feel terrible about and not very manly about is that every day I hope not to work a tough unit with an attendant the inmates will test. And thus test me. What I should be doing is welcoming 3D and hoping for a reunion with Jensen so that I can seize control the moment he arrives and become the heavy and show those assholes that I am the man and they are the boys.

Instead of turning from him and striding to the time clock and elevator, I pansy out, "Do you know who I'll be working with?"

"Yeah, let's see here." Supervisor Taftmont scans down at a grid sheet covering the small desk in front of the time clock. "You'll be with Gerald Jensen."

"Well, is there any way I can work with someone else or go to a different unit. We were there yesterday, and it didn't go very well. I think we're both too new to work a unit like that. We locked up three or four of 'em, but we should have locked up a lot more."

"Oh, okay," he answers like my declaration that just any two greenhorns can't manage 3D astounds him. That the caseworker hasn't told everyone yet somewhat comforts and saves me some face. He glances at the supervisor next to him, a shorter and older leather-jacketed man with a mangy, graying beard and a chain hooked into his wallet. Taftmont is meek and square, like Jensen. Now I too am mystified that administration promoted him to "stupidvisor." The other supervisor looks like a black Hell's Angel who could man 3D alone with no problems.

"So should we pull someone off the fourth floor to do four to twelve?" Taftmont says to the black Hell's Angel-looking supervisor. "How about Otis?"

"Yeah, Otis is strong."

There it is, from a respectable supervisor's lips to my ears: Attendant Dostert is weak.

Two hours with 3D's regular 2–10 in charge flash by, but many inmates grin slyly whenever I step or sit close to them. My co-worker notices and seems to have questions for me and questions for the boys, yet says nothing. Normally off on Mondays, he came in for time and a half to cover someone else's vacation too. Anticipating barbeque sizzling at home and the Bears on *Monday Night Football* up in Green Bay against the hated Packers probably trumps any great worry about what happened to Newjack me here yesterday.

Attendant Otis arrives at 4:00 P.M. He steps to the console, autographs the logbook, and looks to the TV area with a game face. He isn't here to be shamed. Today is not yesterday.

Inmates, be they in front of the television, at the card tables, or behind the ping-pong table, rotate their heads to size up this black man, taller than me, a few years older, slightly slimmer, and a gold hoop hanging from his left earlobe. They have waited, eager to learn if yesterday evening's party will rock on tonight. My being here was half the guarantee. The 8–4 leaves, and Attendant Otis orders all the juveniles into the middle of the block. No flinging discipline forms through the air. He says about what Pruitt said. The boys fix themselves in place and listen. A smirk crackles his voice, like it's our turn to toy with someone. I'm sure the supervisors advised Otis to take over. He finishes his speech and deposits everyone in the TV area. No recreation.

An hour later, Attendant Otis serves dinner. No cookies are snatched. Afterwards, to subtle groans, he extends his ban on cards and ping-pong. No one complains or begs over and over as many did yesterday whenever Jensen or I told them we probably weren't going to gym. Otis returns everyone to the TV area and tells me to monitor from the back row.

He stands out by the console directing cleanup, but the inmates watching television with me are silent. Kitchen help rearranges the tables after sweeping the floor. Then Attendant Otis moves closer to the TV area. "Room eighteen, go shower!" Blowing down the row, he unlocks door eighteen. The 8–4 gave him the keys, not me.

The inmate assigned to eighteen stands up, enters the cell, fetches his towel and shampoo, and aims for the bathroom area. Because my coworker is showering them one-at-a-time, the bathroom area can remain unmonitored. Dragging showers out reduces potential Rec time.

The kid passes Attendant Otis on his way toward the TV area and higher-numbered cells. Attendant Otis struts into cell eighteen. Heads crane behind bodies. I turn and stare too at the open doorway over my left shoulder. We hear the desk skid across the floor and bang a wall. Then a sliding of the bed frame. Then a swoosh of linens onto the floor. Otis exits eighteen, curls right, and unlocks door seventeen and repeats himself.

Twisting around in their seats, the inmates sulk at him. Some glare at me like I'm responsible for Otis being 4–12 today. According to policy and procedure, the 8–4 should have already inspected the cells.

Attendant Otis hasn't checked the logbook though to see if he did. He's inspecting regardless. Blazing out of cell seventeen, his hands are empty—no contraband yet.

"You can't search our rooms for no reason," a round-headed fifteen-year-old, Damien Denison, pipes up without asking me for permission to speak.

Attendant Otis's barging into the cells unannounced does strike me as intrusive and unfair—the sentiment that made me skip the 4K cell inspections a month ago.

Yesterday I'd wanted to confine Damien but he never did anything major—just minor antagonisms all shift long when he cackled like a court jester at everything that wasn't funny, and when his peers mimicked Jensen and me, and we countered with no consequence. He didn't ask just once about going to the gym. Damien pestered me over and over about calling Rec. Fortunately, I wasn't too flustered to conjure up excuses and other lies.

Attendant Otis stops between cells seventeen and sixteen and stares at Damien on a middle row in the TV area. With a smile: "Young man, policy and procedure says that any staff can search any room at any time."

"But you gotta have a reason to do it. You can't just go in our rooms for no reason. You're just doin' it because he got treated! I wanna see a caseworker!"

"Fine, I'll call Mr. Hampton myself, and you can ask him."

This explains Otis's smirk at the console when he arrived—he already was planning to run the cellblock by the book and *treat* them to every last letter of the law. Damien and his friends had indeed treated Jensen and me. The woman caseworker wouldn't have shown up had they not been making Hell on the two Newjacks. Now Attendant Otis too knows I'm worthless. Caseworker Hampton arrives in an hour, be it his regular round or whether Otis has actually paged him. I never saw him pick up the phone. The brawny man about forty in a baggy shirt and uneven goatee moseys from the console toward the line of cell doors to visit the inmates Jensen and I wrote reports on and confined last night.

"Mr. Hampton, can attendants search our rooms for no reason?" Damien quips at him from the TV area as Hampton nears the cells behind the rows of seats.

Hampton is one of few caseworkers that attendants don't peg as an administrative lapdog defending belligerent inmates. I've heard about him placing a defiant inmate in his cell after warning: "We can do this the easy way or the hard way." The hard way began with Hampton pinning him into a wall and then lifting him off his feet and sliding him across the bricks into the open cell. Still, I expect Hampton to gently correct Attendant Otis or backtrack to the console and whisper a reminder of the normal procedure—the 8–4 attendant executes cell inspections between breakfast and lunch. As much as I want Damien Denison to be wrong, I suspect that only probable cause justifies our rooting through cells outside of regular inspections.

"No, they can go through your rooms without any reason, whenever they feel like it. But you'll make a good lawyer, Denison. Keep tryin'!"

Otis grins a few minutes later, "Thanks, Hamp." The affable caseworker is leaving, completing Damien's treatment.

Idiot me still conceives Damien as a victim, a defendant—innocent until demonstrated guilty, like I'm some pity-stricken, justice-trumps-everything ACLU attorney. In court downstairs, he is indeed still innocent until his judge decides that the evidence makes him guilty. But I must act as if Damien is guilty of smuggling and stashing weapons and contraband until my cell inspections prove him innocent. I work cellblocks not courtrooms.

Attendant Otis and I talk after locking the inmates inside their cells for the night. He studies computer engineering a couple blocks over at UI-Chicago. His training for another career in his off time and piloting a cellblock Walton and Pruitt style further dejects me. My time outside the Audy Home is free to meditate on children's attendant theory and practice and to memorize the *Policy and Procedure Guide for Group Services*, which I have read more of, but am still incompetent. I'd love to inform Attendant Otis that I too have an escape plan for another career. But I don't. My vision of mentoring these young legally troubled men embarrasses me now like I've fallen for history's most colossal practical joke.

I explain my frustrations from yesterday and 4K and with attending children in general, particularly when not assigned to 3F. Even working 3K jars away nearly every compassionate and redemptive thought during those eight hours.

"Yeah, some of these kids need to be locked up. That's the only place for them. They can't function anywhere else."

"That's damn near all of 3D." I also tell Otis about my graduate degree in history and how I am possibly interested in teaching, an interest reignited by 4K and 3D.

"Hey, if you have a better offer, maybe you should take it," he answers, looking over at me, seeming impressed by my education.

Here is yet another black attendant not falling down to thwart me from ditching my embryonic children's attendant career and the altruism I'd once idealized into it. From behind the console, we face the line of darkened cell fronts, the glary Plexiglas windows hiding the slayers of my idealism. They're harmless now with Attendant Otis here—oblivious to their dirty deed, oblivious to the fact that I came here to make their jailed existence seem less jailed because I wanted to like them, but now I'm hating most of them.

I'd asked my Western Civilizations professor about job opportunities with a graduate degree in history. "You can't even teach history in a public school with a master's degree in history. You have to get state certification." That is why I'd applied to Teachers for Chicago, and they rejected me. So Attendant Otis, I have no other offers. You're going to be the next Bill Gates while I'll still be here at the Audy Home being treated by Damien Denison.

A supervisor designates me to Medical for my entire next shift. The regular 2–10 is back on 3D. Word about how lame I am must be in everyone's ears because Medical is all but vacation. I'm failing on two fronts. As a volunteer, I liked the inmates and believed I made their lives less depressing for the minutes we were together. Peace and order were a given then. Now, if not paired with a strong attendant, I must establish that peace and order. Supervisors and my coworkers don't care about my idealist ambitions unless I can first help them cement that peace and order we all need not to hate our jobs. They must view me the way I view Attendant Jensen.

I trek the long way around the rectangular hallway to Medical so I won't pass 3D, so the 3D staff and inmates won't spot me. The few respectful residents likely tattled on the assholes. Jensen's and my report copies remain at the console. The staff knows about me being treated.

As usual, the medical shift, checking on kids in their cells, opening doors only for meals or when the recreation attendant arrives to whisk them out to the courtyard for a few minutes of exercise, is eventless and thus relatively enjoyable.

After work, Supervisor Mitchell sits at the front desk, looking very small behind the very long counter. I haven't seen him since the afternoon of 4K.

"Mr. Dostert, how is everything?" he asks in a manner as honest and unassuming as Supervisor Taftmont's.

Mitchell acts like he has no doubt that I've been kicking ass and taking names in the five weeks since my shadow shifts. My mood after 4K obviously wasn't very obvious to him.

I explain that I had my worst shift to date a couple nights ago but sanitize: "We didn't have the control we should have. Some of the kids were pretty antagonistic."

"Right, I understand, Mr. Dostert. But don't think of this as 'I'm in here with a bunch of murderers, rapists, drug dealers, and gangbangers.' They're still human; they've just made mistakes. We all have. Just look at this as a place you come to do your eight hours. Don't worry about it. Rome wasn't built in a day. Don't let them think you're scared. If they sense fear, they're like sharks. They go for the kill."

I don't answer because I am scared of some of the juveniles, scared that these murderers, rapists, drug dealers, and gangbangers, who have made mistakes I've never been close to making, might soon pound on me instead of their cell door windows and send my cellblock up for real next time a stupidvisor teams me with someone like Jensen.

Theory and theory only fills Mitchell's cup of advice. When the 8–4 man departed, leaving Jensen and me to run the show, I wasn't contemplating what all charges the 3D inmates faced, whether they'd killed, robbed, or sold drugs. I didn't care. I just wanted to see the clock read 10:00 P.M. and there be no blood on the floor. How then, Supervisor Mitchell, am I supposed to look relaxed working with a joker like Jensen on a block like 3D?

"Tell you what, Mr. Dostert. I'm gonna bring you up to the fifth floor, show you how we do things up there."

A different supervisor directs me to Medical again the next day. If Medical wasn't painless, I'd be indignant with Mitchell's failed promise to assign me to the fifth floor with him. I begin again with the usual cell row patrol at the first fifteen-minute mark, peering into each window to make sure no inmate requires a nurse's attention. Working Medical for the next ten and a half months, I easily could log a full children's attendant year and avoid staining my work résumé with a truncated entry. Midway down, as if he is waiting for someone, stands a scrawny black kid, his small, rounded face inches from the door window. Our heights are equal. I have no idea why Bryce is in Medical. He looks fine.

Behind the Plexiglas, he tips his chin up. "You from the suburbs?"

When I left Texas, I quit shaving my entire face and sculpted the whiskers around my mouth into a goatee. I'd hoped to look tougher and less suburban. My stubble grew out a rusty red in contrast with the dark blonde hair on my scalp. Bryce's quip takes my mind to a photo of my dad as a Chicago middle-schooler in 1951 before his family moved to La Grange. In that pic, waves of rusty red hair roll across the wide Germanic head that we share—red hair now on my face that Bryce is making an assumption about.

My murmur to black inmate Bryce on the other side of the medical Plexiglas is unintelligible. I don't want to admit that I'm not even from a Chicago suburb but from a suburb of Dallas. My goatee isn't bluffing him.

"You won't be able to handle niggers."

I say nothing but crave conceding that his "niggers" must indeed exist in this facility because the inmates I couldn't handle live on 4K and 3D. Maybe this is history's soft revenge for the one

Christmas when my Chicago-bred grandmother picked up a Brazil nut from a snack dish and said, "We called these nigger toes when I was a kid." Fingering the oblong, brownish seed, she'd voiced no apology. I shuffle out of earshot before Bryce can fire any more questions.

Attendant Chambers, who rescued Jensen and me temporarily on 3D, isn't nearby witnessing this exchange. Medical Movement is the only assignment almost as lax as regular Medical. Once his medicine runs are complete, Chambers can hide out in the Medical break room—an empty cell with a table and metal cabinet crammed with bird-shirts, trousers, and bed linens. Later in the shift, we chat there and I complain about how antagonistically the juveniles, particularly some black juveniles, treat me—my vibe to Otis and Supervisor Mitchell last night. Attendant Chambers turns to me, a light shirt hanging off his thick chest, "Naaahh, these kids aren't tough. Five guys beatin' up one guy? Three guys raping one girl? A carload of gangbangers driving by a house and shootin' up a front porch? That's not tough. Falling asleep every night wearing a gas mask and hugging a gun, waitin' for that siren to go off, and *not* goin' fuckin' crazy? That's tough."

This man fought the Persian Gulf War. Inmates like Riles Davis on 4K, for whom we might need baseball bats to separate, much less smartasses like Damien Denison on 3D, never daunt him. No attendant has died from a punch or shank. Attendant Chambers knows he will caress his wife tonight and jostle his children tomorrow morning. When he departed for Saudi Arabia to garner for America and our allies cheaper petroleum, he wasn't as confident. But to me, Audy Home kids are tough.

12

"You must like being in that room, if you keep actin' up," I overhear a woman. She is seated at a visitation table near me. I'm sitting at the console. The chastisement is for her son, Timothy, "Tiny Timmy" as many attendants dub the runtish eleven-year-old.

Supervisor Mitchell hasn't forgotten his pledge. I'm upstairs now, working cellblock 5G after the three Medical shifts that followed my treatment on 3D. Uncomplicated as Medical is, I am relieved that Mitchell actually is looking out for me. He should—he helped hire me. This block's inmates stand even shorter than those from 3F. I can handle every kid on 5G and will be happy to hide out here as well—hide from 4K and 3D and cheat my way to a completed year of attending children at the Audy Home.

The woman's scold reveals how Cook County has brainwashed even the juveniles' parents about our seven-by-fifteen-foot cells being rooms. Timmy's mother can peer into his living quarters right now because the standard Plexiglas door window spans much of the door. This means that her son, like every juvenile, has limited privacy when standing or squatting over the steel commode and sink mounted to the cell's front wall. Beige brick and mortar compose sidewalls. Mississippi mud brown shellac covers the back wall, all steel up to the window, six feet off the floor. The building's usual mediciney odor, the one Attendant Walton uses breath mints against, trails into Timmy's chamber too. My nostrils grew immune in a week. Detained for nearly a month, Timmy probably can't detect the tang in the air either. He stresses over more. I'll soon notice him pushing his mattress against the bottom of his cell door to inhibit roaches and gray mice from scurrying in while he sleeps.

Timmy slouches back in his chair and stares beyond mom out 5G's front bay window. The clear day grants Timmy a kingly view of the Sears Tower. This may be his closest gaze at the famed landmark. Hearsay is that many of Chicago's youngest poor have never touched their sneakers to a downtown street or pointed their pupils out over Lake Michigan's turquoise waters.

His mother wears glasses and strikes me as in her mid-thirties. Unlike her son, she is reserved, reserved in a way that if ignoring their identical wide brown eyes and plump noses, I'd never hang their fruit pieces on the same family tree.

Timmy's unit houses the shorties—the building's youngest male residents, ages ten and eleven. Maywood should have auditioned me here instead of 4K. Judges spare shorties from jail until last resort, appropriating them to foster-like placement agencies first. Thus 5G often has more cells than boys—the antithesis of every other cellblock. Most of Timmy's peers have already rambled roughshod through asylums like the Saura Center and the Mercy Home for Boys & Girls, which shelter abused, neglected, and abandoned children, in addition to first- and second-time delinquents. "I don't ever want to work with those little monsters," a veteran attendant will swear to me a few days from now in the hallway between 5G and his block. "I prefer the older kids." He likes 4K and 3D over 5G. The smaller the inmates, the less nervous I am. Little monster or not, a punch from Timmy would brush my chest, instead of slamming into my chin or eye socket like one from G-shots Reginald or the fourth-floor inmates. I will even come to like the shorties' dinner prayer: "In the beginning, God created a man." They swallow the *a* and the *man* molding them into a sound like *Amen*. Being young and clever hardly means that Timmy and his peers are booked on petty offenses. "They do the same things the bigger boys do," the attendant doing the fifth-floor medication runs will tell me.

Before this visit, Timmy's mother waited for my coworker, the regular 8–4 attendant, Bradley, a married man with flattop hair who is no taller than she is, to unlock his cell.

Timmy wasn't lounging in the TV area with his cellblock mates.

Timothy is in Confinement, so outside of a five-minute shower and an hour for exercise, he will spend today in his cell. Policy and procedure dictate that confined juveniles enjoy no personal possessions. Timmy's digs yielded several pair of Teenage Mutant Ninja Turtles underwear and baseball and basketball cards scattered on the floor—gifts from his mother during a previous visit or contents of a care package she dropped off for him. Earlier I noticed them wrapped in a plastic bag tagged with his name in the cabinet. In Confinement, juveniles, whether 4K brutes or a handsome kid like Timmy, sit or stand or lie or crouch or pace in their cells the entire day. Restricted spaces with little to grab and twist, push and pull, or build up and tear down are hell for a kid Timmy's age. To head off Confinement-meriting misbehavior, one children's attendant even warns older inmates: "Gentlemen, it's fucked up to be locked up. But it's *really* fucked up to be locked up while you're locked up." No matter how fucked up all this is, Timmy, I'm learning, is often cell-sequestered for serious infractions, like refusing to stand silently during wall time or slapping at a cellblock mate. "Watch him," another 5G attendant has advised me. Timmy doesn't spare the nurses in Medical either. Once, he shrieked obscenities at them when ordered to swallow his twice-daily doses of Ritalin and Prozac.

I scan 5G's other tables of preteen inmates and their visitors. My eyes stop again on Timmy's mother, whose sarcasm seems inhuman. But what *does* a mom say to her incarcerated son? Chew him up one side and down the other for being in jail? Gush over him, guilt-ridden that to relieve himself he must now ask me for permission? Rehash what he did in the real world to be snatched into custody and try to pinpoint where he veered wrong? Impugn the officers who may have picked and chosen which kids sprinting away from the crime site to nab? Blame his under-trained, overworked, under-resourced schoolteacher who couldn't render her classroom fun enough to keep Timmy more fascinated by geographic nations than gangster nations?

Right now—Sunday visitation on 5G—attending children on a real cellblock is cake, finally. Half a dozen moms, one potential dad, a few grandmothers, and other legal guardians autograph my clipboard resting on the console's edge and seat themselves at the table where I direct them and their child who emerges from the TV area. From the dearth of men showing up to see these boys, working visitation at the Audy Home makes me think there was more than one Immaculate Conception. Attendant Bradley is stationed on the back row to enforce our no talking rule—more taxing than signing in visitors. So I should be savoring these grand easy-money moments. Juveniles closest to me have parents preserving them like I want them—speaking in normal tones of voice and sitting in one place. But I don't feel grand. I don't feel grand with the cinch duty because while I control whether a shorty and his grandma converse at the blue table or the green table and decide at what hour I present a kid the toothpaste and clean socks mom brought him, I can't compel this one kid and this one mother to do anything more than languish here, gaping, void of words, through each other. What I want is for Timmy to spill his guts to mom about whatever he did to land in Confinement. I want him to bawl. I want Timmy to pledge over and over that starting now he will be a good boy and won't be in Confinement the next time she visits, and that he will be an even better boy whenever his judge releases him so mom won't ever do another Sunday afternoon at the Audy Home. None of this happens. Instead, Timmy and his mother gape on at each other and then stand up from their table even though visitation hasn't ended.

Attendant Bradley leaves the TV area and motions Timmy back to his cell.

Mom steps to the console. "So why is Timmy being kept in his room?" Her tone is even. No blatant anger at me or Attendant Bradley or the Cook County juvenile detainment system.

"Actually, I just started at two o'clock, so I wasn't here when he went into Confinement. But the carbon copy of his report should be in his room if you want to look at it. We could have him find it if you want."

Timmy's mother turns her head toward Attendant Bradley

bolting Timothy inside his cell. Time remains for her to read and discuss the report with him, but she swings her calm head back around and with nothing more than a nod at me, exits the cellblock.

Some weeks after spying on Tiny Timmy and his mom in their muted state, I draw a fifth-floor Medical Movement shift. Someone is taking today off and I'm still a floater with no permanent cellblock. I make 5G my first stop and call Timmy's name, the lone shorty on my escort list. I let him into the vacant hallway and we head for the next unit. My curiosity about Timmy mirrors that about juveniles of every size and age. Do their charges match their jailhouse demeanors? Timmy doesn't seem wretched and without hope. A recent night he returned my wave as I passed 5G. Some juveniles do "yes sir" and "no sir" me, and then I discover from other inmates that a prosecutor says they've killed two or three people. Or the one on 3G on a night Attendant Edison is absent who hisses "white bitch" when I instruct him to serve wall time. Police, he will say, only snagged him with a few Ziplocs of marijuana. Even 3D's Damien Denison is no AT. For not educating me more about the juveniles, I resent administration. Supervisors know more. Caseworkers know more. Nurses know more. Sneaking into the empty nurse's exam room and flipping through a medication notebook is how I'm aware what pills Timmy swallows. I should know if a kid is mildly mentally retarded and will have a devil of a time understanding why I can't permit him in his cell with his shoes on. The less I know about the juveniles, the harder it is to help them conform. Audy Home ignorance is no bliss.

"So what are you in for?" I ask Timmy.

"A gun case and gang-banging," he fixes his big eyes straight ahead.

In Chicago *gang-banging* means sporting particular colors, flashing particular hand signs, and marauding with those who carry on likewise. All this engenders robberies, muggings, beatings, drug trafficking, and drive-by shootings. Timmy may have created some of the bullet scars, like Medical inmate Ruben's, that I lost count of long ago. I'd assumed that thieving a Game Boy or heaving a shaft of rebar into his school's windows on a Saturday landed Timmy at the Audy Home, not a firearm indictment. The longer I work here, the more of my own ignorance I uncover.

13

To my relief, Supervisor Mitchell keeps me on his fifth floor and returns me to its G cellblock. The regular 2–10 attendant there just acquired his certification as an electrician and is burning through sick days before resigning. Everyone at the Audy Home seems stuck or strategizing for something else. Right now my strategy is to hope that every supervisor is adequately wise and continues assigning me to 3F, Medical, Medical Movement, or 5G. The shorty unit does generate more challenge than Medical duty—we do let the shorties out of their cells. But 5G's regular 4–12 is Attendant Milton, who wrestles the boys into headlocks and bends their arms while they wiggle in laughter. I'm not audacious enough to horseplay with inmates, even the shorties. His forehead and eyebrows compact, Milton is black and five or six years older than me. His casualness works, but I remain stern, afraid the boys, depending on how far away Milton is, will molt into those reputed little monsters if I relax.

Recreation calls us for softball against 3J, the unit whose inmates are closest in age to 5G's. Attendant Milton lines the boys up at the cellblock door. I've worked a straight week here now. Like Walton, Milton knows I must do this solo.

Nothing blows up from unit door to elevator to courtyard and no shorty bat-chases another during our three or four innings. My team never screams at itself. We queue up after the game and enter the building. No one yaps on the elevator. No one squares off in the hallway. Although Timmy is confined again and isn't with us, I feel triumphant for pulling off this non-humiliating elevator trip. We leave the elevator and form only one line because we number a mere fourteen. Wonderfully silent, we round a corner, the trail of little dark heads streaking forward in front of me striding along near the line's middle.

"Can I sleep with you?" one of the shorties shouts.

I spin around. Demetrius, bigger than Timmy, almost 3J-big, is leering into the story-high glass fronting cellblock 5J, a female cellblock.

"Demetrius, back in line!"

His hands are flattened onto the glass like the suctioning feet of a climbing frog scaling a smooth tree trunk. He doesn't move or turn around in response. Demetrius is always either sedate or frenzied, nothing in between. Whenever I've initiated conversation about his favorite non–Michael Jordan Bulls player or what kind of pizza he likes, his chin has flinched side-to-side and his eyes beaded about and never met mine.

"Oohh he in trouble!" "He goin' in Confinement!" other shorties screech.

I should have followed everyone instead of walking halfway between the first kid and the last kid. I would have detected Demetrius peeling off to the girls behind 5J's window. My gaffe was turning left instead of right once out of the elevator. I wanted to take the shortest route but chanced passing the female cellblocks.

Lunging, I clutch Demetrius's upper arm. The twelve-year-old smiles ear to ear like this stunt equals the meaning of his life. I jerk him to the group, no longer a line, but a swarm spanning the hallway, gawking and squealing.

"Line back up! One single-file line!"

We're still partially in front of 5J, and girls are camped at its tables. They see us and this is embarrassing me because the women attendants see us too. They heard Demetrius through the glass. At least, he didn't use "hit" or "fuck"—the regular Audy Home synonyms for sex. Even from a shorty, "sleep with" sounds tamed and rated PG, considering the petitions against Demetrius: aggravated assault and destruction to school property. He ticked them off to me one night when I asked. "Sleep with" seems this kid's last shred of innocence. Or maybe precocious Demetrius knows not to say "fuck" to the girl you want to fuck.

On unit, I dismiss Demetrius from my spot-search line into his cell and lock it. No tattling to veteran Attendant Milton. I know what to do. I finish the search and send the other thirteen shorties to the card tables. I turn around and sit at the console. I pen a juicy yet not embellished report. I state that Demetrius "used sexually explicit language and harassed a female resident." He stews the evening away in Confinement. All other fifth-floor residents will bite both lips if you walk them by 5J and K, thrilled to be granted a glimpse, too smart to go all to pieces like the shorties. Had I not blundered with 5G, later tales of confined girls disrobing and gyrating in their cell door windows as older male juveniles marched by, hooting and grunting during the free strip show, would have channeled me the long way around.

Attendant Milton's managing 5G so well blesses us with time and leisure. One night we chat about his part-time real estate business and marvel at how many millions of dollars basketball player Latrell Sprewell just flushed when he seized his Golden State Warriors coach by the throat. Milton converts the story into a teachable moment for the shorties watching us play ping-pong. Don't be like Latrell—think before you act. Working 5G with him is effortless, like following Attendant Walton around 3G, but Attendant Milton isn't the perfect mentor because while sports and even sitcom repeats may entertain us, they can weary the inmates, the shorties for sure. Antsy inmates of every age badger us: "Did you bring any movies?" The temptation is to sequester everyone in the TV area, plug in a tape, and enforce the no talking rule—an effortless way to kill two of our eight hours, especially with the spastic shorties. Zero rapport cultivates between us, but as I've realized on 4K and 3D, peace and order is a children's attendant's first mission. As with everything at the Audy Home, there are rules. Policy #15.16 describes the "management of music, video, and literature available to residents."

> No music, videos or literature shall be brought into the institution containing profanity, sexually explicit lyrics and/or scenes, gang references, violence, drug usage, lewd or obscene gestures and/or references.[1]

The regulation further mandates that staff carrying entertainment materials into the facility must surrender them for inspection. Still deputy sheriffs never search us on our way up to the cellblocks, nor do supervisors. The few films I've brought in, *Lord of the Flies*, *Dead Poets' Society*, and *Hoop Dreams*, might as well be *Debbie Does Dallas* for all administration knows or appears to care. One fourth-floor attendant, Attendant Tucker told me, totes in rap CDs and blares them from his boom box at the console with inmates leaning on the desk, digging the jam session rife with "bitches," "motherfuckers," and "hoes." A juvenile touching the console is actually a major violation.

One night, an attendant from a neighboring block wanders into 5G holding a video. Seated next to each other on the TV area back row, Attendant Milton and I have Timmy, Demetrius, and all the shorties watching the sitcom *Martin*.

With no reply, Milton receives the tape, stands from our soft staff seats, and walks to the television. Without looking back at me, he plugs it into the VCR. A shapely brunette soon tugs off a sky blue bikini top to call her own bluff at going nude in public. The video is *Jerry Springer: Too Hot for TV*. The shorties issue no sound. To me the naked female speaks of potential intercourse, but I don't want the shorties thinking about intercourse too, or even understanding intercourse. Demetrius has a clue already. I want them to see me react ho-hum to the bare, obvious breasts. If the shorties never realize there is a way to pleasure themselves in a naked female body, despite Mr. Springer's raucous studio crowd howling "Hell yes there is!" coupled with Attendant Milton's hand planted on the television cabinet and eyes burrowing into the screen, maybe they won't have sex very soon. This will statistically lessen the chances of them becoming single fathers, like most of their fathers. Maybe fewer of them will have kids like the kids they are—shorties possibly growing up into ATs on 4K and 3D. Then in one generation we can shutter a few of the Audy Home's twenty-seven cellblocks.

Like I've suddenly remembered something I must write in the logbook, I lurch up and saunter out of the TV area toward the console. An afternoon last month, a former children's attendant turned probation officer whispered to me on the elevator about how "crazy" this facility was a few years ago. Attendants snuck in hard-core pornos for the inmates, he said. I should rat out Attendant Milton. I don't. I'm still too new. And Timmy and Demetrius behave too well with him around.

The 3D flogging is a month behind me, but Attendant Milton takes the day off and Attendant Jensen shows up as my 4–12. He approaches me at the console, smiling. I mumble a greeting. His arrival instead of Milton's prompts a shorty to bounce up from a card table. When Milton is here, no one stands unless instructed or given permission.

Not trusting Attendant Jensen to follow procedure, I say, "Young man, sit down!"

The shorty splats back into his seat, a twinge of surprise on his face. With the cat away, the mice, like they had on 3D, are attempting to play. Perhaps Supervisor Mitchell wants to test me. Taftmont normally manages the fourth floor, so I doubt he is behind this. Mitchell knows if I cannot run 5G with Elmer Fudd, I am indeed hopelessly inept, and he erred unforgivably in hiring me. Assistant Superintendent Davis may kick him off the hiring panel. Attendant Jensen's voice is rare tonight. We have fewer than fifteen inmates, and I loom over them at the tables until dinner to squash their impulse to hurdle up and race off without raising a hand. I send Jensen to the TV area to sit with the others. Like Attendant Otis did on 3D, I dismiss the boys individually to scrape their plates, go to the bathroom, and return to the TV area.

Finally, I'm grasping the 2–10 chronology—recreation and/or television, then dinner, then showers, then more recreation and/or television, and then bedtime—and exactly where the boys should be during every minute. Jensen never supplements my assertiveness with instructions of his own. I'm tempted, once the shorties' day is over and we've locked them in for the night, to tell Attendant Jensen that he shouldn't be here, not on 5G, not on 3D, not anywhere in the Audy Home. You're not being fair to the inmates you can't control because you're so nice that you must try to be mean. To convince him, I might also need to confess that I don't belong here either, that right now I don't feel like my genuine self, the self I was around Jerome and Terry when volunteering with Chaplain Rick. Speaking sternly to inmates, shorties or not, isn't fulfilling. Quit now, Attendant Jensen, before you compromise yourself any more like I am.

For showers, I position myself outside the bathroom area's ten foot wide entrance and bring in the shorties individually from the TV area, where I've stationed Attendant Jensen. He complies like I complied with Attendants Walton and Otis. I could take the boys in threes, but that would begin recreation time too soon. Less free time means less time to potentially misbehave, so I drag out this routine activity. I have no room to gamble. During the entire showering period, I stand, too tense to use a chair. With every bather, I stroll into the bathroom area to scan the mirrors and metal dividers between the toilets. Any soap-scrawled crescent moons or pitchforks or pyramids, and I'll bust the showering kid for gang representation. I may idealize most shorties too young for sexual knowledge but hold no such fantasy about gang activity. Attendant Milton already nailed one for calling someone a "jelly donut"—its initial consonant sounds are code for "Gangster Disciple."

After showers, Supervisor Mitchell arrives on his regular round. All is orderly as if Attendant Milton is here. I relish Mitchell seeing me running a smooth unit, even if one populated only by shorties. His eyebrows are high again scanning around pacified 5G. This is tiny vindication for 3D—suggesting to myself that had Jensen not sunk us from the start and let me be the heavy, the shift would not have gone to hell.

With no emergency, supervisors linger long enough only to sign the logbook with the date, time, their name, and "Rounds" on one of the horizontal lines. Rather than leaving right away, Mitchell reviews shower and bathroom policy and has us testify to the briefing via our logbook signatures. He informs us that the facility is embattled in litigation leveled by a former inmate claiming that several juveniles molested him in a bathroom area.

The $50,000 lawsuit names, in addition to Superintendent Doyle and Cook County Board President John Stroger, the two children's attendants on duty during the alleged incident.

These aren't the first such allegations. Two years before I was hired, a juvenile court judge found two former male inmates, ages eleven and thirteen, guilty of sexual assault, determining that the boys had pinned a ten-year-old boy on a bathroom floor and violated him. A third former inmate, eleven years old, was delinquent of that molestation and another attempted assault. My hope is that they used something other than their anatomies—a pencil's eraser end, a plastic spoon handle—anything but themselves. Were it me, and I could guarantee myself only humiliation with no rectal tearing, I would choose such. I am almost as sad for the perpetrators as the perpetrated. The victim's attorney remarked about the verdict: "It's an indictment of the system. There are too many detainees and there is not enough supervision."[2] Maybe justice was present. Cook County paid this family but now has fewer dollars to hire better people and thus fewer dollars to train better people to do a better job of protecting this family's kid if he is arrested and detained again.

"I know this is what most of us are doing already, but because of this and another recent incident, we gotta remind everyone that two residents can never be in the bathroom area unsupervised," Supervisor Mitchell elaborates next to the console.

"What else happened?" I ask with Attendant Jensen listening in.

The shorties sit at the tables playing board games and slinging cards. They seem oblivious to us. I'm doubly relaxed because a supervisor is here too, a supervisor who likes me.

"Well, a few weeks ago, two girls said they had oral sex in the bathroom for about fifteen minutes. When I was an attendant, I used to take a newspaper or something back there to read," Supervisor Mitchell continues. "Some kids would say, 'You must be gay, wanting to watch us shower.' I said, 'No, I'm not watching you shower, I'm just monitoring you while you shower.'"

Neither Jensen nor I respond.

Mitchell backs away from us. Inserting his key into the lock, he leans against the steel and glass door. "Because I sure don't have fifty grand to give someone."

Neither do I. Nor did I imagine when reading the children's attendant job description possibly having to surrender someone my earnings. There is much here that I never imagined—a runt like Timmy bragging that he lugged a weapon with bullets, a co-worker showing him and others his age a woman's uncovered chest, a twelve-year-old shouting sexual fantasies, and his shorty peers raping each other.

14

"Three mo' niggas to wash they ass!" I hear behind me. Donnell is shouting over my shoulder and stepping out of a shower cubicle a few feet from my roller chair positioned at the mouth of 5D's bathroom area. I'm on shower duty. This is still the fifth floor. Donnell is no shorty though. Cellblock 5D houses the floor's manliest inmates, inmates like Donnell with plenty of facial hair and baritone-voiced enough for the fourth floor. The AT ratio here equals 4K's—where three quarters of inmates are being tried as adults. Supervisor Mitchell has graduated me from kindergarten to twelfth-grade in three weeks. I had no complaint with 5G, but 5D's 2–10 man has two weeks of vacation, and Attendant Bradley requested overtime on 5G, thus converting his 8–4 shift to an 8–10. So here I am.

I spin around to the manly voice. The chair wheels squeak on the slick floor. Mist glistens on Donnell's coal skin above the towel he is gliding over his flat midsection and the muscles bundled up on his legs. I look back toward the TV area. Inmates are stirring in response.

The 4–12, Attendant Marcus, who Supervisor Mitchell says will be a great mentor for me, is off tonight. Otherwise, Donnell would never holler across the unit like this. Despite his testing the Newjack, Donnell's square forehead and steady eyes project a stoicism that recreates, for me, Sidney Poitier from *A Raisin in the Sun*, as though at every moment he is mulling something greater than either of us understands. Over six feet tall, Donnell dwarfs some attendants. Astonishing is his sixteen-year-old physique, sculpted in dips and ridges despite having no weight room in which to pump iron. My straining away at Power House Gym and guzzling MET-Rx meal supplement shakes bulks my shoulders no thicker than Donnell's. As with Attendant Edison asking me to define "nigger," it's almost equally startling to hear a black kid qualify other black kids as "niggers." Blacks were never "niggers" to each other in my hometown of Bedford, Texas, albeit the rare few whom I ever spotted within speaking proximity. Reading in my middle school library that boxer Muhammad Ali had branded rival Joe Frazier an Uncle Tom, a gorilla, and a nigger was baffling. I'd suspected that Ali despised the word, given his Vietnam War draft defiance in which he said, "The Viet Cong never called me a nigger."

Donnell leaves the water running for the next trio, convinced it will remain hotter longer, and strolls down the cell row, shirtless, the towel wrapping his waist. Icy water prompts a lot of juveniles to retort: "Nahh, I'm straight," when instructed to shower. We must then decide whether to let them skip washing, chancing that the cellblock will reek of body odor. No fret about Donnell smelling today. He soaped up scalp to soles. Be it ignorance or prejudice or both, an N-word user washing meticulously surprises me. I'd always assumed a black person uttering "nigger" feels miserably enough about himself and his race that he wouldn't care to be clean. I had intended for Donnell to inform his peers seated in the TV area that another three of them could shower—once closer to them when he entered his own cell.

Tonight I'm teamed with an attendant slighter than me, who speaks a soft Creole accent, instead of Attendant Marcus. Donnell's N-word stymies me such that I spit out no reproach. Three more inmates follow his order and stride down to shower. None of them yell while drying off, and the shift's remainder is uneventful. Perhaps Supervisor Mitchell is correct about the maturity of his fifth-floor boys, certainly these, the oldest ones, even when managed by a Newjack Texan and an undersized guy from Louisiana. Donnell's 5D couldn't be more different from Tiny Timmy's 5G. But I'm not steamed at Supervisor Mitchell, despite 5D's looking just like 4K. No one here is itching to fight or telling me they don't have to follow the rules.

With Attendant Marcus here, Donnell turns even more mannered. While not notably tall, Attendant Marcus resembles in his face and wavy hair a non-superstar Los Angeles Lakers basketball player married to a defrocked Miss America. I'm jealous of Attendant Marcus and how the inmates approach him like he's one of them yet never "act a fool." Being a loudmouthed hoodlum gangbanger in his presence obviously isn't hip.

I hear Donnell though referencing "out west" and what police there do and don't do. He means Chicago's West Side where his Gangster Disciples reign over certain blocks. This veiled gang vernacular is a major rule violation. But Donnell enunciates "out west" in such a mature tone that Marcus and I ignore his subtle breach. Inmates socialize well here despite their size, felony indictments, and gang memberships. One named Richard, charged with aggravated sexual assault, giggles when, in jolly pitches, others call him "Raper Man Rick." Blacks, nearly all from Donnell's gang, dominate this population, so 5D is a POW camp, distinct from the diversity of race and gang on every other block I've worked. In truth, I have been up here before with Attendant Marcus. Between training on 3G with Walton and Edison and becoming a permanent 2–10, I did a few 5D hours as a third attendant. When Marcus arrived, he emptied the juveniles from the TV area and lined their backs to the cell row. Then came his famed line to stem potential defiance that would earn these man-sized kids Confinement: "Gentleman, it's fucked up to be locked up, but it's really fucked up to be locked up while you're locked up." With me as his only coworker, he says it as well. Nothing scary has ever happened. I believe Supervisor Mitchell. And Donnell says "nigger" around Attendant Marcus a lot too. "That nigger got jacked!" Donnell blurts out the next Sunday afternoon in the TV area watching Bears defenders tackle a running back. "That nigger is cold as hell!" rings out a different day when a black sitcom character derides another. For Donnell, "nigger" serves more purpose than merely shower summons. Even around Attendant Marcus, Donnell fires off "nigger" like a first name. For Donnell, a nigger can be a fellow black juvenile or any black person. Other 5D black juveniles employ "nigger" and "nigga." I've heard "That's my nigga!" and "What's up, nigga?" ring out on every cellblock except 3F, reminding me of my white friends and

I being "dude" to each other in the mid-1980s. Other N-word uses though do not flatter. Some are battle cries: "Pussy-ass nigger!" "Bitch-ass nigger!" "Hoe-ass nigger!"

"All y'all step out and go to bed!" Attendant Marcus bellows at the TV area from close to the console and close to me. "Fuck them niggers!"

Fumbling through a spades game at one of the tables, my head whirls around like it had with Donnell's "nigger" line. Attendant Marcus is indeed sending the majority of our inmates to bed early for talking in the TV area. Not every kid was chattering, but the entire group will suffer. Should Supervisor Mitchell or a caseworker ask why most residents are confined two hours before bedtime without authorizing rule violation reports, Marcus will grasp for an explanation. Repeated talking in the TV area really offends him. Kids are "niggers" for doing so.

I think of another black coworker, also close to my age. "You're the motherfuckin' nigger," he'd snapped at a black kid downstairs on Medical after the poor juvenile had called him one. The guy does fourth-floor Medical Movement, so he has adequate free time to linger, duty-free, in the infirmary. Leaning down from a chair along the cell row, waiting for his next medication run, he had ranted on, "You're the one locked up, gang-banging and selling drugs, blowing off school, and makin' trouble for your family." No rebuttal from the young man staring at his cell floor. I'd stared at him and his chastiser who wouldn't let up, as if he needed to prove himself to this medically isolated inmate. "I graduated from high school. I was in the army. I gotta a job. I pay my bills. I support my daughter. I'm goin' to college. I ain't never been locked up. I ain't no nigger!"

In addition to contemplating the N-word and relaxing around big inmates like Donnell, Supervisor Mitchell's 5D experiment is making me think food-thoughts. Outside of fruit, everything arriving on the meal carts appears frozen and thawed, processed, or emptied out of a can. I jot down the 5D menu one night: a square of pepperoni pizza, a 2.75 ounce bag of

Vitner's Sour Cream and Onion potato chips, a Bama twin pack of chocolate chip cookies, and an eight-ounce carton of Vitamin D-fortified whole milk. The next evening yields hamburgers with tomatoes and white onions, French fries, sliced peaches in heavy syrup, more Bama cookies, and more cartons of whole milk. No leafy greens here. Another night: tuna salad with wheat bread to make sandwiches (one of the best entrees I've served up on the 2–10), two four-ounce plastic cups of orange juice covered with aluminum foil, an individually wrapped Sara Lee brownie, a nectarine, and another bag of Vitner's chips, this time BBQ. The most pitiful offering is bacon strips, pinto beans, hamburger buns, the ever-frequent brownie, and four-ounce cups of fruit punch. Murder suspects or not, I don't wish this slop upon 5D dinner plates because these boys cooperate with me even around a fellow rookie from my new-hire group (not Attendant Jensen) on a night Attendant Marcus calls in sick. Big inmates need big meals. Legit meals. The ACA report that Martha gave me stated that the audit team sampled three meals and "found the food to be outstanding." Many juveniles did complain that meals were "cold," yet "the quality of food services appeared to be very good" and the kids "enjoyed the food."[1] I've heard no one rejoice over the bacon-bean burgers. Lunch must suck up most of our food budget because the 2–10 shift also has me dishing out what the Libby brand calls "Garden Vegetable Medley" dumped from wholesale gallon cans, mushy and bland. Inmates pass it over like I do at Jewel-Osco heading for the fresh produce section.

Not all finickiness is the usual "I hate Brussels sprouts." The Gangster Disciples refuse seafood. Legend holds that one of this gang's founding fathers died choking on a fish bone. Hungry kids in jail grow hungrier because a stranger supposedly gagged on a fish rib before they were lusty thoughts in the fathers' minds. Juveniles belonging to other gangs, like the Vice Lords and Black P Stones, shun pork in deference to tenets of Islam. Should one not eat fish because he is a Gangster Disciple, he fills up on rice and mustard greens and waits until morning when it's the Vice Lords' turn to go without because sausage patties cover the breakfast plates. Gang ties are supposed to improve jail life by providing you an ally, but they may bed you with a growling stomach. The older the inmates, the more serious the gang code adherence. No shorty has turned down my hot dogs or fish sticks during dinners on 5G.

Animosity over who receives any leftover food (whatever the quality) can be touchy, particularly on cellblocks with these man-sized inmates like 5D. Seconds usually go to level fours in the behavior management program implemented by Superintendent Doyle during his now four-year tenure. This innovation is so "residents can develop techniques for self-control and develop their own motivation to behave appropriately." The *Policy and Procedure Guide for Group Services* states that rewards attained through cooperative conduct will "enhance their sense of self-esteem."[2] When kids feel bad about themselves, they do bad things. Should an inmate embrace this program and attain level four's gold shirt status, added perks include meal seconds (instead of only one Polish, he might receive two, unless a dedicated Vice Lord and he never bit into his first one), later bedtimes, bonus visits from brothers or sisters, trips to a weight room, participation in talent shows where he might impersonate slain and idolized rapper Tupac Shakur. Genuine assholes right off the streets sprout manners piling up privileges they know will vanish the moment they rebel.

Success on 5D with these task points and gold shirts and extra food doesn't guarantee the same on other cellblocks with equally grown inmates. One night while working Medical, I'm assigned outside transport duty with Attendant Chambers. We climb into the back of a Cook County station wagon. A stout sixteen-year-old sits between us. His shackled wrists rest on his lap. Bandages adhere to his left shoulder under his bird-shirt and the cotton jacket borrowed for him from Recreation. He is going to the hospital for stitches. A supervisor is driving, a burning cigarette dangling from his hand hanging in the cold foggy air out the window over the round Cook County seal painted on the door. Chambers and I are accompanying to reduce an escape's likelihood. Once moving, Chambers asks the inmate if rumors about his cellblock, 5B, going up are true.

"We *did* send it up," he answers with his eyes beating on the seat in front of us. Our cuffed kid admits that he and other juveniles attacked one attendant and 5B's few level fours at lunch today. When cookies, bananas, apples, peanut butter, bread (white or wheat), potato chips, grape juice, orange juice, or fruit punch in tinfoil-covered plastic cups, or milk half-pint cartons are left over at mealtimes, most staff distribute it to that meal's kitchen helpers and any leftover leftovers to the highest leveled inmates. However, according to the rules, level ones can't be kitchen help. Upset with the attendant for picking only fours for the serving and cleaning crew and thus only fours to receive most of the spare goodies, the ones, twos, and threes retaliated. "He gave them all the extra juices," the shackled inmate explains to us.

The story circulating has mutinying juveniles dashing to their cells, mistakenly left open, to weight socks with bars of soap and swing-like medieval lances. The targeted children's attendant will miss a month of work. In the fray, a fiberglass chair's bottom edge gashed our passenger's shoulder.

In the hospital exam room, a slender doctor—her skin snowy from what I suspect is hour after hour under fluorescent lights—readies an antiseptic swab near a counter along the wall. I stand nearby, close enough to intervene should the inmate make any move. I'm not sure why, but Attendant Chambers has stepped outside the room. The doctor asks the boy how he was cut.

Deadpan again, "Fightin'."

"Maybe you shouldn't be fighting. Don't you think?" she pipes and walks over to him seated on a short metal stool.

The inmate turns his face from his wounded shoulder as she peels off the gauze Audy Home nurses had applied in order to access the slit flesh. Like in the car with Chambers and me, his eyes point down and away as if surrendering eye contact will disgrace him and equal an admission that what he did was indeed wrong.

Not suppressing his indignant impulses in order to accumulate task points, wear a different-colored shirt, and eat heftier meals is a matter of pride.

From several feet away, I look on at this chance couple—a white woman bound for moneyed social class and a husky still-handcuffed criminally accused teen with an inch of Afro who is willing to bleed and maim for extra grape juice that he would never drink, only then to be confined.

The wispy, blonde doctor doesn't badger the sullen boy's cop-out to violence as conflict resolution, nor does he lash back at her snide dismissal of his bitterness over 5B food and beverage injustices.

The simmering peace delights me. Attending children at the Audy Home hazes my workweek with wave after wave of racial animosity. But for this minute in this shift, I pretend that wealthy white working America and poor black incarcerated America can have a conversation, albeit three lines, without erupting in hostility and reciprocal hatred. For his restraint, I almost want to petition for a Confinement sentence reduction for this kid. Even though he apparently attacked one of my colleagues, right now I'm not condemning him to a full five days of cell time.

"Whose life you trying to ruin now, Mr. D?" I hear from behind me.

A month has passed since my two-week stint with Donnell, Raper Man Rick, and Attendant Marcus on 5D, but I remember this voice—gravelly and cartoonish. I'm back on the third-floor, so Supervisor Mitchell's coddling me isn't permanent.

"Yours, Chance!" I turn around and return the jest to Gregory Chance, who has just returned from a court hearing, escorted by a Movement and Control children's attendant through the hallway toward an elevator back to 5D. Everyone calls him Chance. Gregory loves talking to adults and always chirps something jovial. Chance fills out at nearly Donnell's size and carries what I am certain is at least 175 pounds on his rock-hard frame. A mischievous jabbering smile seemingly betrays any darkness of soul. Forever wiggling are Gregory's shoulders while his eyebrows quiver, such that a couple of 5G boys teased him about taking Ritalin when Attendant Marcus ducked into the block one night with him tagging along to speak to Attendant Milton.

Chance is an AT, and I've listened to his name being connected to "double murder." My second night on 5D, I overheard a different AT bragging after phone time how he'd just been informed that the police raided his "crib and found the AK-47." Chance was no choirboy among choirboys. He hinted at his charges being grave when I asked him about playing high school basketball after leaving the Audy Home. "It's too late, Mr. D. I'm already too far into the gangs."

For his court appearances, armed Cook County sheriff's deputies shuttle Chance and every other AT in vans with wire-meshed windows to the Cook County Criminal Court located next door to the Cook County Jail, "the County." His court notices remind him to supply his attorney, most likely a public defender, with the "*full* names, addresses, and phone numbers (if they have a phone)," of any witnesses potentially helpful to his "vindication or reduction in culpability." The sheet wisely defines *Stipulation*, *Finding of Probable Cause*, and *Finding of Urgent and Immediate Necessity* but not *vindication* or *culpability*. Back in 1985, administrators reserved one cellblock for ATs—4D. Soon three more fourth-floor units E, F, and G, received such inmates. Everyone called these blocks "the county units," in that they were an extension of the county jail. Cook County Jail—North. That first year some one hundred Cook County youthful offenders were automatically transferred to criminal court. By the early 1990s, the number had tripled.[3] Now only one cellblock never houses ATs—5G. Twelve-year-olds can't be tried as adults. ATs even live on 5J and 5K. Girls kill and tote guns and thrash the tar out of people too. Before ATs meet their first grownup cellmate down at 26th and California, they can't lie about legal predicaments because local media quotes their complete names. Sometimes I encounter an infamous inmate and then read his headlines, like Gregory Chance, whom caseworkers had initially placed on 4G, where he slugged and bickered. On 5D though, Chance earned level four and kept his gold shirt for several weeks. One evening though during my stint, he'd "snapped" and rushed an inmate with expletives, suspecting that he dialed up his girlfriend during phone time. Attendant Marcus dashed out from the console and coaxed Chance into his cell for a cool-off. He ordered the other sixteen-year-old into his cell too, motioning me to lock him in. The boy had squared his shoulders and egged Chance on.

"Why you wantin' to box?" inmates at the card tables had quizzed Chance's adversary.

Seemingly bewildered that his actions triggered such an imbroglio, his eyebrows lifting and his forehead wrinkled, he answered, "Over a bitch that I fucked that he says he fucked."

If Chance has two murder cases pending, why stress over a girl he likely will never see again? Greater concerns should woe him—like doing fifty or sixty years downstate. If a jury convicts Chance, Illinois law mandates that he serve at least 85% of his sentence. A forty-five-year term will dress him in state garb for thirty-eight years and three months even if he plays angel at the big house. Chance occupying himself with a bygone sweetheart may numb this fact. I want to believe that Chance thinks this young lady more than a "bitch" to be "fucked" despite his boast of physical nakedness with her. I want to believe he is a good person—he follows my instructions. Maybe Gregory does care about the girl. Maybe that is why he wanted to box.

"I'm goin' to the county Mr. D," Gregory says from behind his cell door on Medical. His seventeenth birthday is days away. I don't ask why he's medically isolated. Nothing looks wrong. Some ATs do stew away their final days before transfer here in Medical because administration fears them acting out against regular staff or other inmates. Such defiance from Chance would surprise me. Either way, our time is finishing because in the eyes of Illinois criminal justice, Chance is almost a man and soon can no longer be incarcerated with boys.

"How long you gonna be down there before your trial starts?"

"A long time, maybe a year, it takes a while for double murder."

For once I have an identical story from the juveniles, my colleagues, and the juvenile himself. I could ask Chance right now if he really did kill two people. But if he says "yes," then what do I say? And if he says "no," do I believe him? And what does it matter whether I believe him? He could have been playing me all along, kissing up to me in hopes of an eventual favor, but he isn't begging for anything right now, locked in medical isolation—an Audy Home short-timer. I don't ask. I don't want to know. If he says yes right here in front of me, I might recoil and condescend. I want our connection to remain. I like pretending that Chance is just a kid I know and am cordial with, a kid whom I don't leave work every day cursing out in my head. Administration won't confirm to us what any kid's charge is, as if every inmate on every cellblock has committed the same crime or no crime or every crime. Such info isn't included on the roll board either. I assume the policy owes to admin's believing that we aren't disciplined enough to treat alleged child molesters the same as alleged stabbers and shooters.

Chance leaves for the County. My curiosity surges about whether he was telling me the truth. Was our connection genuine enough for truth? On an off day, I visit a library and type his name into an online *Chicago Tribune* archives search. Eight months ago, the *Trib* ran: "16-Year-Old Charged in Fatal Shooting at Liquor Store." It was Gregory.

> Detectives investigating a slaying on Chicago's West Side arrested a suspect Saturday after watching a videotape of the incident taken inside a liquor store. A security camera at Personal Buy Low Liquors, 4241 W. Madison St., captured the fatal shooting at 8:40 p.m. Friday of customer Michael Robinson, 42, of the 4300 block of West Washington Boulevard, police said.[4]

The feature adds that a judge also denied Gregory bond and charged him with another homicide. Reading this, I recall kidding Chance one afternoon on 5D when he'd been kicked out of school before class ended. Attendant Coleman from the school area had escorted him back to unit and locked him in his cell—no more level four and gold shirt and staying up past 8:30 P.M.

with Attendant Marcus watching extra television and eating left-over brownies and oranges from dinner. The stout man lingered after securing Gregory's door. Incensed, Chance was pacing the cell and bumping the door window with his forearms and shouting.

"Chance, I can't talk to you if you cursin'," Attendant Coleman said, a few feet from his Plexiglas. Something had happened in class.

Gregory composed himself after some minutes. He stopped in front of his window. Attendant Coleman nodded to me, as if to say he'd done his job, now it's mine to keep him calm, and left. He had to be back downstairs before 3:00 P.M. when the school day finished.

From the console, I meandered over to Chance's cell front. Now knowing that his 5D angel figure could sprout horns in other locations, I'd remembered the double murder rumor and tossed out the possibility that Gregory had merely thieved something.

"Yeah, I stole a bike," Chance answered, still standing and flaring his eyes through the door window past my shoulders through the 5D common area and into the airspace over the rec yard as if he could see all the way thirty blocks "out west" to Personal Buy Low Liquors, and right then was watching a reenactment of his actions there.

15

Today, I'm working the 3E console with Attendant Hammonds, who works 4–12 on 3E every shift. The regular 2–10 attendant is on vacation, so I'm here, still floating. Since my flameout on 3D, if someone like Edison, Otis, or Marcus won't be my coworker, supervisors only appear confident enough to assign me to 5G and Medical. Block 3E is new, but Hammonds, over six feet tall with a square face channeled into a jutting chin, reminds me of Ken Norton Jr., the Dallas Cowboys linebacker whose boxer father broke Muhammad Ali's jaw. Every indication is that Hammonds is another Edison, Otis, or Marcus. I feel neutered once again, knowing that supervisors don't trust me, like they're cheating for me in which cellblocks they assign me to and with which coworkers—protecting me from certain inmates and protecting certain inmates from each other. So far, 90 percent of my shifts have come on the same third of the jail's total cellblocks. The continued floating means that supervisors haven't settled on a place for me. Even between annual or biannual shift bids when attendants win particular shifts on particular cellblocks, supervisors do leave new staff on certain blocks where bids will open. A guy from my new-hire group younger than me and at least ten pounds lighter is doing 8–4 on 4H—a very thuggish block, I'm hearing.

After dinners of Polish sausages and seafood the Vice Lords may or may not dig into, but before showers and lights-out, cellblocks can host special programs. Once, tutors from a church visited 5G to read and play Chutes and Ladders with the shorties while Attendant Milton and I chatted about barbeque joints in his South Side neighborhood. These are the only such volunteers I've seen, aside from well-dressed mostly early twenty-something males in the third-floor hallway, whom I suspect are my successors from Good News Jail & Prison Ministries, Chaplain Rick's organization. They still bring Bibles, but Bibles handed to them from a different Protestant minister. The cancer blinding Chaplain Rick since youth killed him before my first day as a children's attendant. Nothing extra ever happened for Donnell and Chance or even for 3G boys during my evenings there. The younger the juveniles, the more savable outsiders conjure them to be.

The special program called Law-Related Education has just ended, but some juveniles commenced whispering long before—which has irked Attendant Hammonds to bark, "Fellas, listen up!" Four students from Loyola and Northwestern Universities have guided willing juveniles to hold up character placards: *District Attorney*, *Defendant*, *Plaintiff*, *Public Defender*, *Witness*, *Prosecuting Attorney*, and *Judge*. Other kids posed to their sides and voiced courtroom role-play lines from paper sheet scripts, most in monotones despite the dialogue's obvious modification for these young actors. The remainder watched this special program from the tables.

"They're only trying to help. They don't have to be here. You need to be taking this more seriously," Attendant Hammonds lectures.

Our guests haven't yet stepped completely through the door, so I know the law students can hear him. His words must dishearten, like their own scripted words were dispatched upon deaf ears. I hope they're mildly depressed, that they're not just here because a professor is making them be here. I'd have been depressed if Jerome had begun whispering and staring around our tiny room during my New Testament readings and the discussions I followed them with. Nothing from the boys here on 3E. If not for their disinterest, I am sure that Attendant Hammonds would already have granted the standard go-ahead for cards, chess, and ping-pong. "Hey, I was poor growing up in the hood, with no father, and my mom on public aid. But now, I'm living the American Dream. I gotta wife, two kids, a house, two cars, a dog, and a nice vacation every year," my coworker goes on.

Block 3E compares to 3K and houses only three boys facing AT charges. I'm bigger than everyone by at least my neck and head.

Most units hold far more Automatic Transfers. This unit's eighteen other inmates are arraigned in juvenile cases that will never be public record. They probably will see the light of a free day before they are old enough to join an armed force. There is time and chance to regenerate, hence Attendant Hammonds's homily.

An inmate snaps, "You were lucky not to get caught up."

"Lucky?" Hammonds leans forward in his chair as if he is on fire to stand up and bolt right at the kid. He repeats his argument and applies it to the kid's logic: "I grew up here in Chicago, in the hood, with no dad, and my mother on welfare. But I stayed out of trouble, so there wasn't anything for me to get *caught up* in. I decided to avoid the gangs, learn proper English, and respect my mom. How is that lucky?"

"We're just bein' real," another blurts.

"Real? What's so *real* about being stupid and ignorant by not speaking proper English and quitting school? What's so *real* about shaming your parents by getting locked up over and over? Gentlemen, think about your neighborhoods." Attendant Hammonds pauses. His jeans and collarless shirt betray the seriousness of his expression and the seriousness of his message. No comeback from the "bein' real kid" or any other kid to this the first seemingly premeditated admonition I've witnessed from a children's attendant about the inmates' lives outside this building. Most staff just worry about what they do around them during their shift inside this building with no obvious care to what happens after their release.

"How often do you hear gunfire? How many people do you see standing on the street corners selling dope? How often do you see the police?"

A collective murmur, "All the time."

"How many banks are in your neighborhoods? How many currency exchanges?" Attendant Hammonds taps his sentences out like soft drum beats. "How many pregnant girls do you see? How many good jobs are there in your neighborhoods?"

More silence, but some eyes find Attendant Hammonds. None are finding me, and I wonder if they secretly are cursing Hammonds for selling out, "acting white." Should I soon work 3E without him but with another Newjack, will the inmates lash out at me to lash back at this lecture? Will I have to prove myself, like I had with the shorties and Jensen? I'm finally matched with a strong attendant who already controls the inmates but also tries to show them a different way—the reason I took this job. My worry that I can't yet likewise establish total control on these older cellblocks is squelching my own humanitarian impulses.

"Sure, you were livin' large on the streets. Hell, on the bricks [not being incarcerated] you had it all! Riding around with your boys, smokin' your blunts [hollowed out cigars repacked with marijuana], drinkin' your forties. Goin' to your girl's house. Hittin' it [having sex] when you want to. But in here, you can't hardly scratch your head without permission. Now you gotta ask someone just to go to the bathroom! What kind of way is that for a human being to live? Can you remember anything from five years ago? How about a year ago?"

No reply. Attendant Hammonds adds, "This should be this best time of your life. Before you guys know it, you'll be twenty-five years old and still locked up." Hands slide over tabletops. Pupils bore into walls, the dull scratched floor, or neighboring bodies. A good five or six inmates point their eyes at Attendant Hammonds. Wheels seem to turn in their heads, weighing pros and cons of his counsel, unexpectedly cognizant of their devil-made-me-do-it slumber. I lounge at the console next to Hammonds and watch. He is saying to the inmates what I want to say but never do. No way can I preach to an entire cellblock of black and brown kids that they shouldn't steal cars and skip school and sell drugs. What would I answer if they shouted out that my neighborhood had no drugs to sell or gangs to join?

"Right now you should be worrying about passing classes and preparing for college. You outta be concerned with finding a part-time job and helping your families and communities. You shouldn't be worried about standing before a judge, begging for your freedom. This morning I wasn't sweatin' over a trial. I didn't have to deal with any judges, lawyers, public defenders, or district attorneys. Guess what my biggest problem was today?"

No inmate ventures any guess.

“Whether I would have enough time to get to the pet store and buy my son the goldfish that I promised him.”

Attendant Hammonds and his wife are planning a Pennsylvania vacation to check out a children’s clothing ad posted on an interstate billboard featuring their six-year-old son. When this little boy turns twenty-five years old, college and neighborhoods with more banks than currency exchanges will be actual options for him and his younger sibling.

After showers and lights-out, I depart, happy that someone is trying to help the juveniles but sad that I have no guts to orchestrate my own special program.

Down the hall on a different night, I’m monitoring overflows on cots. My coworker is a very tall man with a shaved head and glasses. Block 3J with Attendant Avery is another safe move for supervisors—the shift was quiet, easy money for me. An hour before my shift is to end, a more average-sized man from 3B arrives with more overflows to bed down on the blank cots we have set up for them. These two friendly black men with shadow beards have trained me in handshake maneuvers that might elicit odd expressions if I attempted them with white friends. Outside of my volunteer sessions here, back in college when the ratio was one to five, being the only white person in a room of dozens was new to me before becoming a children’s attendant. With this ratio now at one to nearly thirty, someone in that thirty pretending that I look just like them is great comfort—comfort I needed more of back in week one.

The 3B attendant lingers, leaning on the console, and the three of us complain about the maddening number of detainees we suspect are in custody for months and months and even years awaiting trial on AT drug cases, contrasted with kids linked to crimes like murder and assault—acts rendering them more perilous to society.

“It’s too good to resist,” a 3B inmate raises his head up off a cot and squints at the console. The fifteen-year-old with thin shoulders has overheard us. “It” equals drug booty.

The visiting attendant spins around, eyebrows lifted and

forehead wrinkling. "Son, the way you guys are acting, no wonder white America thinks we're all gangbangers, drug dealers, thieves, and hoodlums! I came out of all that and look where I am. Am I selling drugs? Am I gang-banging? I hardly ever saw my dad. But I'm not locked up!"

In other words, *If you young black men live by the notion that drug money is easier and more profitable than an honest day's work, everyone will always peg us for scum.*

To the inmate, he then admits growing up on the South Side while certain family members associated with Black P Stone gangster icon, Jeff Fort. I love this rant. I think it's what these kids need to hear and who they need to hear it from, but the cynical boy's head plummets back onto his flimsy, green mattress before the 3B attendant finishes.

"I used to have a dope house," quiet Attendant Avery chips in without changing his seated body posture in the console's roller chair, his flabby midsection pooling around his lap.

Hours ago I'd cringed seeing his physical shape, but our shift went smoothly. The 3J near-shorties followed his every order. They don't distinguish muscle from flab.

Avery glares at the cot row through his glasses. "And you're right, the money is real easy. I had all kinds of loot. I could've wiped my ass with fifteen hundred."

The dissenter, apparently curious again, props himself back up on his elbows. Others squirm as well on their mattresses. Attendant Avery waits. More heads upright.

"Would any of you have quit dealin' making that kind of loot?"

"No," is the answer from four or five.

"I had it all, but I quit. You know why?"

Attendant Avery doesn't wait for any hovering head to answer. "One day a girl came to our crib beggin' for a hit. She was a hype but flat broke. She said she'd do whatever we asked, just to get a rock. My partner said she had nothing he wanted, so she wasn't getting any." No cash. No crack cocaine. "I thought he was gonna send her away with nothin'. Then my guy spotted his German Shepherd in the backyard. He told her if she gave it a blowjob, she could have a rock. She did. And when I saw that, it fuckin' hit me. Next time that could be my mom, my sister, my aunt, my cousin, my girl suckin' a fuckin' dog's dick—just to get high."

The boys looking at Attendant Avery stare at him as long as he keeps staring at them. I'm staring at Avery too. What words can I fire out at Audy Home boys so that fewer women in their home neighborhoods debase themselves with dogs?

16

In fourteen weeks of Attending Children, only two days—4K and then 3D with Jensen—register as utter throwaways when I wanted to apologize to the juveniles, to my superiors, and to the taxpayers who fund my salary. The two weeks on 5D, which included a shift with a fellow new-hire when the cellblock didn't go to shit, have upped my confidence. Running a smooth 5G the night Jensen covered for Milton did likewise. I've also executed half a dozen Medical Movement shifts with not one juvenile, including the fourth-floor broods, raising any hell in my ten- or twelve-juvenile hallway transport lines. Preemptively, I threatened write-ups for any illegal talking in line when I arrived at their cellblock doors for the escort. The 4K and 3D floggings nearly seem a worthwhile exchange for their lessons learned. And in a vicarious way, the impromptu special programs on 3E and 3J, when my coworkers of similar upbringings as the inmates lectured them about why they need to change their lives, are encouraging too.

My optimism is peaking such that I have volunteered for overtime—$105 take-home per eight-hour shift. This will help me shovel more dirt onto the memories of 4K and 3D. I figure I've neutralized half of one of those bad days by pulling 5G with Jensen. Doing overtime on a new block somewhere possibly with another new attendant might satisfy me that I am closing in on even ground. Meek-mannered Supervisor Taftmont solicited me for his upcoming shift, and I needed to prove that I don't beg off every challenge like I did that potential second 3D round with Jensen. Overtime could be anywhere in the building. I approach Taftmont at the front desk. It's October and Sunday right before 6:00 A.M. "Dostert, 3A," he says flatly. Again, no smirk, just like he'd pointed me off to 3D as if every cellblock in the jail is the same and every attendant who might work with me on those cellblocks is the same. My stomach muscles tense up and in. I don't ask who will be my 8–4 coworker. It's not 3D or the fourth-floor, but it's also not 3F, 3J, 3K, 5G, Medical, or Medical Movement. I've yet to do a full 3A shift, only a partial shadow one night when Attendant Edison was off.

Breakfast is a pleasant bore with the 12–8 man in charge and then in saunters Attendant Newton, 3A's regular 8–4 children's attendant. Newton is strong, I've heard, and he is here, so I won't have to grow any more hair on my children's attendant chest today. A plain man in a Bears jersey, he hardly looks upbeat, but I like non-smilers here. Physically, he is no more intimidating than me but obviously possesses the magic I'm trying to develop—a control of the inmates with your eyes and your mouth. He takes the console, and I take the TV area with all fifteen inmates—a luxuriously low resident count. A campy action movie plays, but it's a relief that this overtime won't pose any great obstacles. The inmates, none appearing younger than thirteen, hardly move in their seats much less break the no talking rule and challenge me to stop their misbehavior. I'm cheating again—leeching Attendant Newton's influence in commandeering this silent TV area. Were Attendant Jensen sitting at that console, the inmates would be yakking, and being new to this cellblock, I'd have to answer their challenge and silence them on my own. To prove I'm not Elmer Fudd, I should hope for a second crack at 4K or 3D with an Elmer Fudd. But for an easy $105 instead, that challenge can wait. Within the hour, my head twitches right. Steel snaps against steel, and the unit door bangs shut behind a tall gray-suited stranger. Attendant Newton cuts off the television, training his eyes on the console panel. Our tall middle-aged visitor looks past Newton with no greeting either, strides by the common area tables, and rounds the glass partition to enter the TV area. Breezing up the rows, he stops in front of the blank screen and thumbs open a Bible. Special programs go down on Sundays too. I try to meet eyes with the man, but he glances at his Bible pages and then at the boys between us. A surprise to me, he offers no joyous vibe, only an unfilled stare. Little changes when he opens his mouth.

A few minutes into the sermon, Reverend Henderson frowns at an inmate with an inch of spongy Afro, Lamar, on the second row. "Young man, will you please step out."

I don't know what he has done.

"You said the same thing last week," Lamar groans in a groggy voice, just loud enough for me to hear from my perch resting along the back wall. I always position myself on the TV area's final row so as to monitor every inmate at every moment.

"Young man, I said when I started that everyone has to stay awake, or you'll have to leave, so you need to step out," Reverend Henderson answers.

Apparently, Lamar, lanky and fifteen years old, in jeans and a baggy red sweatshirt, had nodded off. He writhes higher in his cushioned lime-green chair with wide plastic arms, one of several that isn't plastic-coated fiberglass. He dons no bird-shirt or khaki pants because he is "on Intake." Lamar and every other juvenile here and on 3B were just arrested. They wait for a judge to indict them and thus be assigned to a regular cellblock or have their cases dismissed and be released. If indicted, we will fit them with bird-shirts and Audy Home trousers.

Lamar turns a consternated face to me. "Is he staff?"

Napping in the TV area doesn't violate our rules, only talking. Honestly, I'd rather juveniles drift off into sheep-counting realms and thus not worry about them socializing or brawling. Lamar is correct. Our guest isn't on Cook County's payroll. Still I urge, "Just sit up and listen. It's not gonna hurt you to pay attention."

Positioned straighter, Lamar's head tilts to one side. His semblance of interest must satisfy Reverend Henderson because he eases off his demand and Lamar stays put. I feel good for moderating the dispute. Being a children's attendant can be summed up as conflict resolution. Conflict between juveniles. Conflict between juveniles and me. Conflict between my coworkers. Conflict between my coworkers and administration. And now, conflict between a juvenile and a pretentious volunteer preacher who won't preach to an exclusively volunteer audience removed from the cellblock like I had. My participants never lost consciousness. A couple minutes later, Reverend Henderson frowns down at the middle of the boys whose first row is a couple yards away. He halts the sermon. "Okay, son, you need to leave right now!"

Sighing like a whistle petering out, Lamar erects himself without another full glance of his craggy face my way. No protest of his second excommunication.

My instinct is to command Lamar back into his soft seat and remind Reverend Henderson that like his congregation member stated, he isn't a paid staff member and that I wield the final say in where juveniles sit and whether they sleep.

Lamar bolts from the TV area before I can redirect him. He slumps into a plastic chair at a table near Attendant Newton and the console.

Newton says nothing to Lamar, perhaps thinking that I kicked him out for talking.

Lamar plunges his face into folded arms.

I turn my head to refocus on Reverend Henderson—the most formally dressed person I've ever spotted in the jail. Most attendants and even some supervisors don jeans or track pants. I wonder if Henderson intends his black shoes reflecting the overhead fluorescent lights and burgundy tie matching the handkerchief in his jacket breast pocket as part of his presentation—the glossier his guise, the more inmates will believe what he says. No one pays Henderson for his homiletic efforts. He points this out to us. Sunday mornings are free for him to bring our juvenile detainees "a message from God" because God "has blessed" his limousine business.

Aside from television, meals, and being excused to the bathroom area, a weekend sermon from Reverend Henderson is all Lamar and these fourteen other street-clothed 3A juveniles can expect. They cannot attend the weekend Protestant and Catholic chapel services downstairs. Tiny Timmy and Demetrius weren't birthed into lockup life here or on 3B because shorties go straight to 5G. Timmy wouldn't last long in fisticuffs with Lamar.

Intakers miss more than church. They leave the block only for court appearances and medical attention. No school. No recreation. Even bathroom breaks on 3A and 3B are scheduled, not whenever a single juvenile requests. Starring in a *Tribune* headline like Gregory Chance, or not, few juveniles spend more than a week on Intake as has Lamar whose judge likely already evaluated the evidence against him, decreed it non-incriminating, and exonerated him. Thus caseworkers have not transferred Lamar to a regular cellblock. Instead, he waits on Intake for mom, dad, or a legal guardian to claim him. If no one shows within seven days, caseworkers will designate Lamar to the Illinois Department of Children and Family Services. One Intake attendant dubs such limboed DCFS kids "wasted sperm" because "nobody wants them."

With Lamar anathematized, Reverend Henderson explains that his limo company cleared almost a thousand dollars last night. "So I've come to teach you brothers the word of God, so you can be obedient to God and live righteously and successfully. My father told me: 'Son, you're killing time and pretty soon time will kill you.' Like many of you, I didn't listen to my father and mother. Now that I'm fifty-seven years old, I know what he meant. My body holds two bullets." From his Bible, he draws some yellowing folded papers—court notices and legal documents testifying to wayward years, and holds them high like sacrament offerings for the inmates to witness. In 1956, Reverend Henderson says, he was locked inside the actual Arthur J. Audy Children's Home and later did hard time at Cook County Jail and state prisons. "The other day, I saw a man in a wheelchair trying to wheel himself up a hill in the cold and wind. I can't help but think that the man was being punished by God." Unless the reverend resides in the far northern suburbs near Wisconsin, Chicago is hill-less. Henderson adds that his aunt lives in a mental health institution—another example of divine judgment. "You don't want to be punished by God too." If his audiences will "live righteously while still of sound mind and health," they can escape God's earthly fire and brimstone.

Without Audy home garb, Henderson's Intake congregation

sports five or six colors—potentially five or six different gangs. These 3A boys though could all be wearing plaid and corduroy for the zero attention they're granting enemy uniforms while Reverend Henderson talks on. His presentation is stimulating me though like a smoky Sumatran coffee. If God flogs us down every time we stray, dear reverend, why aren't we all cramped into wheelchairs and atrophying away in psych wards?

"Ask and it shall be given to you. Seek and you shall find. Knock, and it shall be opened unto you." Reverend Henderson's feet slide on the floor, reading Jesus's words from his black Bible. "Ask God to meet your needs, not your gang leader or drug dealer. Whatever you wanna be, a doctor, a lawyer, a teacher, a carpenter, a businessman, a politician—ask God for it!"

The inmates sink deeper in their seat cushions and stare behind Henderson to the blank television. I scan the common area. Lamar's head still lies on the table by the console while the reverend goes on, "Young men, I want you to be successful. God wants you to be successful! God wants you to be the lender, not the borrower. He wants you to be the landlord, not the tenant. We've got some future millionaires right here in this room!"

No juvenile moves. No one seems enthused at the idea of becoming a millionaire. Myself? I want to lurch up and shout: *So reverend, famished people in Angola shoo flies from their mucus-caked nostrils languishing in line for a bowl of high-protein gruel, and our fellow Chicagoans freeze themselves ashen on Lower Wacker Drive because voices warn them not to check into Pacific Garden Mission, but God wants the rest of us to summer in Loire Valley chateaux? Saint Peter obviously forgot to "ask and seek and knock." I doubt many denarii tumbled from his pockets when a crucifixion mob flipped him upside down!*

Reverend Henderson directs the boys willing to "give their lives to Jesus" and "go to church" in their free civilian life to raise their hand. I hope they all sit like statues, but not because I disagree with the prayer. We all must repent. I guided Jerome and Curtis and the other boys in similar petitions of repentance.

Four 3A inmates throw a palm up, bow their heads, and murmur through a recipe repentant prayer with the reverend. I hear nothing about the cross of Christ and the crosses he asks his followers to live with on their bleeding, raw backs. Henderson's cross is hollowed balsa wood stuffed with greenbacks, one he twirls like a cheerleader's baton. Here on 3A no one prays only to God. They pray to Henderson too, unknowingly inducting themselves into the army of this man's ego.

As the reverend starts for the door, two inmates turn and ask me for permission to leave their seats and speak with him.

I can't think of an excuse to deny them.

In a low pitch, as if he doesn't want Attendant Newton at the console to hear their exchange, Henderson converses with them near the glass wall, his back to Newton. From my view in the TV area, the cellblock door frames him as he scribbles on a note pad and then leaves.

The door clangs shut, and Newton dismisses Lamar to the TV area. The two questioners follow. In front of me, the other juveniles stir in their seats, seemingly grateful they remained awake, anxious to resume the movie.

I'm sure they want to finish it before the food cart returns, knowing that after lunch, we will shut off the videos and turn on the National Football League. And if the Bears are playing a night game, it will be tomorrow morning before the boys can watch anything with gun battles, car chases, and explosions again.

Another Sunday, I draw 3A for my regular 2–10. I arrive and Reverend Henderson is driving his entire congregation from the TV area to the meal tables to which he'd banished Lamar. Maybe all the juveniles dozed this time. Reverend Henderson usually waxes eloquent during traditional church hours. Perhaps a serendipitous hundred bucks to whisk a CEO or dignitary to O'Hare Airport this morning proved too tempting. The common area chairs he plants the boys on are the usual fiberglass, coated with slick, hard plastic—not conducive for napping like the two sofas and multiple soft chairs in front of the television. The sermon cranks up. His message remains: God wants to bless you and make you rich. Lamar, the "wasted sperm," is gone now, but he was right. This guy does repeat himself.

A rangy sixteen-year-old with cornrow hair braids catches my eye. He is leaning toward the reverend, elevating his haunches off his seat and jutting his torso over the round table like a praying mantis poised to snare a fly. Henderson isn't soliciting any show of hands, but this kid raises his and chops the air around his head, "My mom was off livin' with her boyfriend, my dad was never around, my brother was locked up. No one took care of me! I was all by my damn self! If I hadn't learned how to use a gun, I'd be a dead nigger right now! Where was God then?"

Reverend Henderson is wordless. I wish he had relocated his pulpit sooner so that more 3A inmates would have remained awake on these hard chairs and thus challenged his bullshit health-and-wealth gospel. This kid's question vexes me too, and I'm game for the rev's answer. Volunteering here, I'd dreaded this theological quandary and avoided reading my inmate friends biblical passages like: "He shall provide all your needs according to His riches and glory." What would I say to a kid demanding to know why God placed him on Earth with a mom who extension cord-switched him when he cried?

"God is the same yesterday, today, and forever," Reverend Henderson answers. Only his chin and lips move. The hands cupped under his Bible don't shift. "Give God a chance." Then he folds the Bible shut, turns around, and strides past Attendant Newton and me at the console, departing the cellblock. No heads bow for prayer today.

We all sit without moving for several seconds until another kid complains about Henderson. Attendant Newton nods. "Yeah, all the times I've seen him in here, he's always talkin' about his limo and painting companies. But I've never seen him offer any of you guys jobs, or even bring in some job applications."

We idle for more seconds, silent. I can't think of anything to say either. Attendant Newton, wearing another Bears jersey today, interrupts the contemplation, "Okay, you two right here, stand up. Go to the TV area," pointing to a couple boys close to him.

They do. Then he sends the remainder of the juveniles, two at a time, back around the glass wall to seat themselves in front of the square screen. I nod at Newton and stand up myself. I follow the last pair of inmates, flip on the television, and plunk down with them on the rear row. Plunking down with us is the angry boy's questions about God, his mother, his father, and his gun. They must wait. Maybe he will be stewing on 3A again next Sunday, and like Lamar, be able to hear Reverend Henderson pontificate twice.

At least now, I'm aware of one special program that doesn't envy me and expose me as an even more incapable mentor to help inmates see something in the world besides guns and gangs and girls. Listening to and watching Reverend Henderson, I feel valuable. For the first time since fraternizing with Jerome and Curtis and Thaddeus and Lemmuel during my Chaplain Rick days, I feel like one of the inmates, like for these few minutes here on 3A, I might finally be existing with them, living on their side.

17

Halfway between Halloween and Thanksgiving, I land on 5G. I'm confident from piloting the hushed evening here in September with Attendant Jensen—the hushed evening witnessed by Supervisor Mitchell. I'm even more confident because my first real fight is behind me. Working 3E without Attendant Hammonds, an inmate who, to that point in the shift, hadn't smiled or frowned or spoken a word that I'd heard requested to leave the TV area for the bathroom area. When I said yes, the fourteen-year-old, tall as me but fifty pounds lighter, stood up and strolled to the back of the TV area. Five or six chairs past me on the last row, he pivoted right and fired a haymaker down at a kid on the second to last row, missing. I rocketed up and with both hands yanked him by his non-punching arm and, like a swing dance partner, spun him around and squashed him into the cell row wall, shielding him from the group with my body. The targeted boy could rush in for a sucker blow but didn't. The attendant at the console didn't bolt over to assist. I was in control. My first punching fight lasted one punch. Another reason to relax here on 5G is that Timmy is gone, moved to a different cellblock. So even though Attendant Milton is taking off again, I'm not stressed that Attendant Avalon, fortyish and portly, is here for the 4–12. I know little about her, but she grins less than Jenson, is an inch taller, and weighs much more.

After dinner, two shorties in a TV area center row pop up during *Martin*. Shoulders and chins tremble. They frown. Compared to the one here with Jensen, this young shift is already a failure. The first sign of a strong children's attendant is that your inmates don't challenge each other around you. Your influence and control makes them forget about ever being angry at one another. Both these boys are new from when I last worked 5G.

They don't know about the quiet shift I commandeered without Attendant Milton. My looks alone aren't enough to scare these two into good behavior.

"Hey sit down!" I snap right away.

They threaten and flinch and glare. Attendant Avalon and I spring out of our seats and grasp at the boys. We bang into empty and occupied chairs, which scrape the floor.

One of the combatants, round-faced Nick, likewise barely taller than the bend in my elbows, knocks my forearm from his torso and fists at the other kid. So much for now being on the juveniles' side.

Lunging around me to grab Nick by one arm and yank him to her side, Attendant Avalon wants to restrain him with the official Audy Home method for incapacitating a violent juvenile—the Crisis Prevention Institute hold from training class resembling a shared potato sack race that is our last resort when verbal de-escalation strategies prove vain.

Nick twists and flails between Avalon and me, clawing back at his adversary. We can't quite wedge him between our hips to fold his torso in half and eliminate his center of gravity, so we grab Nick any way we can. Restraining Nick "by the book" isn't working even though he is half the size of the 3E inmate whose aggression I extinguished by myself in three seconds.

This should not happen. Nick was supposed to freeze when I yelled. He doesn't know about 3E bouncer Attendant Dostert either. Avalon and I should drag his pudgy little ass to cell seventeen or eighteen—Confinement cells, but we don't. Nick is my first true restraint, the only kid I've touched my hands to for more than a few seconds. I want this over with. We're aiming for his original cell, number five, behind us as Nick thrashes and croaks out "No!" without moving his lips far apart. His enunciation makes me feel bad, like I'm doing something wrong, something abusive. But he is the wrong one.

I let go of Nick and key open his cell door. Attendant Avalon still clutches him at the armpits, his back against her front. I remember his feet. Even a shorty, if irate enough, feasibly can dislodge his door window pounding it with sneakered feet.

"His shoes gotta come off."

Squatted, I cup his shoe heels and wrench them off individually without untying the laces. Nick's body coils like a barber's pole stripes in Avalon's grip. His socked feet flap at us. The door is open. Attendant Avalon lumbers in and shoves Nick's body away from hers. Free, he grips the bottle of shampoo on his desk, socked heel-pivots, and hurls. The bottle glances off Avalon's forehead, and with yet enough force, whacks the Plexiglas door window behind her.

"Ooohh! Did you see that!" a kid behind us shrieks. Another doubts my masculinity: "He shouldn't be makin' a lady do that!"

The "lady" ducks around the Plexiglas as Nick slings his brush and soap bar. I heave the door closed and lock it. The soap and brush clatter to the floor. Nick bull rushes and slaps the window. Tears speckle down his cheeks. Attendant Avalon and I swivel around. Shorties are flying about, escaped from their chairs and jabbering away.

"Okay, sit down, sit down. And don't talk! There's nothin' to see!"

Kids love to watch each other lose their wits. The boy Nick attacked has wandered back to his seat, but we don't confine him. He never swung back at Nick. We're grading on a curve. Attendant Avalon and I sink into our chairs, mine inches to the right of Nick's door. My heart thumps from the physical engagement but more from my crushed idealism. Working cellblocks, even the one I thought was manageable for a white Newjack, is a different universe from being a volunteer. Working with Chaplain Rick was like looking at the ocean through a drinking straw. My eardrums pulse. My arms fidget. Nick boils in his cell window. His hand slaps on the window grow into fist pounds.

Several shorties on chairs in front of us twist their heads around to gawk at Nick's tantrum. "Turn around, there's nothing to see!" I thrust my face at them as if being closer will intimidate them into following my instructions.

Nick attacks his Plexiglas and yells for twenty straight minutes. Everything is crashing down on me. I should quit now, and I should have quit at Martha's bullshit spiel about how "this place works." I should have quit after 4K and 3D. Three strikes should put me out.

"Okay, you have rec." Attendant Avalon and I finally decide to remove his audience, if only the backs of heads. Most of the boys zip through the space between the cell row and the glass partition into the block's middle two quarters, the common area, for cards and ping-pong.

I follow. Attendant Avalon stays in the TV area to enforce no talking for boys watching the recently tipped-off Bulls game. *Martin*, the sitcom, has ended but not the discord kicked off during the show—one child openly defying two adults. Only half the previous gawkers sit near his cell, but Nick keeps his position in the door window to shout and pound more.

Monitoring those at the card tables, I begin ping-pong with one shorty. I want 5G to look normal. I ignore Nick—all the consequence I can muster.

Similar to the 4K meltdown, attendants pass through the hallway with their juveniles in quiet lines and leer at me swiping at the ping-pong ball. They hear Nick beating and screaming and see that I can't do shit to stop it. My manhood deserves doubting. I'm doubting it too.

Half an hour into Nick's fury against his Plexiglas, which some card-playing shorties ignore while others giggle, Attendant Peña, a thinly mustached attendant from 5F, shorter and slimmer than me, his arms showing no sessions in a weight room like mine, taps our glass door. This is worse humiliation than Caseworker Jamison showing me up on 3D. I need intervention with one shorty as well—not just a couple dozen middle teens, several of them ATs.

I let in Attendant Peña. His gelled hair shines. "Can I see your keys?"

I hand him the ring and wander to the console like I have something to do. I can't idle nearby like a dunce and watch. From the console, I watch anyway.

Attendant Peña's boot heels patter on the slick floor in a stalk past the card tables. The card players' eyes follow him. Nick sees him too. Peña is humble in size but moonlights as a security guard at a Southwest Side mall where, from what he says, shoplifters may equal shoppers.

Nick flees to the rear of his cell.

Peña rams the master key into the door and jerks. "What the fuck is your problem!" booms off Nick's back wall and out into the common area and toward the console, shaking my eardrums. His question is as much for me as it is for Nick. Peña blows into the cell, and I can't see or hear him, nor can I see or hear Nick. Watching someone correct my failure is humiliating. Peña rants more, curses more, backs out, and leaves.

The Come to Jesus meeting with Attendant Peña permanently chases Nick from his cell door window. He repents of his sin and lives righteously (and quietly) for my shift's remainder. I can't look directly at his quieted cell front—my flashing beacon of failure. From the corner of my eye, I don't see Nick, so he is likely lying down or squatted against the back wall. I want to do something and make it look like I'm working and doing my duties and everything is under control, so I resume ping-pong with the same kid.

Ten minutes into ping-pong, Vernon, already confined, peppers his door with Nick's same side-fisted strikes. He yells, "Send it up!" but I won't blast into his cell and curse bloody murder like Peña. I loathe abandoning composure even more than listening to Vernon's cacophony.

Vernon's feet and vocal cords tire before Attendant Peña hears him, or maybe he does hear him and, for whatever reason, doesn't return—*Dostert's a lost cause and it will happen again and again until shift's end. I have my own block to manage.*

Soon I hear flushing. I turn to my right. Vernon is stuffing bed sheets into his toilet. His flushes come and come until the commode overflows its steel bowl and runs under his cell door toward me at the ping-pong table.

I do nothing. Attendant Avalon in the TV area glances left and notices the cascading water. She does nothing. We know nothing to do. To move across the cellblock and down the cell row to conduct the every-fifteen-minute Confinement log observations, we step around the toilet water slick. Standing, Vernon's squinty eyes smirk victory through his Plexiglas.

The black Hell's Angels–looking supervisor stops in on his last round. We called for him an hour earlier to discipline Vernon, but he never came. He sees the water. I'm sure he recalls my wimping out of 3D with Jensen.

Sauntering to a corner of the cellblock, the stout and squat man grabs our broom. Then he opens Vernon's door and swishes the broom straws through the water against the floor. His wallet chain jingles. The toilet puddle flows back into Vernon's cell. The supervisor's head twitches over his shoulder at me. *You are fucking worthless. I wish I could sweep you away too.*

Vernon shrinks from the grisly-bearded man, scooting off to lean against his rear cell wall. I'm ashamed that Vernon wouldn't back away from his door while I was standing there. "Sleep good," the supervisor says while locking Vernon's door.

I go home and don't sleep well. Now 4K and 3D are nothing. The 5G shift I did with timid Attendant Jensen might as well never have happened. Because I can't restrain a shorty or even shut one up inside his cell, a lady took a shampoo bottle to the head. Black Hell's Angel supervisor had to swab the floor of my cellblock.

18

The time clock supervisor sends me to Medical. Word must be out that Dostert is worthless, worthless even on 5G. Only Supervisor Mitchell knows about my smash-success shift there with Jensen and the smooth 5D shift with the other rookie, but now every supervisor must know about last night's shorty drama. Black Hell's Angels supervisor probably advised them: *Keep Dostert off any regular block unless you put a strong attendant there, 5G included.* I should be handing this supervisor a resignation letter. True and profound is my insult to the facility and Cook County taxpayers in letting the shorty cell-block go up. It was only two of the shorties who went buck wild, but no real man should need outside help to reign in any pair of shorties. I feel embarrassed to be here, like I'm insulting every real man in this facility doing whatever he has to in order to keep supervisors and neighboring attendants minding their own business. I want them to think of me as a real man too, as someone who can do what they do, but dropping my composure and saying words I've never said would make me feel like less a man, or rather less an adult for somehow not figuring out a solution void of profanities and physical intimidation.

I'm glad for Medical. Coming in today gives me one more day of pay if I quit after this shift, but part of the shorty block is waiting for me here on Medical—Timmy.

Two days ago, Thursday, I'd found Tiny Timmy locked behind Plexiglas during one of my breaks doing third-floor Medical Movement. Standing in front of Timothy's cell, I looked at him, his legs folded under him and his face inches from his door. "How come you're down here now?" I was curious why Timmy was suddenly housed in Medical. Nothing appeared wrong. I wondered the same thing last night, but "on Medical" was all any 5G staff could tell me.

"For something B did." By "B," Timothy meant Attendant Bradley.

"What happened?"

Timmy shoved the carbon copy of our standard yellow rule violation report under his door. I squatted and picked it up. According to Bradley's account, Timmy had defied orders the night before and ignored a directive to enter his cell.

"Is this what happened?"

"No," Timmy mumbled, his eyes flaring away from mine.

I bent down and slipped the paper back into his cell, hoping we could brainstorm how not to repeat the mistake. Maybe he would be more transparent with me than he had been with his mother that 5G visitation day. I probed more, but Timmy admitted nothing. A Close Watch notice taped to the brick wall next to his door mandated that two staff members be present when unlocking Timmy's cell. Dr. Jacobs walked up in his usual white dress shirt and solid tie. I asked, and he clarified his special edicts.

Timmy has triggered this transfer to Medical and earned Dr. Jacobs's special edict by accusing Attendant Bradley of molesting him, informing a caseworker that he awoke with blood on his underwear. According to Timmy, Bradley opened his cell and assaulted him after he fell asleep, having mouthed sexual suggestions before lights-out. The caseworker, a mandated reporter of possible resident mistreatment under the Illinois Abused and Neglected Child Reporting Act, called the DCFS abuse hot line and initiated an investigation.[1] Now if two attendants breathe into Timmy's open cell, he can't level accusations without each of us having an alibi. Timmy's quarantine also separates him from Bradley until DCFS investigators determine if his account has merit.

Only two children's attendants manage Medical, so it is inefficient for both of us to monitor the same location, like the TV room. And as a Close Watch, Timmy can't be locked in there alone without one of us sitting in the hallway monitoring him through the Plexiglas—he might pull the TV over onto himself. "That's some bullshit, man!" Timmy shouted when I'd informed him of the decree later in the shift when he asked to watch cartoons. A kid in an adjacent cell soon ridiculed Timmy's rape tale through their shared wall. News this exciting spreads like stomach virus at day care, even on Medical where juveniles share little face-to-face interaction. Grilled as to how he slumbered while "bein' raped," Timmy insisted, "I'm a heavy sleeper." Dr. Jacobs believes that Timmy plotted to be transferred off 5G. The boy has little regard for Attendant Bradley, who has already confided to me that he stripped Timmy to his underwear whenever he shouted in his 5G cell and kicked the door. When practically naked, few juveniles continue to scream and thrash. As soon as they pacify themselves, they receive their clothes back. Even on Timothy, it worked. No such instincts though welled up in me yesterday while under Nick's and Vernon's onslaughts against their cell doors and my eardrums.

"Timmy, you need to stop with that door!" I snap on Sunday on Medical where Timmy remains and I'm assigned again.

Being sent to the building's easiest cellblock again is a secret relief fresh off the shorties diminishing my manhood. Now I'm afraid even of 5G, afraid that if Attendant Milton takes another day off, some of the shorties will send the block up on me again.

Timmy is cramming chunks of mattress sponge into the crevice between his cell door and doorframe, trifling annoyances compared to what Nick and Vernon did to me from inside their cells two nights ago. Still if Timmy persists, consequences will follow, I promise. A Medical Movement attendant, on break, wanders up.

"I don't care! I'm goin' home on the eighteenth!" Timmy jeers through his Plexiglas at us and rips more green pieces from the foam mattress.

If he packs the space tight enough, we will struggle to unlock the room at dinnertime and in case of emergency. The glow on

Timmy's face broadcasts how proud he is that filling the gap with debris agitates us. Until now, Timmy has never aimed any trouble at me. I've only listened to stories and read reports about him and his trouble. He shouldn't harbor any revenge. Such is the most exasperating part of being a children's attendant—kids punishing me for their years of affliction, be it from Mom's man friend who whipped the backs of their legs with a phone cord, the police who billy-clubbed them after they quit fleeing, the gangsters who forbid them from playing tackle-the-man in Gage Park because it was their roost, or even my fellow attendants who forget their names and favorite juice types despite serving them lunch five shifts a week. Timmy is doing a marvelous job of dirtying his blue trousers and white socks shuffling about the cell on his hands and knees. Even his owl-faced white bird-shirt is dingy.

Visitation begins in half an hour. Four inches of snow settled yesterday, so Chicago is cold and white. The Medical Movement attendant and I voice our doubt that many parents, grandparents, and legal guardians will be braving the bluster. Without special permission, no one else can show up. All we fancy is to hush Timothy between now and 4:30 P.M. when the last visitor will leave. Attendant Peña is two floors away, and like me, the other Medical attendant may not have the stomach for a rampage like Peña's if Timmy assails his door with fists and feet. We hope someone will visit Timmy and squelch any disquieting rage.

The more we order him to leave his door alone, the more chunks of mattress Timmy tears off and flings around his cell. "The judge said I'm goin' home on the eighteenth, released to my dad!" Timmy continues. Translation: I'll be gone in forty-eight hours and can handle whatever discipline you dish out in the meantime.

"You're gonna lose all your shit if you don't stop!" my coworker at this moment threatens to confiscate Timmy's mattress and linens.

This man is big and solemn enough to intimidate most inmates, certainly a shorty. I'd be happy to work 4K or 4-anything with him. I hadn't strategized a mattress hull and blanket removal. There isn't much else to induce Timmy to quit—the boy has lost his television privileges. Policy and procedure prohibit us from spanking him or denying him food, even an orange or a butter pecan cookie for dessert. One fifth-floor attendant does admit that he "Jenny Craigs" confined juveniles. I won't do that, not with Tiny Timmy. Unlike Jimmy and Vernon, Timothy hasn't antagonized me enough. I might consider cheating two certain dinner plates if returned to 5G. I'd be even less of a man though, my neutering by two shorties completed.

"You can't take it!" Enough cat-and-mouse. I have a witness in case Timmy goes physical on me. I key the door and pull. Timmy has jammed it. I can't open it. The Medical Movement attendant takes a turn and needs thirty seconds to wrest the door loose. A dozen mattress scraps flutter to the marble-hard floor as the door swings open.

Timmy's grin is whipping into a grimace because I'm crouching down, grabbing his blanket and destroyed mattress, and yanking it out from underneath him. The bedding wadded up against my chest screens Timothy's legs and feet from my view as I back out of his cell. I see only his angrily creased face. I've bested a defiant shorty, albeit one who isn't pounding his door and screaming. Manipulating Timmy's environment though to foil his creative impulses with sponge pieces does not solve his actual problem. I turn to the other attendant. He nods and leaves for his next medication run. I drop Timmy's linens into a pile on the hallway and lock his door. With the broom and dustpan from storage down the hall, I return to Timmy's cell. He scoots away from the window when I push in the key and reopen the door. Kneeling, he eyes me while I sweep out the mattress remnants along with trash leftover from lunch—empty milk cartons and two Sara Lee brownie wrappers. Maybe someone bribed Timmy with an extra brownie to go easy on the mattress and door. Perturbed as I am, I don't relish the boy crawling in squalor.

Timmy saddles off to the back wall of his suddenly barren cell, save for the sink and toilet. He is still eying me. I lock his door.

Being a Close Watch, Timmy's cell was fairly empty to begin with. In his initial interview with Dr. Jacobs, Timmy spoke of suicide, prompting the stubble-faced man to label him a Close Watch long before he accused Attendant Bradley. That is why Timmy has no bed frame to set his mattress on or sheets to cover it with.

Swift was our purging Timmy's cell. Outside of a fuzzy cotton blanket and decimated mattress, it contained no furniture and few personals—no desk or chair or books or magazines, only some playing cards. Timmy likes to play solitaire on the floor. We let him keep the cards.

"When do I get it back?" Timmy lurches up onto his feet.

"When you can act right!" I leg down the hallway to stow the broom and dustpan.

There, Timmy. Who says we can't snatch something from you? This is hollow gratification though. My altruistic mission in relocating three states north to be a children's attendant now amounts to matching wits with an eleven-year-old over chunks of mattress sponge on the only cellblock I've yet to be chased out of.

Timmy curses me and his stripped cell. Stashing the broom in the storage cell down the hall, I can hear him. His tirade pulsates louder as I head back for the sign-in counter when our first visitors, a man and woman in their thirties, hit the block and spot Timmy squatting on his cell floor glaring through the door window. They hear the boy's "bullshits" and "motherfuckers." His eyes go to them. "On his way to prison," the man says to the woman with a glance at me and signs my visitors' log in front of Timmy's cell. They move down the cell row toward their son's chamber. Medical visitation is different. We arrange chairs in cell doorways for parents because the unit has no open space, only a hallway.

"You see that lady that just walked by?" Timmy wags his head side-to-side, as if he wields X-ray vision through his walls into adjacent cells.

Perhaps Attendant Milton's showing 5G the Jerry Springer tape did Timmy no favors either. From the counter, I notice the couple's heads tic left because they hear him too. They move on to their son's cell, and I begin walking up and down the cell row during visitation, monitoring the five total parents and guardians who have shown up.

Even though no one is visiting him, the longer Timothy seethes in the stripped cell, the less frequent his profane shouts. Slouched against a sidewall, Timmy peers out his cell door window, eyes shifting to track everyone happening by. Timmy is creeping no closer to a Wally and the Beav way of life. I am flinging no starfish back into the sea, but all is calm on Medical. Timmy isn't kicking his door, and although he possesses only toilet tissue with which to stuff his commode, he isn't stuffing and flushing. Medical is under control because of me. I can cash my next paycheck in better conscience—a few molecules of my manhood reclaimed.

It's 9:00 P.M. Visitation is long over. With Medical still quiet, I locate Timmy a mattress more intact than the one he pieced into his doorjamb. He deserves new bedding—like Sea World workers tossing the dolphin a sardine every time it soars out of the water and through the rings. As I learned in training, I'll reinforce the desired behavior. Timmy is giving me what I want, so I'll give him what he wants. I drag the new mattress in front of his cell where his old blanket and mattress are still heaped in the pile.

Timmy stands up, his eyelids high and arching up into his forehead. This is a dehumanizing process—treating a human being like Pavlov's dog.

Supervisor Wilkins, a thick and tall woman near forty, ambles into Medical. "No, he doesn't get a new one. He can have his old one back."

Timmy tore the vinyl cover off his first mattress, she reports. I still think he merits a different one in exchange for four hours void of yelling and whacking Plexiglas, but this leather-skirted woman nearly my height is boss. I say nothing and step aside.

She opens Timmy's cell and with a foot pushes his original

mattress back inside. After throwing his blanket onto the cell floor, she bolts the door.

"Man that's bullshit!" Timmy slams the door with the soles of his socked feet—not our desired behavior.

Supervisor Wilkins reopens his door, crouches down, jerks the old bedding away, and relocks the cell.

More kicks. More expletives.

She watches Timmy for a moment and then exits the unit. He bangs on and yells more until the woman returns with two sets of shackles—handcuffs linked by eight to ten inch chains. Only the superintendent, assistant superintendent, floor managers, and supervisors can authorize mechanical restraints—handcuffs and leg irons. Shackles are not to be "placed excessively tight," nor applied in such a position to "cause cruel or unusual punishment."[2] Chains in hand, Supervisor Wilkins opens Timothy's cell and drags in his old mattress and blanket. She motions for Medical's mandated female Medical attendant, a jolly woman whose hips span mine twofold, to help her pin Timmy down on the shredded mat.

"Bitches, motherfucker!" Timmy wriggles his arms and legs to hinder them from chaining his hands and feet together. He doesn't.

Two big-boned women subduing an undersized fifth-grader seems extreme. Even in pity, I can strategize no other options. Timothy is thrice-incarcerated. Once inside the detention center. Then inside a cell. And finally shackled inside that cell. So in the words of 5D's Attendant Marcus, life is "*really* really fucked up" for Timmy now. A kid this young articulating this crudely is extreme too, but the Audy Home extracts the worst from many of us, and not only from the juveniles. Flashing me his identification badge, one children's attendant confessed: "I used to talk like a church boy. Look at me now. Don't I look a lot more than nine years younger there? I never cursed before coming here." Maybe I should have cursed on 4K and 3D and then at Nick and Vernon like Attendant Peña did. I wouldn't have liked myself for doing it, but I might have avoided the ultimate children's attendant failure—your block going up or someone else storming in because your block sounds like it is going up. During my shadow-shifts, an attendant in his mid-fifties told me, "My favorite word is *motherfucker*. That's when the boys know I'm serious."

The women exit Timmy's cell and I linger nearby.

He tries to stand. He can't. The chains attached to his wrists are tangled with those attached to his ankles, thus binding his feet to his upper torso—an accidental hog-tie. Squatting, Timmy contorts all four limbs, his stuck-together fists bobbing below and above his chin, as if miming a protest expression. The chains clink and Timmy mashes his wrinkled forehead against the cell door window and scowls. His eyes move about like flashlights in the hands of a kid frightened of the dark. A playing card, which slipped underneath his door, catches Timmy's eye just as the juvenile to whom I've relegated the nightly cleaning duties finishes a push-broom lap from the other end of the thirty-cell corridor.

The boy swabbing the hall whisks the card into a pile of trash against the wall.

"Gimme my red card!"

The sweeper halts and looks to Attendant Jarvis, a Medical Movement attendant sitting at the counter a few steps from Timmy's cell. Six-foot three-inch Jarvis, once a soldier stationed in Germany, is the attendant I witnessed trading "nigger" barbs with the inmate here last month. Attendant Jarvis frowns at the sweeper. Timmy sees this and more four-letter words spew from his creviced face. Then he rocks back on his haunches and slams his door with short, hard kicks. He is small enough and the metal links between the cuffs are long enough for him to fire off abbreviated blows. Supervisor Wilkins is still close. "You wanna be shackled to that toilet?"

She knows that chaining a kid to a commode not only will jeopardize her job but also subject her to criminal charges. Shackles are never to be "fixed to any object."[3] The supervisor is feigning, anything to coax the boy into stopping, yet fantasizing about doing something masochistic to him. I felt likewise earlier today when Timmy smiled at me and kept jacking with his door. Right then I felt like unwrapping Timmy's next dinner cookie and making him watch me eat it if assigned to Medical again.

Timmy blasts the door even harder, clattering the giant Plexiglas sheet in its steel frame.

Supervisor Wilkins opens the cell and instructs Attendant Jarvis to pick the boy up, "Let's go." Maybe Wilkins doesn't trust me for such duty. She must know about 5G going to pieces on me in that flooded racket.

Jarvis follows her, his arms cradling shackle-bound Timmy like an infant.

"Make sure you finish up," I say to the inmate who has begun the sweeping.

Timmy has created a terrible disruption, and it is bedtime, so Supervisor Wilkins has few alternatives but to relocate him to a cell where cell door kicking can't entertain like on Medical. Moreover, like on 4K when one inmate starts beating a cell door, others, previously sedate, often join the attack. Wilkins could open Timmy's cell and sit with him through his crisis, but such practice would engage too many staff members every time an inmate explodes.

At cellblock 3B, adjacent to Medical, Supervisor Wilkins and Attendant Jarvis free Timmy from his mechanical restraints and imprison him in another empty room. Instead of a regular Plexiglas window nearly the span of the door itself, Timmy's new cell has a metal door. Its window is about five and a half feet off the floor and not much bigger than two legal-sized envelopes. With no bed frame to invert and scale, Timmy cannot see out the front or back of this room. Unusually hostile juveniles land here. Everyone calls it putting them "behind the steel."

After an hour, Supervisor Wilkins leads an unshackled Timmy back to Medical cell four. I expected her to leave him next door overnight, but his tantrum ended after several kicks against the steel barricade. Wilkins hands him a pen and the yellow violation form that Attendant Jarvis completed. Tightlipped, Timmy autographs the clip-boarded report to acknowledge receiving a duplicate. I doubt Mom will see this one either. Timmy then grasps the carbon copy from the supervisor and tiptoes into his cell. He squats on his original ragged mattress and glares through the window into a now swept clean hallway. Timmy's red-backed face card is long gone.

A few days later despite being assigned a different cellblock, I stop at Medical. Timmy sits on crossed legs almost exactly where I saw him last. Instead of cell four, Timothy is camped on the floor of cell two. Looking at him, I hope I wouldn't ever torment him at dessert time. No temptation right now—he is calm. I ask what happened, remembering Timmy's prediction to be released to his father on the eighteenth. These words out of my mouth reassure me. I haven't hardened. I still care enough about this boy who scoffed at my directions to ask him a question.

"My Dad didn't come to court, so now I go to Placement," Timmy chirps as if the idea of living in a group home doesn't grieve him a bit.

His indifference to Placement, real or unreal, does grieve me, even if new mattresses are dispensed far more liberally there. When first assigned to 5G, I expected the shorties' innocence and malleability relative to the older juveniles to revive my original Audy Home mission. Now even the shorties appear beyond hope, and I seem hopeless in managing them anywhere but the contrived reality of Medical.

19

"Now they pissed me off!" Attendant Littleton turns to me at the 3J console. I move my head but do nothing nor say anything. Littleton is permanently assigned here and I'm still floating. To our left down the 3J cell row near the bathroom area, deafening noise throbs from doors one, two, and three. Something sounds like it is cracking and breaking.

Littleton springs off his chair and blazes back to the doors. He warns the three confined twelve-year-olds inside: Keep up the ruckus, and I jerk everything out of your cells. From here, I can see two of the three boys—scrawny by anyone's estimation, more annoying than threatening. Unkempt and shaggy hair, not gang code styled or shaved, crowns each head. Arrested and indicted yes, but none strike me as chronic hell-raising bad kids. I know that look, the one where right away an inmate makes me imagine all sorts of turmoil and mayhem—him smack in the center robbing and maiming and striving to kill, or actually killing. Not these three though.

So my exile to the third floor, be it Medical, 3E, 3F, or 3J, continues. The third floor is where is I should have been all along, had Maywood and Taftmont not put me on 4K and 3D, prompting Mitchell's spiriting me upstairs. Whether or not Supervisor Mitchell has wind of Avalon and me on 5G, he and I are even now. I've screwed him back for hiring me by letting 5G degenerate into noisy watery discord.

Something else I've figured out is our options when confined juveniles kick or pound their Plexiglas and scream profane words behind it: (1) tolerate the noise and write another rule violation report, which might elicit additional disciplinary measures, usually more Confinement days, (2) contact a supervisor to transfer the inmate to a steel-doored cell, (3) cuff him inside his original cell, or (4) alter the cell's environment, motivating the juvenile to less aggression. If a supervisor isn't around, some attendants extend option four—like what Attendant Bradley did in stripping Tiny Timmy to his briefs.

With three truly bad days now, I'm content, if possible, to every day luck into a cellblock with a strong attendant and let him run the show. *Don't send me somewhere where I must be the heavy.* Once ensconced though on a unit with someone like Edison or Hammonds or Milton or confident in my own self on Medical, my entire six-month children's attendant life cycles through my mind, and a nerve goes raw. How much of a man am I if kids, be they ten or thirteen or sixteen, can make me want to quit because my eight hours were torturous, and I dread eye contact with supervisors and coworkers the next day? As long as children can torment me, I'm a child too. What those real men like Edison, Hammonds, and Milton do, I must learn to do. Not today though because Attendant Littleton, the 8–4, gives off no rookie air. Ten years older than me, serious with glasses and a chest thicker than his stomach, Littleton will handle this. Block 3J won't go the way of 5G with Nick and Vernon.

"Send it up!" The 3J trio synchronizes its battle cry between strikes on their windows.

Yell. Pound. Pound. Yell. Yell. Pound. The din from at least one cell collides with the bathroom area wall hiding its full view from us, echoing louder down the row.

Heads of 3J's non-confined inmates twitch up with each door kick. They check out the three cells and then us. *What are you two gonna do?* Littleton and I have them sequestered at the common area tables in front of us for this unit's traditional after-school quiet hour. They can only complete homework (about half have worksheets of some kind) or read—no conversation, drawing, board games, cards, ping-pong, chess, or checkers.

"Send it up!" Bang and kick. Kick and bang. "Send it up!"

Attendant Littleton turns my way. "Lemme see them keys!"

I pull them from my pants pocket because his shift ends in a few minutes. He doesn't want to accidently depart the cellblock with them.

Littleton bounds down the cell row and opens door three. He rips the kid's blanket and sheet off his bed and slings it out of the cell—what he promised. The green vinyl mattress is next. Then he shoves the bed frame through the doorway, stands it upright between cell fronts along the row, and relocks the door—approved option three. Per the usual consequence of Confinement, a different attendant has already confiscated everything else: reading desks, chairs, magazines, family pictures, and extra socks. The personals are bagged, tagged, and locked in the unit cabinet. Littleton levels the identical consequence on cells one and two, so each boy has nothing to sit on, save for his steel commode and nothing to lie on, save for the slick floor. The cells are empty, save for the boys.

I face the three cells from the console and can see two of the inmates standing in their windows turning their necks to see their peers in the common area. Littleton heads for the console and sits down in the other chair.

"Maybe that will shut them up."

For about thirty seconds, the boys are quiet. Then comes, "Send it up!" Whacks on the doors. "Send it up!" Whacks on the doors.

We look at each other. More whacking and yelling. Attendant Littleton keeps his seat. Most of the inmates stare at us, then down at their book or magazine when we glare at them. The racket clangs on for at least a minute until Attendant Avery, the 4–12, steps into the block. He sets his duffel bag on a small desk next to the console. The boys' cacophony is obvious to Avery, the attendant who recounted his dope house and the woman blowing his partner's German Shepherd for a pebble of crack cocaine.

"Kick it again!"

A single strike rattles a Plexiglas window. Every kid at the tables looks at us.

"You got the keys?" Attendant Avery swivels toward Littleton and me.

I hand the ring to him. Avery didn't hesitate or even make eye contact to see if I was going to do something about the boys' yelling and beating because I've been here two hours already, and he just arrived. Avery must see me as a clueless Newjack he needs to override.

Littleton leaves, and Avery stalks to the three adjacent cells, his feet sliding along the floor as if he wants to be noisy and draw this spectacle out—force the other kids to witness his intervening in this bad behavior.

He opens door three—closest to the console and TV area and easiest for the non-confined boys to see from the tables. From the console, I watch too. Attendant Avery, like Littleton, is permanently assigned to 3J. This is the path of easiest resistance—letting someone else do the work, someone framed by confidence and composure, the perfect plan formulating in his mind whenever an inmate acts with defiance or obnoxiousness, like Attendant Otis egging on 3D's Damien Dennison to tattle on him to a caseworker.

"Take off your pants, shirt, and socks and give 'em to me."

I can't make out the kid in cell one now, but in less than ten seconds, he hands Avery a wad of clothing, which Avery drops onto the inmate's bedding already piled outside his cell. Next come the other two boys, who back away from their Plexiglas windows while disrobing. None refuse like Timothy had when Attendant Bradley stripped him. Avery just stands in the doorway, waiting for the surrendered clothing. Attendant Walton never outlined this strategy for inducing inmate cooperation. The boys in cells two and three hand Avery their clothing, which he likewise tosses down. Sheets and blankets, now topped with khaki trousers, bird-shirts, and the kids' own socks further cluttering the few feet of floor between their cell fronts and the bathroom area, cause me to think of an exploded laundromat.

Attendant Avery turns his head toward cell one and says, "If you can shut up, you'll get your shit back after dinner," a hint of fatherly concern edging into his tone. *I don't hate you, but fuck with me and you'll regret it.*

Ninety peaceful minutes pass. We serve dinner. Afterwards, Avery exits the block to wheel our food cart to the elevator for cafeteria personnel to retrieve it. I stick to the console and eye the rest of the boys in the TV area. If they talk, I can cut off the television with one flipped switch. The underwear-only boys are calm. They've been calm every moment since their involuntary voluntary strip-downs. They notice through their door windows that Attendant Avery is gone. They can test me, the Newjack seen on their block only a couple times and always with a stellar coworker.

After several minutes, Avery steps back inside the cellblock. He knows that I'm a Newjack and knows the boys know I'm a Newjack.

"They beat on the doors?"

Compared to earlier while Littleton was here, the boys' strikes were bumps and brushes, but the sting from Nick and Vernon humbling Attendant Avalon and me while we wrote reports and waited hours for Supervisor Lankford lingers. I tell the truth, "Yeah, there were some love taps, but I couldn't tell from which room, or if it was from all of them."

"Drraawwers!" Attendant Avery swings his head at the confined boys' cells.

From behind the console I stand and toss him the keys.

The television is still on, but our fifteen non-confined inmates rotate their heads right from their seats to follow Avery sauntering for the cellblock's opposite end. They behaved while he was off unit.

Almost stooping to look each inmate in the face, my coworker unlocks the doors one at a time. A wavering hand fingering a pair of boxers extends from each doorway. No fight this time either. Avery drops each undergarment on top of everything else heaped on the floor and relocks the cells. Turning on a heel, he heads for the TV area, "Rooms sixteen, seventeen, and eighteen, shower time!"

Avery portioned out the dinner plates, so doing showers falls to me. I push the console roller chair in front of the three Confinement cells directly across from the bathroom area. The first trio of boys meanders past me, gawking over my shoulders into the cells. The three confinees have wrapped themselves with toilet paper loincloths cradled in place with both hands.

“Go on, take your shower!” I snap above their giggles.

Fortunately for Avery and me, supervisors making their rounds proceed only as far as the console and sign the logbook. I doubt that undressing kids to their underwear lands within policy and procedure. I know that making them naked doesn’t. I’ve come across no instruction in the guidebook on how to calm celled inmates who scream and pound. Avery’s method works. The three wispy youths are ghost-quiet during showers and card time. At lights-out, Avery returns the three confinees everything—mattresses, bed frames, bedding, bird-shirts, pants, socks, and drawers. Sitting at the console, I hear them with no cue from Avery vowing how never again will they make noise in Confinement.

Soon I’ll hear about a stripped but still screaming and pounding juvenile in an empty 3A cell and an attendant opening the door and hurling a pitcher of icy water into the brick chamber and then saying, “You’re a bad motherfucker now, huh?” to the bare, shivering kid. Like these on 3J with toilet tissue swaddled loins, he too halts his racket.

Becoming a man at the Audy Home requires doing what my parents taught me a man, a child having grown into a moral adult, never does—employ a bad means to justify a good end. They preached that it was my choice all the time to choose what was right and to thus grow up. Now I must resolve how to grow up into what I believe is a genuine manly children’s attendant—one who preserves order by thwarting the inmates from humiliating him but executes all this while still himself being mature and moral.

20

Attendant Bradley expects a sluggish response from DCFS inquisitors regarding Timmy's rape accusations. The Illinois child abuse hotline averages over a thousand daily calls. This government agency whose decrees result in suspensions and firings unnerves many attendants. "They'll take a kid's word over yours," I've been warned. Much to Attendant Bradley's satisfaction, DCFS rules Timmy's claim "unfounded" fewer than ten days after the allegation. Inmates accusing us of mistreatment, even with subsequent DCFS not-guilty verdicts, do not return to our cellblocks. Dr. Jacobs and the caseworkers can thus hold Timmy in Medical or transfer him to 3J where one of the three naked-for-an-evening kids isn't much bigger than him. Dr. Jacobs suspects that Timmy had wanted to change blocks because "some of his gang buddies" are housed on 3J, hence his assertions against Bradley. "Instead of him responding to the system, Timmy loves seeing the system respond to him," Dr. Jacobs tells me. He keeps Timothy in Medical for three more weeks, but shortly after his twelfth birthday, Timmy has his preferred living arrangement.

"Where's Timmy Tyler?" I wonder aloud, reporting to Medical one early December afternoon. I'd expected the boy's bug eyes peering at me through cell door number two.

"On 3J and already in Confinement," a fifty-year-old regular Medical Movement attendant wearing boots and a black leather vest says. Last night, this small man with glasses escorted Timothy from a locked 3J cell to Medical for dosage. I haven't worked 3J since Timothy's transfer there. The attendant reports that kicking resumed, Timmy dislodged his first 3J cell door window from its steel frame and staff members moved him to a different cell but to no effect. He kicked on, but the Plexiglas held.

Supervisors and caseworkers are shackling Timmy more too, but I hear that he thrusts his wrists into the air, taunting whoever threatens to cuff him. Timmy has discovered how to wriggle out of his fetters. For Timmy as Houdini, supervisors revert more to steel-doored cells. Within policy and procedure, this is all we can do—subtract privileges and increase his time caged inside various cells. Aside from earning a later bedtime or quarters closer to the TV area, we wield little else to motivate Timmy to change. I've never seen him, nor any other inmate, scheduled for regular therapy or counseling.

Wherever I work, I forever wonder about Timothy, hoping he will conform, as if his fate here will mirror mine. If Timmy can behave, then I can too. I can be another Attendant Tucker, never cursing or stripping inmates or throwing cold water into their cells. I can't resist quizzing coworkers with Timmy-relevant knowledge—like Attendant Simons who mans 3B, where Timmy often ends up behind steel. While he drives me to Union Station again for my train home, I ask him about Timmy's stints there after all his Plexiglas damage on 3J. Simons tells me about a recent incident when he heard a meek tapping sound from behind Timmy's steel door. The noise surprised Simons because Timmy usually yells when he wants something. Simons left the console and opened the cell to find Timmy standing at the front, panting with vomit speckling his chin and shirt. Simons escorted the faint boy to Medical, where nurses let Timmy suck air from a ventilator for an hour. Then he returned behind the metallic door with the envelope-sized window. Simons admits, "It's probably the only time I ever actually felt sorry for the kid."

At Timmy's next court appearance, a judge *continues* his case. Timmy will spend the winter holidays detained. His claim to be indicted in "a gun case" still disheartens me. Perhaps Caseworker Hampton will sympathize and disclose what administration won't. After work, Hampton spots me on our way out of the building. "Aggravated assault, so he could've used a gun. He had to use something." Everyday physical attack must be a bare-handed one. I tell myself that Timmy fabricated the gun part to thump his chest as a badass but in reality had brandished something less lethal, like a rock or a bat—my ploy to believe that Timmy will eventually, like I did at his age, be excited about his history fair project, tingle nervously about football team tryouts, and query his English teacher why e. e. cummings wouldn't write capital letters. I want my childhood for Timmy.

The violent nature of Timmy's offense, particularly for a then eleven-year-old, and his misbehavior under our care induces more court hearings, motions, continuances, and requests than the average detainee. Yet after five months of detention, half of it being locked up while he was locked up, and one medical attendant deeming him "a bad little motherfucker," Timmy is again contending that freedom nears. It's been two months since his father didn't show, and Timmy's story now involves him being sent home to his mother's custody, instead of to Placement.

On my way to a different third-floor cellblock, I pass 3J and notice a plywood sheet standing in for a front windowpane. Days earlier, Timmy committed a major rule violation but entered his cell cooperatively until Attendant Littleton began confiscating his personals. A local charity had distributed transistor radios on Christmas Eve—a present that Timmy disassembled. Before Littleton could snatch all the strewn radio components off the floor, Timmy grabbed one of the magnets and zinged it out of his cell doorway. His throw struck the bay window and cracked its glass. A supervisor shipped Timmy back to 3B. Maintenance workers removed the damaged glass and installed plywood.

Timmy then calls Attendant Rucker, the attendant unlocking his steel door at breakfast time, a "fat bastard." Timmy said the man shorted his food plate. Rotund and under six feet tall yet easily weighing three hundred pounds, many staff joke that Attendant Rucker struggles to fit through cellblock doorframes. "The kid's right. What can Rucker say, 'I'm *not* fat'? He *is* a fat bastard," Attendant Simons later comments to me. Finally, a second sympathizer for Timmy.

On the eve of Timmy's next court appearance, I volunteer for graveyard overtime on 3G. Tiptoeing onto the sidewalk's snow and salt just after 6 A.M., eight-Fahrenheit-degree air whipped by the wind knifes at my pores, and my face stings like someone has splashed me with acid. The parking garage across Hamilton Avenue obstructs the sun's warming beam in its climb above Chicago's plain running up to Lake Michigan, lending the crunchy mix under my stiffening feet an even darker tint. A couple hours from now, the sunlit slush will be brighter, and moms and dads, Timmy's mother among them, will slog their way to this glass entry-exit, hoping to depart this arctic January morn with their vindicated sons and daughters. After Timmy's hearing, Attendant Haines, another regular 3B staff, opens the boy's steel door. Timmy is finishing his five-day Confinement sentence for breaking the glass. Haines asks Timmy how he fared with the judge. The man has three small children of his own and often motions Timmy aside if he sees him in the halls being escorted to Medical for his meds and gives him pep talks about avoiding trouble. Not everyone thinks he is a bad little motherfucker. Timmy calls Attendant Haines his "personal caseworker."

Timmy cries and tells Haines that his mother has abandoned her custody rights and turned him over to the Illinois Department of Children and Family Services. Timmy says it is his punishment for the shattered window. Otherwise Timmy could have left with her, Caseworker Hampton later confirms to me.

After more than five months of detainment, Timmy is no closer to returning home than he was the day of his arrest. Whenever the court finally releases him, be it from the Audy Home or from Placement, Timothy won't go home. DCFS will find Timmy a home. So neither Attendant Bradley, Dr. Jacobs, myself, nor the obese man who wouldn't furnish him enough scrambled eggs is Timmy's worst enemy. A caseworker transfers Tiny Timothy back to the fifth-floor but not to 5G and Attendant Bradley. Normally 5A houses no twelve-year-olds, but administration grants an exception. While older, 5A inmates are undersized, many fourteen, a few fifteen.

Into the New Year, Timmy's judge ships him to Placement—a group home somewhere on the city's South Side. Haines, Simons, myself, and Caseworker Hampton expected him to be detained much longer. We suspected Timmy's judge would nail him with damage to county property for what he did to the window. Mom was harder on him than was his magistrate. I want to curse Ms. Tyler for her cold, hard heart and champion Attendant Haines and myself as more loving influences in Timmy's life. She laxed into the easy route, opting for the path of least resistance—a mindlessly excessive punishment benefiting only the punisher—what I am striving to avoid and thus facilitate my own moral maturity as a children's attendant. Ms. Tyler is no woman. Like Timmy, she too is a child. I must concede though that this child knows much more about Timmy than me.

"Timmy Tyler is back?" I stammer out loud, swinging around to coworkers, having just reported for medical duty, a name at the top of the fifth-floor meds list stopping my eyes.

"Yeah, he's back. Came in this weekend," the fifty-year-old medical attendant answers, his boots scuffing on the floor. He hasn't forgotten Timmy either.

If juveniles find obedience in lockup arduous, Placement is worse. Such facilities often are not secure—few barriers to keep jumpy boys like Timmy from dashing off premises. If a kid manages to behave there, a judge might release him outright to his parents, legal guardians, or DCFS. Should he really act a fool at Placement, not only will he be banished back to the Audy Home, his judge might hit him with another indictment.

Timmy's name on the medication list surprises me. Three months have passed since his departure. His conduct improved once on 5A, and I planned on never seeing him again.

Caseworker Hampton soon verifies that Timmy ran away from the group home and was arrested again.

Timmy is lucky.

Just weeks before the window incident, Timmy and an equally runtish 3J Close Watch kid pranced in adjacent cell door windows and shouted after lights-out. No 3J attendant remembers what initiated the slam session, but overflows lying on cots near the cells savored the boys' sexually oriented banter degrading the other's mother, giggling instead of drifting off to sleep, as did juveniles housed in cells on either side of the two ad-libbing standup comedians. Attendants then extracted everything from both cells. The duo though needed no vinyl mattresses and scruffy blankets to frolic in their darkened door windows, executing their vulgar exchange, "back and forth, like a tennis match," according to Attendant Simons. He was there delivering his overflows to the 3J cots. "Were they enemies?" I quiz a 3J attendant who had a front row seat at the console for the duel. "No, they fed off each other."

A judge frees Timmy's verbal adversary soon after the late night insult contest. An evening not long after his release, he sits with two men in a parked car. Someone approaches the car and opens fire, killing the boy. The *Chicago Sun-Times* reports the thirteen-year-old's death in its Metro Briefs column.[1] "He was safer in here than he was on the street," Attendant Avery says when we talk about the murder.

I remember the slain kid, Carltell. His final words to me: "Mr. D., you locked me up!"

Before Dr. Jacobs had transferred Timmy to 3J, I'd worked there again and this boy scoffed at my order to serve wall time for talking in the TV area. Attendant Avery then grimaced: *Stand up for yourself! Don't let him do that!* So I barked at Carltell to step to his cell. He did. Something of a stroll, but he complied. I bolted Carltell behind his Plexiglas and wrote a report to justify the early bedtime—everything I should have been doing since day one on 4K but didn't because Attendant Walton never advised me: "If a kid refuses to follow instructions, immediately tell him to step to his room." No inmate ever refused his instructions. Weeks after confining Carltell, he and I passed in the hallway, our blocks marching opposite paths. The soon-to-be deceased boy, very boyish looking even for thirteen, spotted me and blurted his "locked me up" comment enduringly, as if he was proud that I'd confined him. Reminding me of his transgression and my imposed consequence made Carltell feel good—bad attention is superior to no attention. Without saying anything, I glanced over my shoulder. Carltell's pug nose and still mangy Afro were cocked likewise over his shoulder at me. *Hell yeah, I locked you up! Follow my orders the first time you little punk asshole!* At least on the outside I was being a man, the moral children's attendant I wished to be, even if on the inside I was cursing Carltell during the Confinement-triggering incident and then again weeks later when not even assigned to his block.

Now this shorty is buried in a cemetery, but I don't lament locking Carltell up. I'm glad I granted him no second chance to step to that wall for wall time. Five months ago, I sympathized with Calvin staring through his Plexiglas at me on that first 3G shadow shift with Attendant Walton. I wanted to free Calvin for cards and television. Confinement was the Gulag. Now it's opening an umbrella in a thunderstorm.

Studying the *Sun-Times* clipping and then musing with Attendant Avery, I don't picture slain Carltell's family at the funeral and meditate on their grief, trying to participate with them and somehow rendering the boy's passing less tragic. Instead I relish how cellblock 3J will be easier if I work it again soon because the kids will know that I won't take any shit from them, like I hadn't taken any shit from this kid who was just shot dead in a car in the dark. Retaining my dignity by not taking shit from children, especially shorties like Timmy and Carltell, now seems my only possible mission here.

21

The leniency of Tiny Timmy's judge is corrupting our caseworkers. They have pared down Confinement sentences since Timmy's departure for Placement. Possessing lethal contraband, cursing out staff, and brawling with each other, offenses formerly meriting five days, now bring only three, two, and occasionally, a mere day of lockup. I mention this to a coworker who comments on Superintendent Doyle: "Yeah, he thinks this is some group home or summer camp. It's not. This is fuckin' jail, and it outta be run like one." He believes Doyle is instructing caseworkers to reduce such punishments ahead of slowly and subtly eliminating Confinement all together. I'm not happy either. Had Carltell on 3J not known that multiple Confinement days loomed if he defied my order to step to his cell, he would not have done so.

I do appreciate one recent Doyle innovation. The day after Tiny Timmy's assault on his Medical mattress and cell door, I gathered with twenty-five other attendants and caseworkers for lunch near Doyle's office in a conference room normally emanating the same accosting odor as the cellblocks. Instead, I whiffed appetizing aromas seeping through torn aluminum foil covering pans of baked chicken, black-eyed peas, and mustard greens. The free meal—a food service offering not culled from the juveniles' menu like at the other few staff functions—was an honor. A caterer delivered coconut cakes for dessert.

We all wanted to know who had won the Do Right Foundation Program Proposal Contest. Grasping to recreate the relationships from my Chaplain Rick volunteer days, I had tendered a plan to create level-four reading groups. I would recruit willing older juveniles, perhaps Donnell and Chance from 5D or the mature AT chess players on 3G, to read and discuss adolescent literature, maybe even Malcolm X's autobiography and Martin Luther King Jr.'s "Letter from a Birmingham Jail." To open, Doyle stood in front of us and invited Assistant Superintendent Davis to "say a few words."

A children's attendant at the actual Arthur J. Audy Children's Home in the late 1960s, Fred Davis becoming the superintendent's next-in-power culminated a demanding administrative ascent. Despite a prominent limp due to a degenerative hip, Davis once subdued belligerent juveniles as an attendant, caseworker, and then supervisor. Many attendants though warn me not to bring concerns to Davis's attention. "He's forgotten where he came from," Attendant Chambers says. "He won't do anything to solve your problem," according to Attendant Haines. Some mock Davis, a heavyset fifty-something man, certain the vacant superintendent position was his for the taking five years ago were he more educated. The county board commissioners hired Doyle, a fitter and college-degreed man, from a juvenile facility in the Bronx, New York.

Before his younger boss reassumed the wood podium to announce winners, Davis remarked how the wide range of personnel who submitted proposals, twenty-two in all, pleased him. The surprisingly high number who "served under an administration that did not encourage this kind of activity" equally impressed him. By "activity," Davis meant this very contest enabling us to institute our own special programs and provide juveniles alternatives to staring at the television and bickering over kings and aces. Davis alleged that the previous superintendent, James Jordan, would not have endorsed this initiative. Winners were due cash prizes and funding from the Do Right Foundation. Various staffers wanted to teach juveniles to cook and interview for jobs. An ex-marine attendant envisioned 5:00 A.M. boot camp calisthenics for older inmates, rationalizing that thriving in military environs fosters kids' self-esteem and attaches them to something. This is why, he preaches, they enlist themselves in gangs—poor self-image and nothing communal in their communities or familial in their families.[1]

Many colleagues who worked for former Superintendent Jordan vow that Doyle and Davis, whom several call "Uncle Jesse and Fat Freddie," have already instituted too many changes. Relative to Jordan's administration, they swear "the kids practically run the facility" as evidenced in Doyle's apparent assault on Confinement. As the original Audy Home's final superintendent, James Jordan became the first superintendent at the new Cook County Juvenile Temporary Detention Center in 1973. None of the attendants I've met who served under Jordan admit to being happy their old boss is gone. Plenty go the other way. Before hearing an older black attendant reminisce, "Mr. Jordan ran this place like a plantation," I assumed that like Doyle and Davis, Jordan was black. I hadn't seen a picture of Superintendent Jordan, but the seeming implausibility of a black man managing a plantation forced me to ask about him. Superintendent Jordan was white. With the way Confinement is evolving, I'm beginning to agree with one black colleague who warned: "When Doyle first got here, he'd walk onto your unit, ignore you and your coworker, go shake hands with the kids, and then leave without even speaking to you. That shows he doesn't give a shit about us."

Since Christmas, I've been working 3G every day and the unit now has a much tenser mood even with Attendant Edison still being the 4–12. My third-floor carrousel through Medical, 3E, 3F, and then 3J following the shorties' triumphant coup against me on 5G has returned here—a cellblock far more challenging than any of those. One afternoon, as my shift ends there, another black coworker beginning his shift airs similar venom: "Jordan never said to hit the kids. But he said do what you have to do to keep them in line. Kids knew exactly what they were supposed to do, and if they fucked up, they knew what would happen. No one had any say but him, from the inside or the outside. But he was a good man. He supported his staff. This new guy doesn't." Even after five years, Doyle remains "new." This particular attendant bid for the overnight 10–6 shift to dodge administrators despite his ample seniority to land a 6–2 because Doyle and Davis are snooping around at that time. This 10–6's smooth face shows little stress for one attending children for twenty-five plus years.

Maybe there is something to the graveyard shift. No inmates. No administrators. Just you, bolted cell doors, and the night log sheet.

Attendant Rollins, who does 4–12 on Edison's nights off, echoes these two: "I'm a lot more loose now than I was back then. I'm a lot easier on the kids than I used to be." Attendant Rollins did ten years under Superintendent Jordan.

"Really?"

Sitting behind the console and easing his tall, flat head back, he goes on, "Uuhhuh, back then you didn't have these grievance boxes on the units and have DCFS investigating every last damn little thing you did. When Mr. Jordan was here you knew that if a kid came at you and you defended yourself, they wouldn't ask questions, as long as you wrote a good report. Now you can't hardly touch a kid without DCFS breathing down your neck trying to give you twenty-nine and pending, even if the kid attacked you! It's like we're the criminals now instead of the kids; they get treated better than we do. And hey, the kids know it too. See all these broken windows?" His eyes shoot beyond the console to a cell midway down the row. The door is rare in having real glass, but it's cracked. An inmate slammed it with his chair. Rollins then points at a fist-sized cluster of cracks defacing the glass barrier dividing our hallway from the recreation yard, courtesy of a softball bat. He swivels his head back to me, "That didn't happen when Jordan was here. The kids were scared to pull any shit like that."

"So was it really like a plantation?"

"Yeah, it was."

So Jordan's tenure rendered inmates slaves and children's attendants the slave masters, but Doyle has inverted the hierarchy. Part of me is curiously jealous about the Jordan days. To know that I wouldn't worry about being fired if I lost my cool and did punch or knee or elbow an inmate who attacked me, would help me relax. It also would, I'm sure, prompt me to let down my moral guard and, because I could, protect my reputation by greeting any physical disrespect with disproportionate retaliation. Respecting yourself after an assault is a challenge unless you can avenge the assault—take both of their eyes for your one eye.

Rollins reminds me of Attendant Lathon, a man with toffee-shaded skin and sporting enough bulk and inches over six feet tall to set himself at an advantage in manning any cellblock. "It's like a resort," he summarized life at Jesse Doyle's Audy Home during a conversation my first week in the building. I've frolicked at zero retreat spas, save for childhood summer vacations at a not-for-profit Colorado family summer lodge. I never though think "resort" each day that I plod into one of these brick and steel shoe boxes for another eight hours of safety and security. Zero hot towels or Swedish massages here. "They get three meals, a warm bed to sleep in, recreation, clean clothes, a shower every day. It's too easy," Lathon ranted on, his forehead wrinkling. Attendant Lathon was present during the Jordan days but drew no paycheck. An afternoon twenty years ago, fourteen-year-old Lathon and a female cousin idled on their front stoop. Local thugs happened by and Lathon retreated into the house and returned with a baseball bat. He scored no blows, but a neighbor called police. Kid Lathon still gripped the bat when officers arrived. They brought him to the Audy Home. "Now there's hardly any reason for them not to come back. When I was here, they made it so hard on you that you never wanted to come back! My first night here, the staff threw peanut butter and water in my room to attract mice and roaches. I didn't sleep for three nights!" Under Doyle such behavior intervention would trip off the grievance process. "And back then you didn't do wall time on the wall. They put your ass in the middle of the unit, facing the windows where everyone could see you. And there was no forty-minute time limit, you stood there as long as they wanted you to, no matter how many people walked by in the hallway laughing at you. I was miserable! I wanted out real bad! And when I got out, I stayed out. I've had no problems since." Lathon's eyes scowled away from me toward 3G's empty end, as if he had something to prove in telling this story. Current administrators intentionally fashion jail life cushy, he swore. The larger our juvenile population, the more easily these men in suits can justify their positions with salaries tripling and quadrupling ours.

We harbor other misgivings, misgivings that children's attendants probably voiced during the Jordan era. Because so many despise Superintendent Doyle though, I suppose these same complaints ring much louder now. We hate our job title and believe *Juvenile Detention Officer* a more becoming title, like equivalent positions in other states.

In agreeing with such complainers, I've finally embraced what I am—a jail guard, and what I am not—a Big Brother like when a Chaplain Rick volunteer. More greenbacks wouldn't hurt either. I started at $26,010.40 annually, which after federal and Illinois taxes, pension, and mandatory union dues portions out to $761.38 two Fridays a month. Rent on my single-bedroom apartment off a noisy stretch of Joliet Road is $550. A badge, we believe, will fit, and we should be armed, if only with mace. No matter how badass you are, if six or seven boys from fourth-floor or certain fifth-floor cellblocks with the wrong attitudes set their fists, elbows, and toe points on you, good luck driving yourself to the hospital. So shrinking Confinement sentences is just the beginning of our qualms with Doyle and Cook County.

A Thursday 3G shift in late January with Attendant Rollins is over. His waist wider than his mushy shoulders and being shorter than half our inmates, Rollins can't strike Edison's militant, chiseled pose or even the beefy if unwieldy intimidation of Attendant Lathon. But tonight, Attendant Rollins and I haven't banished many kids to the wall to count bricks for smarting off to us or leaving their assigned area. Only one threatened another with, "Man, I'll beat yo' ass!" He served his wall time statue-like, so I let him off with that. I could have written a report and locked him in his cell pending Confinement, but wall time has elicited our desired behavior. Without Attendant Edison on duty with me, this is a great night.

Before I leave, I stride past cells on the block's north end. Rollins and I have just locked the juveniles in. I'm yanking each cell door handle to kill my worry that we missed a deadbolt, and a juvenile will escape his cell while Rollins is alone—a juvenile who, unlike Arthur, may seek more than a less nasty drink of water. Around door twelve something smells. It isn't the shoes lining the cell row. I spin and holler to Attendant Rollins because the keys rest in the pocket of his faded green sweatpants.

He ambles over. We sniff at several adjacent doors. Rollins opens twelve. Nothing. Thirteen. Nothing. He pulls back door fourteen and smoke streams into our faces. I despise few smells more than burning cigarettes, but Attendant Rollins sucks on Salem 100s. Sometimes he lights up on the cellblock after lights-out, chancing that a supervisor won't saunter in. I appreciate him staying with me to puff away though, instead of sneaking down the hall to a staff bathroom. If the juveniles battle royal, I'll have a comrade with whom to battle the riot.

"Pack it up!" Attendant Rollins squares off with the fifteen-year-old a foot away from him, slouching in the doorway in boxer shorts and his white bird-shirt. Smoky wisps frame his blank face. His hands are relaxed. He's already flushed the butt.

Shane and his apathy are to gather his bedding and tramp down to the last cell on the row, number eighteen. Inmates loathe this cell—3G's automatic Confinement room. Pinched into the corner of the building's outer perimeter, it is smaller than 3G's seventeen other cells and the only one sealed with a steel door. Therefore it's our darkest cell because the bathroom area shields direct natural light from beaming into its tiny door window. Eighteen's sole interface with the sun is its back wall window fronting Ogden Avenue. Attendant Edison calls it "the dungeon."

"I don't care. I'll get out tomorrow," Shane, an inch of Afro foaming up off his scalp, quips and tips his chin up.

He rotates around and pulls his bed sheets off his mattress and saunters out of the cell. The bedding drags the dull floor. Rollins follows complaint-less Shane to unlock eighteen and bar him behind its steel door. Word must be spreading about Confinement's downward-spiraling sentences. Usually, Shane contests our every instruction and consequence. Dungeon time isn't fazing him now. He doesn't seem a bit fearful of the report we will write.

During every Sunday visitation session that I've manned 3G, no parent or guardian has come to see Shane. An uneven scar juts down one shin from a bullet and resulting surgery. His explanation for the scar tissue was yet another, "I got shot." A hitched gait sticks him out on the crowded basketball courts downstairs. Were I a detached social scientist reading about Shane, I would pity Shane and excuse his antagonism to factors outside himself. I don't pity him right now though because Shane is here in front of me, as he has been every shift for a month, forever debating and mouthing off when he suspects Attendant Edison won't hear him. He's done significant wall time. Now he has just shown up every 3G attendant who worked today and missed the cigarette and match or lighter stowed on his person or hidden in his cell. I fantasize at the thought of this bastard stewing away in the dungeon.

Rollins offers to write up smoking Shane, so I can clock out on time. He guarantees to include the boy's predicting to be released right away. Possession of cigarettes and matches, forget lighting up, warrants at least two Confinement days. We hope Shane's smartass declaration gains him a third day in our dingiest cell. The Audy Home goads us to such—wishing bad upon kids who have already had more bad happen to them than the rest of us combined. I'm no Mother Teresa after all.

I work 3G again the next afternoon. Shane is locked up but not in eighteen. Someone has returned him to his original cell, granting Shane more natural light and a view of the console and common area instead of the bathroom area. I want to know why but don't probe, happy enough to see Shane still behind Plexiglas. Around 7:30 P.M. a caseworker strolls in and stops at the console. He requests Rollins's report. I give it to him. It's not Caseworker Hampton. Without a word, this slim goofy overdressed man, whom I've yet to hear a respectful word about, scans Attendant Rollins's violation form and glides over to cell fourteen. He unlocks the door and invites Shane out. Two or three days of Confinement have eroded into twenty-two hours.

"I guess we might as well have smoking areas on the units," I say to Attendant Edison as the caseworker leaves.

He looks angry as sock-footed Shane dances through his open doorway and into his sneakers heeled against the brick wall. Shane smirks at me and heads for the tables. If he hurries, Shane can enter himself in the next game of spades. Congratulations Superintendent Doyle, Shane and I both are harder now.

Monday morning I join the nine other children's attendants from my new-hire group for our third cumulative week of classroom training. I've been the unofficial 2–10 on 3G for five weeks, so each day I worry about Edison or Rollins taking vacation and my having to work with an attendant like Avalon or Jensen. For this week though, I vow to forget that stress and enjoy these five vacation days.

Shane skipping out of the dungeon after twenty-two hours still infuriates me. Class itself converts the infuriation into downright fear because Trainer Thompson tells us during Gang Awareness, "As soon as the elevator door opened, I heard it."

His slacks and tie seem impractical at the Audy Home. Most children's attendants dress in jeans, shorts, jogging suits, T-shirts with rappers' glittery silhouettes, gym shoes, shiny gold chains, diamond studs and gold loop earrings, Lugz and FuBu hats and jerseys, some even skull caps. Thompson though served eight years as a children's attendant and caseworker. Now in his dressier duds, he choreographs for us the varied ways—hand signals, code names, fashion statements like rolling up a particular shirtsleeve or lacing shoes in a deliberate pattern—that juveniles proclaim gang allegiances. If not curtailed, cellblocks can erupt, he cautions, like the one he heard going up as he stepped off that elevator.

Thompson reached the cellblock door and saw a trash can arch across the unit. A Vice Lords faction had amassed on one side of the rectangular steel and brick arena, the Black Disciples (the BDs) marshaled on the other. They were taunting each other and hedging closer, chaffing for hand-to-hand combat.

Trainer Thompson's war story raises another concern about shrinking Confinement: furniture. The standard plastic-coated fiberglass chairs in their various playground primary colors furnish every block but one. The flat bottoms can slice flesh, like one had on the inmate riding in the station wagon with Attendant Chambers and me. Every block features at least thirty potential slashers—their two narrow edges functioning as legs. Even the smallest Audy Home boy I've seen, a dark-haired kid tinier than Tiny Timmy, brandished a regular chair, a chair nearly as big as him, when a bigger shorty shoved him to claim a seat close to the television. Unit 5A though has much lighter chairs. They resemble rubbery plastic patio fixtures from Target—truly a snap to grab up and sling, but they can't bash a window to shards or slice into a limb. A sliver of the facility's $22.7 million annual budget should be portioned out for more forest-green Target deck chairs.[2] The easier it is for us to maintain safety and security, the easier it will be to, in Assistant Superintendent Davis's words, "help the children." Five years have elapsed since the new 5A chairs were introduced. I heard that right after Chance and Donnell left for 26th and California, one new 5D kid busted out an entire glass wall swinging a chair at another juvenile. I ask Trainer Thompson if 5A's refurnishing will happen elsewhere. His answer: "I don't know."

Intimidated further about the added prospect of cellblock civil war and the lingering weapons juveniles can wage it with, I write Superintendent Doyle to voice collective children's attendant concern about dwindling Confinement sentences. Prisoners of war shorten the war. The longer they are imprisoned, the sooner the war ends. In my letter I recreate the 3G smoking incident and quote Shane verbatim. I stress that inmates will attack and brawl and brawl and attack if certain they'll only do a day behind their Plexiglas—pithy consequence for blood revenge and street cred.

I push my letter under the superintendent's office door on

Wednesday morning before class. I don't expect to hear from Doyle because Attendant Tucker has composed similar notes and says that Doyle ignored them. Like Attendant Walton, Tucker is a Children's Attendant III, so he trains new hires and functions as a supervisor on days when enough of them take vacation. A recent employee of the quarter, administration has never subpoenaed Tucker to a hearing, much less suspended him. About Tucker, one staff lauds: "He never has to put his hands on the kids; he does it all with his mouth and his pen." Tucker completes rule violation reports, instead of screaming in faces. His most recent letter occurred after 3F and another unit clashed. Tucker, the children's attendant from the other cellblock, and the lone Recreation staff had to quell the fracas involving nearly fifty juveniles. No injuries, but the incident prompted Attendant Tucker to plead to Doyle for more personnel in the gymnasium. By Tucker's account, he pled to no avail and no response. Despite the bad press on Doyle and his staff, I harbor slight hope that Doyle will at least read my letter. Without my thinking the question, much less asking it, a couple black coworkers have already promised: "Administration won't fuck with you because you're white. They'll be too scared that someone at city hall will take your complaint seriously."

Thursday afternoon after class, Superintendent Doyle stands in the hallway outside our training room requesting me. Unlike Attendant Tucker's letter, the superintendent is indeed taking my complaint seriously. Depressed that my cynical colleagues have pegged Doyle correctly, I follow him to an empty office.

His forehead glinty, Doyle sits down behind the desk, and before I'm all the way in my chair, he fires off, "I got your note. So where else do they lock kids up as often as we do here?"

"I don't know. This is the only residential facility I've ever worked at."

"Well being locked in a room is not good for a young person. We have to find ways to modify the kids' behavior other than simply locking them in their rooms for days on end."

His question condescends, but his answer isn't outrageous. Indeed this is the point of behavior management—inducing desirable behavior with desirable rewards, so as to ensure civil and peaceable cellblocks. Solitary confinement certainly harms the soul. I think of the Rhesus monkeys that scientists insulated from each other and their human providers; they regressed into writhing, desperate creatures, no longer even primates.

Doyle goes on, "Right now, 10 percent of our population is in Confinement. The national average for juvenile detention facilities is well below five. All I want to do is bring our facility into conformity with the national average so we won't face litigation from the ACLU. If they sue us and win, they could place a monitor on every unit."

For an administrator ridiculed mentally challenged for his gullible view of dysfunctional kids and the physical dangers they present, Superintendent Doyle right now appears smarter than his reputation. Few attendants, myself included, expect such cunning, particularly to shield us from more scrutiny. Doyle has done nothing but increase scrutiny. Still, I'm damn sure Shane lit up before 10:00 P.M. with Rollins and me on the block because he anticipated scant few confined days if caught. Another half hour and Rollins would have been alone. Two noses smell better than one, especially when that one nose is a smoking nose.

"But what else can we do to keep the kids from running the facility other than putting them in Confinement?" Behavior management works with some inmates but not all, and we need that most menacing of swinging sticks, Confinement, to motivate the others to conform. My parroting "kids running the facility" impresses me, like I'm standing up for the wronged and the voiceless. I hope this line insults Doyle because I too am starting to believe that the inmates will soon checkmate us if his plan succeeds. Shane is the mild beginning.

"If a kid *really* wants to smoke or if two kids *really* want to fight, whether it's one day or five days of Confinement is irrelevant. We have to find other measures to discipline misbehavior, as opposed to just locking them in a room."

I feel like arguing back that it is relevant—I will enjoy up to five glorious fight-free days while those assholes count bricks inside their cells. My safety and the non-fighting inmates' safety should out-prioritize nurturing the defiant ones. But this confession would embarrass me.

Doyle launches into federal statutes regulating the isolation of juvenile detainees in cells. He concludes, "Before I got here, they were putting kids in the Hole for up to thirty days, which is illegal. And really the way we do Confinement now is too. So eventually, I want to reduce Confinement to a max of one day because additional Confinement time requires authorization from outside this building. That way we'll be doing it legally."

The Hole is a single basement cell furnished only with a bench, sink, and toilet—all steel. No one treads near the Hole in a shift's regular course. According to Attendant Haines, present during Jordan's last years, "It was for the kids who drew blood or attacked staff." I've seen the Hole only because, earlier in the week, someone convinced Trainer Thompson to show it to us on our lunch break. The subterranean holding tank has two windows, neither with natural light. One window is in the door, small as the ones in the steel-doored cells upstairs. The other is the size of a medium pizza box in a sidewall, which allowed an attendant in an adjacent cubicle to observe the inmate. Holed inmates missed school, softball games, gym time, spades, chapel, and television. Once hired, Doyle eliminated cellar isolation and restricted all Confinement sentences upstairs to a five-day max. Now his sly and steady assault on that maximum enrages us.

I say nothing to Doyle's federal laws bullshit and evils of the Hole because he is offering zero alternatives to cell isolation. Shifting against my cushioned seat, I don't care about federal laws. I hate coming to work. The building's edgy tone and Shane the smoker are frustrating me enough that I haven't initiated my Do Right Foundation Reading Groups. I was a winner and accepted a $150 check. I hoped this diversion would be my résumé insurance—what would keep me here a full year. No one has inquired yet as to why I'm not showing up early on Saturdays to gather inmates into my club in the same visitation rooms where I once met with Jerome and Terry and Lemmuel for Bible lessons. This is what I promised Doyle I would do when I was summoned to his office for a brainstorming session. I'd conceived, drafted, and submitted my proposal during the smooth stints on 5D and Medical Movement before the 5G disgracing and the current stress over Confinement. I've deposited that $150 and will not give it back. Donations from rich people who work posh jobs with zero interactions with gangbangers, drug dealers, murderers, rapists, and thieves are what sustain the Do Right Foundation. Because of my fret and sweat, they don't have to work at the Audy Home themselves or worry about criminal youth marauding into their neighborhoods. I feel that rich people owe me some of their money.

"We have to find other ways to modify the residents' behavior and use Confinement, not as punishment, but only as a last resort," Doyle goes on. "The only time a resident should be locked in a room is when they become a threat to their own safety or that of staff and other residents. Even then, they should only be confined for twenty-four hours. And only under extreme circumstances should a resident be confined for more than a day, and if so, only with the proper authorization."

Doyle's theory is sensible and one I wish my coworkers could consider. I concede Doyle's idealism—even the most violently rebellious inmate should always exist in community regardless of his heinous deed toward me or another inmate. But damn the ideal! Shane is proof. He didn't fear being busted and thus didn't fear bartering for contraband in a deal that going awry could have erupted in fisticuffs or shankings. Doyle has provided us no heads-up about Confinement policy's transition, nor have I been coached to employ his hypothetical ways that supposedly will prompt kids to conform without throwing them into temporary virtual solitary. I agree with my coworkers on Doyle being a dope, at least a half-dope. Why implement a good policy without implementing good support for that policy?

Superintendent Half-Dope then advises me to inform inmates, "Smoking is unhealthy." This from a superior earning a salary four times mine. I've already overheard kids fantasizing about "rolling a big fat one"—a big fat marijuana joint—once their judge releases them. Contracting lung cancer in thirty years is nothing to Shane. "Your job is not to make your day easier by locking residents in their rooms. Your job is to help the kids. Sure it would be easier to keep them locked up all day, but that does them no good," Doyle adds. "It doesn't help a kid change his behavior."

Superintendent Doyle, right now I really don't give much of anything about helping the kids. I just want to prevent chaos and tick the clock through my eight hours—enough eight hours to, in five more months, equal a full children's attendant year and not scar my employment résumé when I quit. Kids smoking when they want and trafficking contraband with no threat of discipline will usher in violent, injurious chaos. Shane probably inquired about his contraband supplier during the card game that he joined right after the caseworker let him out of his cell so shockingly early—curious if the kid was still incarcerated, curious if he would see him again soon downstairs in the classrooms or gymnasium to purchase more cigarettes. You should walk me through every feasible scenario and present your alternatives (if they exist) to Confinement and enlighten me on how they will work, both for the inmates and me.

Doyle only asks if I have any other questions.

Maybe it's because I'm new, maybe it's because this meeting is a surprise that I couldn't prepare for, but I'm too timid for more serious challenges. I answer "No" and walk out of the office lacking a single Confinement substitute, a substitute that won't overlook the fact that an inmate, a boy, just called me, a man, a "punk-ass bitch" because I ordered him to the wall for talking without permission or to his cell for inciting his cellblock mates to a group disturbance. I walk out of the office with nothing new to help me "help a kid change his behavior," knowing for sure that I no longer want to help Shane.

"You must be someone!" a black colleague jests the next morning before class, having noticed the superintendent in hall yesterday. "Usually Doyle sends for you, rather than him come looking for you."

I feel like someone—someone I don't want to be—the white

Newjack that administration is indeed treating better than respected black veteran attendants like Tucker. Before this job I'd chuckled when hearing that whiteness in America grants advantage. Slavery and segregation are over. "It's hard being black," a fellow children's attendant about my age has informed me. Honest empathy impossible, I'd nodded to be polite, never expecting my white privilege to bore its way into a place where nearly everyone else isn't white. This privileged peering into Superintendent Doyle's incompetence with Confinement policy reform is blasting the altruistic ideals I once aspired to here at his jail toward the realm of the comic and the deluded.

22

Whenever I work 3G, Attendant Edison directs me to perform the strip inspections after Sunday visitation. I'm proud that Edison doesn't have to run the entire show. Such disrobings go down in the bathroom area, given its seclusion.

The *Policy and Procedure Manual for Group Services* instructs me to: "Ask the resident to remove all clothing."[1] I have him remove each piece individually but quit at underwear. Cavity searches are for nurses, should a supervisor deem necessary, like Supervisor Hilliard decided with the one inmate setting the mini-bonfires in his cell. To me, shoes are the first stitch of "all clothing." With rubber gloves between my hands and the inmate's sneakers because feet treading streets day and night turn pretty ripe, I press two fingertips along each seam and corner to remove the insoles, which may cover up folded up dollar bills, razor blades, or matches. I've added this step since the night Attendant Valdez coaxed a 3E boy into giving up a five-spot concealed beneath his insole. I'd missed the stashed cash hours earlier, searching the inmates after visitation before another kid snitched to her. There is worse contraband to overlook than currency notes hidden in shoes. Several colleagues recount an AT riding in a van to 26th and California who seethed something like, "I ain't goin' back to the Audy Home if my judge don't release me." The children's attendant squeezing the wheel pulled over and searched the cuffed and shackled kid. Planted in gym shorts beneath the sixteen-year-old's jeans was a snub-nosed .44 pistol loaded with hollow-point bullets. In five previous 3B days, the boy had stowed the gun undetected. Police hadn't discovered the weapon in their street pat-downs and Intake staff downstairs bumbled around it during their once-overs. I have yet though to ferret out a firearm here in the 3G bathroom area.

Rubber slaps tile when I drop the shoes onto the floor and tell the inmate to peel off his socks, turn them inside out, and hand them to me. At each subsequent command, inmate edginess can fester, as if this undressing and exhibiting ritual screams that I don't trust him not to have something hidden with which to hurt me. *You're afraid to touch me*, their faces scoff back at me and my gloved hands, gloved hands which exaggerate my skin's lightness and their skin's darkness. I hold the socks with one hand and zip my other hand down them like ringing milk from a cow's teat. Bird-shirt is next, which the inmate turns inside and out, shakes, and drapes over his shoulder. He removes his pants and hands them to me. I yank out the pockets and trail my thumb along the waistband, probing for tears that create openings to hide a cigarette, match, shank, or chalk-stick for writing and drawing on cell walls. I shake them hard. The maneuver may spirit out contraband morsels I've missed otherwise. Nothing floats or clatters to the floor. Lastly, I instruct the inmate to snap the top of his underwear against his hips. If the elastic traps contraband, it will cascade down his legs to the floor. Hot goods present or not, I avoid seeing him stark naked, unlike during shower duty. Every strip-searched inmate I send to the TV area, I send without being absolutely satisfied that he ferries no short, slender makeshift weapon or incendiary device. Only him yanking his ass open will settle that.

Contraband undetected in strip searches or cell inspections, the inmates traffic primarily in the school area. In the jail's quarter century, I'm sure thousands of joints, cigarettes, dollar bills, pencils, pens, lighters, matches, and skin mag centerfold shreds have journeyed down our elevator shafts, transacted owners, and floated back up to the cellblocks. In the middle of shoes thwacking during one after-school spot search, a jingle sounds from the 3G floor. I step closer to the juveniles' line. A four-inch steel rod the diameter of a car antennae lies between a hefty six-foot tall inmate's socked feet. He strikes me as fourth-floor material although he isn't an AT and hardly ever talks, but he could hone this little bar against his brick cell wall a few nights in a row and puncture a windpipe or barter it to someone who will while barely breaking a sweat. I write up the inmate's lethal contraband and lock him in his cell. He had to slam his shoes together before lunch after returning to unit with Attendant Walton, so the rod was purchased in afternoon class. The same fool caseworker that forgave Shane's smoking after fewer than twenty-four hours of Confinement releases the massive inmate before dinner when he stops by and I give him the metal rod. I am still waiting on Superintendent Doyle to provide those alternative interventions to locking kids up for multiple days. I don't wish to make any kid a Rhesus monkey if better ways exist to preserve safety and security. Until Doyle explains himself, I say confine away. If not, why won't this man-child buy another shank at school tomorrow?

The 2–10 shift affords far more Sunday post-visitation strip searches than everyday cell inspections—policy and procedure obligating the 8–4 attendant to the latter. But as Attendant Otis taught me on 3D, we can barge into a cell or cells any time we please, so I should have barged into ox-like Terrence's cell and torn it apart to see what other potential shanks it harbored. The caseworker never did. At one time in this jail's history, there were not as many such potentially shank-bearing cells for us to barge into though, however frequently executed our barging—scheduled or spontaneous. Daily populations have doubled since 1988, when fewer than three hundred and fifty inmates resided here.[2] Back then, 8–4s escaped sifting through all sixteen or eighteen cells because empty cells required no inspection. On certain days now, over seven hundred juveniles jam the facility. During construction though, outsiders balked that its cell count would be excessive. "You do not run your entire building at full occupancy at any time," Superintendent Jordan contended to justify the expanded size compared to the original Audy Home designed with only beds and bunkrooms instead of cells and cellblocks. He sought to prevent ever having an inmate for every cell. "We can't anticipate what laws may change. We must make sure the building has provisions to meet the exigencies of the twenty years ahead."[3] On most nights I work, some seventy-five overflows sleep on cots. The once excessive digs are now too small. We inspect every cell because every cell incarcerates a juvenile. This World War II vet was a prophet. "Jordan got the last laugh. He's probably laughing in his grave," Attendant Simons says when I quote the former superintendent from an archived *Tribune* article.

As Supervisor Hilliard taught in orientation, inspections of these five hundred cells must be "systematic, thorough, and objective." We shouldn't allow a cooperative inmate to stockpile extra bars of soap but write up a different inmate for one too many pairs of socks because he lied to a caseworker about us punching him. The bed frame, mattress, pillow, sheets, blanket, walls, sink, toilet, desk, chair, ceiling, and floor are to be examined. All "openings, cracks, crevices, grooves and ledges" merit exploration too, especially the crevice formed by the back wall and its glass window—a perfect cache for cigarettes and shanks, or rolled up dollar bills that inmates can swap for cigarettes or shanks. We're to canvass the walls for loose bricks or mortar but leave cells "as orderly as possible."[4] These kids are in jail, but still we shouldn't toss their bed sheets onto the floor or not reroll a pair of their socks once confident they veil no weapons or joints although Attendant Otis never remade those 3D beds.

Smells can expose the success or failure of our searches. Later in March a foreign odor brews up after lights-out. It's not Salems. Rollins is off and Edison has called in sick. A different 4–12, Attendant O'Neal, and I sit at the console. The shift has been easy though. O'Neal, about my size with sharp eyes and a penetrating voice, was an officer of some kind in Florida and aspires to be a policeman here in Chicago.

Keys in hand, Attendant O'Neal strides over and lowers his shaved slick head to sniff around the doors. He pulls on number seven. Even from twenty feet away, the intensifying scent has me imagining emerald green leaves, not parched brown leaves like in regular cigarettes, incinerating. I twist my nose. Door seven stands open wide and the creeping wall of green-smelling haze all but nudges my roller chair into the glass wall behind the console.

In my life, I've smelled marijuana once—several months ago on Medical when an inmate smuggled in a joint and match stashed inside the cast on his broken arm. Having just been to court, he admitted to bartering for the pot in the waiting room. After dinner he lit up in his cell, enveloping the Medical corridor with the most pungent smell ever to my virgin nostrils.

Hair nearly touching his shoulders, cell seven's slender white teen stomps out from its wafting smoke. His gold level-four shirt ripples as he roves around like performing in a stage play, darting cue point to cue point. We have no overflows on cots, so the buzzed inmate enjoys plenty of roaming space. Other than myself, Attendant O'Neal, and any roused juveniles now glancing through their cell door windows, the pot smoker entertains no audience. From the console, I can see a towel rolled up longways like a joint lying on the floor where his locked door stops. The juvenile has soaked the linen with water from his faucet and lined the doorframe bottom. With near zero ventilation in his cell, he re-inhaled his secondhand smoke for a stronger high.

"You just lost your level," Attendant O'Neal backs up.

The kid storms by, shaking his shoulders and arms.

"You gotta move down." Say goodbye to residing near the TV area and falling asleep watching the news through your cell door window.

"I don't give a fuck! Fuck level four!" he peels off the shirt and slings it at O'Neal, who shadows the bare-chested boy around in front of the cell row.

The man's demeanor impresses me, no trembling in his voice over the fact that he might have to restrain this sixteen-year-old if he remains in the common area much longer. O'Neal's is the commanding disposition I'm desperate to grow into. I keep my seat and watch my trim and muscular coworker herd the skinny kid into a cell farther from the TV area and closer to the bathroom area. The inmate in that cell receives a free upgrade to Kid Mary Jane's vacated digs. Another confinee already occupies the Dungeon.

Back at the console, Attendant O'Neal says, "Damn, that shit gives me a headache!" The inside of my own head coils and corkscrews too. This inmate's attitude has been souring. Police arrested him, the *Tribune* says, with another teen (housed upstairs on 5E) in Kentucky driving an Oldsmobile stolen from the other boy's grandmother. She refused to let them borrow her car, so one of them, or both of them, apparently beat her to death with a saxophone. A rare criminal couple—one white and one black, both from the same gritty south suburb near Indiana's steel mills. The weed-tripping 3G boy claims he was only riding in the hot car. After a few court hearings and a judge informing him that he is an AT, he realized he might as well have bludgeoned grandma with the brass piece too. This made him start hating the world.

Days later, I pass the boy's cell. Instead of Plexiglas, rare wire mesh forms cell seventeen's door window from my chest-level up. The inmate lingers close to the screen and feigns a cough. Spittle sprays my forearm.

I look down.

He laughs.

Now he wants to say "fuck off" to everything, not just his level-four gold shirt and extra apple juice. I deserve to be spit on because Illinois law deems him as complicit as his pal, even if he never touched his black friend's grandma.

Our scheduled picking and poking around these five hundred–plus cells trolling for illegal and nasal-contorting smokeables, also ensures that juveniles do not accumulate too many personal items. A sheet of white paper taped onto cell-block walls lets inmates know what they are allowed:

1 one toothbrush,
2 toothpaste—tube, not pump,
3 one plastic hairbrush,

4 hair grease/gel—no larger than eight ounces, no pump,
5 one face towel,
6 one bar of soap,
7 one small radio—no antenna or attachments,
8 four extra batteries,
9 five envelopes and stamps,
10 five pair of socks,
11 one roll-on deodorant,
12 five pair of underwear,
13 three paperback books,
14 three magazines, and for female inmates
15 three bras.

Anything else, excluding homework, letters, and five family pictures, we can decree contraband. I've met no inmate amassing the maximum envelopes or books. Parents surrender underwear and socks, soap, or shampoo for their children downstairs at the front desk before visitation.

After another Sunday 3G visitation I bust the staples on a paper bag care package and remove the top of a bottle inside. Something protrudes from the shampoo. I squeeze the plastic cylinder and jab at the protrusion with my long Toyota ignition key. Submerged are several cigarettes and several matches cocooned in cellophane. Front desk personnel hadn't opened the container. The smuggled items I retain for a supervisor but present the inmate his shampoo while saying nothing about the cigarettes.

Tobacco and lighters are far from the sum total of what steals onto our cellblocks. During another 3G Sunday, a bright-faced young female signs the visitor list on my console clipboard and eases herself into a chair across a table from gold-shirted Hector, my favorite inmate on the block. The asshole quotient on 3G has radically increased since training days with Attendant Walton. Inmates are larger and several blatantly antagonistic. One called me a "white bitch" because I confronted him for talking in line and made him serve wall time. I wrote him up, and he served Confinement only until the next afternoon. He never did it again, but I still wanted him in that cell longer even if Superintendent

Doyle was correct, at least with this kid and this offense. Nothing more was needed to modify his behavior although Doyle never would have approved him in the cell to begin with because he wasn't a threat to me. No children's attendant with any self-worth will let a boy curse him out and not put him in a cell.

Temporarily though, I can forget such angst with short-haired Hector who addresses me as "Mr. Dostert" instead of "Hey," ensuring that I'll never ignore his requests. His voice is a normal tone, never a shout, and never barking a criticism or complaint of anyone or anything. He is smaller too. I never tell Hector to do anything because he's always doing what he should be doing. This girl must be his sister or cousin because Hector is a level four and has earned a special visitor. Then their giggling faces lean closer across the table. I stand and see the girl's stomach bowing out. Later in the day, I quiz Hector. He confesses that she is pregnant and that downstairs she'd claimed blood relation. Front Desk staff checked her identification against the approved visitors' roster about as painstakingly as they examine shampoo bottles. Policy and procedure says I should contact a supervisor. But Hector is cool air in a stuffy room, one of few inmates who reincarnate the kids from my Chaplain Rick days. Hector sways me from resolving myself, exclusively, to: *Now that I'm around Chicago's juvenile detainees longer than thirty minutes a week for Bible study, let 'em all rot the hell away in a penitentiary for fifty years until they're too feeble to wreak more havoc!* I'll wait and see if Hector sneaks her in again. If this were Damien Dennison or a cell door–pounder on 4K or Shane the smoker, I'd race to a supervisor with my rule violation report.

The court releases Hector before next Sunday and its visitation period, but I can't forget him smuggling his pregnant girlfriend onto 3G. And if a whole person can waltz in this easily, how simple must it be for joints or razor blades or dollar bills hidden in shampoo? Inmates squirreling it all away from us in their cells and on their persons is probably the more challenging crime.

23

Back in Bible college, before and after my first volunteer evening with blind Chaplain Rick at the Audy Home, Chicago's flagship news radio station often woke me with how many Chicagoans had been stabbed, bludgeoned, gunned at, or gunned down the previous day. Setting my alarm to WMAQ 670 AM instead of music or sports talk became compulsory. I listened when not in class or studying too, and specifically for children: the latest gang-beating victim, the number of youth the city's police arrested during school hours at drug dens on South Langley Avenue, and to which hospital an ambulance had ferried a parentless (I assumed) teen in whom a liquor store owner just buried a bullet. These facts evolved into matters of strange importance and contemplation, as if my being aware of these smoldering lives somehow mitigated their smolder. I knew it didn't. But living the easy life in that posh River North nook of Chicago as if everyone in the city lived like me seemed wrong. What I wanted was to help yet knew of no way to help other than volunteering with Chaplain Rick and, crazy as it sounds, listening to the radio. Six years later, I still can't turn away from Chicago's bad news. Even after wallowing in the bad news all workweek, I still tune in WMAQ on my off-days.

Two afternoons before slipping my letter under Superintendent Doyle's door, I was driving home from the Stone Avenue Metra stop following training class when WMAQ announced the murder of two boys standing at 50th and Paulina Streets near the Apostolic House of Prayer Church.[1] The *Tribune* prints what appear to be school pictures of the victims, Delvon Harris, fourteen, and Robert Owens, fifteen, next to half-inch headlines. I bring the front page to training. Coworkers and I pour over the story and the two faces posing somewhere between laughing and smiling. Below them, Delvon's cousin, Angel, crouches over the muddy curb where the two dropped and presses her face with both hands above a rumpled yellow police ribbon.

The feature offers no likeness of the suspect whom police are said to have nabbed dashing away from the kill-site carting a .38-caliber snub-nosed pistol with five spent rounds and one live. Police disclose that the boy, ten days before his thirteenth birthday, confessed that he had "wanted to go out and shoot somebody" as part of a gang initiation. The paper also quotes Teddy, an admitted Latin Saint explaining that Patrick, who lived with his father, disabled by a stabbing, and younger brother, had tried "to prove he is down. He wanted it for the longest time."[2] Administrators from Seward Academy, Patrick's 94 percent Hispanic public school four blocks north of the death scene, disclose his five suspension weeks for replicating gang symbols on his folders and raving about joining the Latin Saints. For Patrick, this was complicated. Patrick is a non-Hispanic Caucasian. This is another of Chicago's color surprises for me. Before this print story, I pegged the two deaths yet another cliché—black-against-black urban bloodshed.

If Patrick was thirteen, prosecutors could petition the judge to transfer his case to criminal court and arraign him as an adult—a Presumptive Transfer. Our caseworkers worry that knowledge of Patrick's case will endanger him in our vastly black population, so they put him on Medical. Even in the quiet safety of this basement classroom, I want to see Patrick. I want to see a twelve-year-old murder suspect.

Patrick remains on Medical for only a week and then is transferred to 3F, Attendant Tucker's unit. "Yeah, we got him," Tucker tells me outside the building after work. Training is over, and Tucker soon takes vacation, leaving for Tennessee's relative warmth on a Greyhound because he hates driving. I land on 3F and will see this just turned thirteen-year-old murder suspect while catching a break from 3G and its huskier, nastier current inmates. Despite being average age and height for 3F, Patrick outweighs his cellblock mates. His buzzed head is globe-round and his shoulders' width rivals mine. With almost blonde hair and skin paled like someone growing up under the perpetually cold gray skies of the former Eastern Bloc, it's unlikely that Patrick, at first glance, would pass for Hispanic. I wonder if this is why he killed—the Latin Saints wouldn't trust him as one of their own until he engaged in something vicious.

Even if they want to, inmates on 3F can't intimidate Patrick given his size, but socializing elsewhere is problematic. The boy's mother confers with administration, and they order us to hold Patrick out of school. While his peers are in class, Patrick idles upstairs, lolling at one of the tables outside the TV area. I arrive at 2:00 P.M. and he is flipping through books and magazines or sketching pictures. I sign the logbook as he lays his head down on the pages and papers, waiting for the cellblock to return from the school area. The 4–12 children's attendant accepts movie requests from Patrick, offering to rent videos for the boy to combat school day boredom. This man, the same black man who warned me back in September not to make attending children my career, knows of Patrick's indictment. We all do. "Again?" I hear him answer Patrick's request to bring back *Scream 2*.

Patrick's mother further requests that her son not mingle with the general population during recreation or church. Permanent 3F attendants tell me that she claims other inmates are plotting to hurt him. When Patrick's cellblock mates march off to chapel with one of us, Patrick remains on unit. If Recreation schedules 3F for basketball or softball against 3J, Patrick can't participate. He watches more television, draws, or cleans. Patrick does maintain one of the more spotless 3F cells. Intellectually, I should hate Patrick for what he likely did to Robert and Delvon, for heaping up more white-black animosity in America, for how differently I fear every black inmate at the Audy Home who knows about Patrick's case may now view me. Patrick has reminded them that even if his murder was fundamentally to impress Hispanic gang members, whites continue to kill blacks, right here and right now in Chicago—not just a million years ago in grainy lynching stills from Jim Crow's South. A killing is a killing. Black inmates may link me to this contemporary racial assassin and thus to those who noose-cinched their ancestors' necks. Yet no fiery rage at Patrick wells inside me. I didn't see him shoot Robert and Delvon. I didn't watch them bleed and exhale and then exhale no more. I've shared no breathing space with their weeping families. So far, Patrick hasn't made me hate my job. He hasn't called me "Opie" or "white bitch." Wrong as this seems, feeling rage at Patrick is difficult.

"His mom requested it because she feared for his safety. But if you look at all the reports, it was Patrick doing all the fighting," 3F's regular 8–4 attendant tells me. "He's been written up at least eight times and he's only been here two weeks—all for fighting and gang-banging," Attendant Tucker noted before his vacation. According to Caseworker Hampton, Patrick also instigated "a gang fight" in the gym one Saturday afternoon about a month after his arrival.

Father Kelly, the facility's Catholic chaplain meets regularly with Patrick off cellblock down the hall in the same rooms where I met with inmates under Chaplain Rick. On another day I'm assigned 3F, Father Kelly returns Patrick to the cellblock, where I greet them at the door and direct Patrick to the TV area. Then I lean my head into the corridor so inmates sitting at a card table near the console won't overhear me. Softly, I mention the media reports of Patrick's gang ties. "Yeah, he's a Saint," Father Kelly says. As a volunteer, I visited with several inmates at a time, but Father Kelly counsels Patrick in a group of one. Maybe he thinks the boy needs confidentiality should he talk about that .38-caliber pistol which police extracted from his jacket.

The meetings with Father Kelly, who publishes a newsletter entitled *Making Choices* and distributes copies on the cellblocks, don't convert Patrick into an Audy Home Saint. His misbehavior persists, and 3F staff confine him over and over. With me on duty though, Patrick never rebels or smarts off or goes hostile. I wonder if this is because I am white, and none of the other 3F staff are. Days and weeks of detainment are warping Patrick's story too. Attendants on 3F tell me they overhear Patrick bragging to other juveniles that he did kill Delvon and Robert. Next he claims to have only been "holding the gun." The *Tribune* then reports two teenage female witnesses: one claims she saw a twenty-one-year-old male rip off the shots; the other echoes that the man was with Patrick, but she can't identify the shooter. The accused adult confirms that he had accompanied Patrick to the scene, provided him the gun, but departed before rounds rang out. The state's attorney refuses comment. Patrick's public defender alleges a setup because both girls provided her a contrasting tale—the man fired the shots, shoved the pistol into Patrick's hands, and fled in a car.[3]

Curious if the boy will corroborate his own life story from the *Tribune*, the opposite way it happened for me with Gregory Chance, I approach Patrick. Attendant Tucker is taking a second week off. Right now Patrick isn't in Confinement but doodling at a table because all his cellblock mates are in class. I meander over from the console after signing the logbook.

"So where'd you go to school before you came here?"

"Seward," Patrick looks up, answering in exact accord with the media news. Without prompting, he also names the school that expelled him before he attended Seward. Nothing on why the previous school kicked him out. I don't ask.

But I do ask, "You going back to Seward when you get outta here?"

"They probly gonna keep me 'til I'm twenny-one. I wish I could beat the case, but they got too much evidence on me." Patrick is correct. If convicted, he won't be incarcerated beyond his twenty-first birthday because he was younger than thirteen the day of his alleged crime.

I can ask Patrick who fired the gun that killed Delvon and Robert. But I don't. Our interactions are amiable. I'm curious, yet know all I want. No point risking Patrick not being quiet the next time I order him to, merely because I'd harassed him with everyone else's question. This foray to 3F is quite indulgent—a relief from the far more challenging 3G, where I worry each day between two and four o'clock about the odd chance that Edison or Rollins will call in sick or use a personal day. The longer I'm employed at the Audy Home, the higher a priority smooth simple shifts are becoming. It's about saving me now, not the kids. I feel like a failure and a hypocrite, like I haven't truly known myself until I became a children's attendant.

"Hey, make sure you guys clean this off," I say to three juveniles instructed to swab 3F's bathroom area floor and sinks.

I figure someone inadvertently brushed soap or toothpaste against a steel divider anchored to the tile floor between two toilets, creating a white splotch. I move closer to the chest-high steel fence. Rather than a blurry abstraction, a capital S and N flank a cross—each letter hovering below the rung. I summon a cleaning designee over and point to the design.

"That's Patrick's. That's how he makes his set," a slender kid says.

S for Saints. N for Nation. Earlier today Patrick possibly was excused to the bathroom area, and unsupervised, soap bar scrawled his *Nation* onto the toilet partition like unincarcerated gangbangers all across Chicago inscribing tenement breezeways, alley walls, and the sides of parked eighteen-wheelers. Patrick just hadn't wielded a magic marker or spray paint can.

"Patrick, who told you to come over here?" I ask the next evening while monitoring inmates stacking extra mattresses in cell number three. My coworker and I can't assign it to anyone because a jagged metal bracket protrudes from a back corner where a steel beam and brick column converges. Patrick is supposed to be tidying his own cell.

"No one," he looks away. He knows he broke a rule. "I just wanted to see if my writing was still there."

A few weeks ago, cell three was Patrick's cell, perhaps before someone spotted the protruding metal.

"Go back to your room and keep cleaning."

Patrick does so with no guff—a potential double-murderer boasting about his deed is letting my directive go down like cool rain on a parched lawn. In his short life, Patrick has defied many orders. I swing back and forth on Patrick. Why does he follow my directives but not others from parents, teachers, and other children's attendants? In dissimilar environments, does he follow and defy different commands, including one to shoot two people?

I wait for the other juveniles to finish organizing the mattresses. I step into Patrick's former cell. High on the wall above the steel toilet and sink almost to the ceiling, etched in four lines of white chalk, is his writing. Patrick must have pilfered his chalk stick from a classroom before Mom axed his going to school. Or he traded a dollar bill or twin pack of chocolate chip cookies for it at dinner without us noticing and that night mounted his sink and scripted away. Each line runs four or five bricks long containing: "Almighty Saints," the gang's trademark halo symbols, more S's and N's, "Joe-Joe" (Patrick's nickname cited in a *Tribune* article), and inverted Gangster Disciple pitchforks. To blaspheme other gangs, kids draft their symbols upside down.

A year has passed since discovering Patrick's writing on his cell bricks, and I'm reading in the *Tribune* online that he attended his verdict hearing with a bruised left eye. By his mother's account, other juveniles had finally succeeded in beating him. Patrick was deemed guilty in both killings, and the judge sentenced him to five years at the Illinois Youth Department of Corrections.[4] Patrick wasn't as bad off as he feared—just wrong about being held until he is twenty-one.

In my closet I find the *Tribune* front-page section with Delvon and Robert's faces. I've saved it. I hold the unfolded paper inches from my own face and study theirs—soft with curious eyes, Robert's trailing off to the left away from the camera as if even this most basic of attention makes him uncomfortable. I try to conjecture what force intersected their lives with Patrick's, but the minutiae of Patrick, Delvon, and Robert and how they met, soon translates meaningless. If Patrick killed? Why Patrick killed? Two kids are still dead. A boy I knew, a boy who always did what I told him to, will be warehoused away for five years. Then the death count may be three.

The rest of America never meets the majority of Audy Home residents, hundreds and hundreds never verbally accosting visitors like Tiny Timmy had with his four-letter word show on Medical or garnering newspaper and TV news infamy like Gregory Chance or Patrick. When a squad car plunges them into our underground portal and police prod them, handcuffed, onto an elevator and up to our cellblocks, most Americans have no clue what life becomes for them and for those of us who must care for them and yet must also care for ourselves while caring for them. Whether or not anyone else ponders their sad life stories below block-letter headlines or tunes in WGN News to learn whom the residents of our home have supposedly just shot or stabbed or raped or beat down, here they sulk in front of us. They arrive in clothes that don't smell like fabric softener, shouting "pussy-ass motherfucker" and other phrases never tearing at my eardrums before I worked here. To the world, these kids are gone. But we all will see them again someday, even those of you who don't attend children at the Audy Home. In time G-shots Reginald, Riles Davis, Damien Dennison, Gregory Chance, Donnell, Shane the smoker, and Patrick, and even sooner Tiny Timmy, Nick, and Vernon must fit into a community somewhere—no Illinois judge gives any kid death or life imprisonment. But I cringe at these boys becoming adults in the free world and cringe at being one of the adults sharing that free world with them.

24

The night Attendant O'Neal filled in for Attendant Edison on 3G wasn't Edison's only call-off. He's phoned in sick now for multiple consecutive shifts. I don't know why. Neither does Supervisor Wilkins, but Wilkins and other supervisors send me to 3G anyway. Random attendants of random competency fill in for him. Each afternoon at the time clock, I still dread hearing "Dostert, 3G," a relapse to being scared of 4K and 3D. I've experienced no terrible nights on 3G, at least not 3D-terrible or 4K-terrible or 5G with Nick and Vernon. Everything "works" as Martha idealized, yet with certain Edison fill-ins, 3G carries on too loudly, too sassy, too argumentative, too slow to comply. Eating me still is the question, *If I couldn't control all the shorties every time, how will I control* 3G *every time?* While here, Hector was a radical exception. Each day I wish for: "Dostert, Medical" or "Dostert, 3F."

It's later in March, and Attendant Walton is training a new female attendant. I arrive at my usual 2:00 P.M. Walton leaves. Right now the woman is with the 8–4 attendant and most of the juveniles at school. One non-confined juvenile, Kenneth, is on unit with me. A Movement and Control attendant just returned him from a court appearance. Kenneth missed school today. In an hour, the 8–4, the inmates, and the new woman attendant, who today is wearing leather trousers, reach the hallway outside the cellblock door. Sitting at a card table, Kenneth sees them. "Man, she need to take them pants off!" Kenneth leaps up from his seat where he has been vegetating, staring out the windows or at the walls. His head is slick like he shaved it with cream and a blade. He is fifteen with bulges in his shoulders, and I'm not much huskier.

No heads in the hall turn. Kenneth's horny declaration hasn't penetrated the glass wall. I don't counter. I fight bigger worries, like who will show up for 4–12. The inmates enter the unit orderly with the woman and the 8–4 who conducts the spot search.

Afterwards, I tell Darren, a different loudmouth heading for the TV area, to lower his voice, and he smarts off. I instruct Darren to serve wall time. His body isn't track star honed like lustful Kenneth's, whose illegal words I did ignore. I'm not ignoring these words from Darren, who sports more the stout but self-conscious neighborhood bully look. Unlike when alone with Kenneth, the 8–4 is here now if anything goes physical with Darren. Darren stops walking toward the TV area but refuses to turn and face the bricks. I change wall time to cell time. Darren refuses again.

The 8–4 man, at whom I've never seen an inmate jeer, watches from the console. I repeat myself several times until Darren complies.

I follow him to his cell. "Take off your shoes and step in!"

Darren swivels his shoulders and looks right at me from the doorway, "I got somethin' for you!" Then he steps in and turns around, glaring.

I lock the door. "Okay I'll write that down too!" He's looking at me through the Plexiglas. I turn and stride away to the console.

In my report I quote Darren's threat and then phone a caseworker. Within half an hour, a three-hundred-pound man with a boyish face and hair short as mine eases through the cellblock doorframe and reads my violation form, which I left lying on the console. He walks back to Darren's cell, opens the door, and steps in. I can't see him or Darren for some minutes.

The man backs out and waves me over from the TV area. I stand up and saunter down the row. Darren now stands in the doorway. The caseworker is in front of one doorframe post. I'm at the other. We're arranged like points in a triangle.

"So, Mr. Dostert, this is what he said to you?" the caseworker, several inches taller than Darren and me, flashes his eyes at my report in his hand.

"That's what he said."

He turns to Darren, "Why'd you threaten staff?"

"I didn't say that."

"Then what did you say?"

"I said, 'I got somethin' to tell you.'"

The three of us are quiet for several seconds.

"That's some bullshit right there!" the massive man drops his hand clutching the report. The paper crackles against his leg. "Mr. Dostert, if you hear anything from him the rest of the night, call me! If he breathes, coughs, cries, burps, farts, anything! Call me!"

The caseworker is dressing Darren down where all of 3G can see and hear from the card tables and TV area, to legitimize me to them. He wants the other inmates to see him supporting me, to see him confirming that Darren belonged on that wall and now belongs in his cell. I wish all caseworkers were like Hampton and this guy. What I really want though is to never need a caseworker to legitimize me because all the inmates do what I tell them to before wall- or call-time.

Today being Thursday, I already know I'll be working harder than usual and mustering additional vigilance—I have Attendant Rollins, as long as he doesn't take off, instead of Attendant Edison regardless. And now I have to muster additional vigilance to monitor any more stealthy threats from confined Darren. But I don't want to work harder and muster more vigilance than usual because today is my mother's birthday. I have moved to another state and missed my mom's birthday for this kid to threaten me.

At 4:00 P.M. the tight-trousered woman trainee leaves, and Attendant Rollins arrives with another trainee who will shadow him. The man has heft yet reminds me of the Michelin Tire man—big around the middle and a soft voice. As I've heard juveniles say when they dislike something, *Fuck that!* My future coworkers include a woman bent on strutting her figure around boys she is old enough to have mothered and a man meeker than Attendant Jensen! I go home and write a resignation letter. My last day will be in three weeks, a few days after my own birthday. I will turn twenty-seven on an off-day, reveling in the fact that only two shifts of attending children at the Audy Home remain on my life calendar. Then I'll look for a job in the suburbs near my apartment where no spiteful juvenile delinquents lurk to ruin my career, even if no career awaits me there. I've long been pondering a close by Italian restaurant with merlot bottles in the window for this very day. I can be a waiter again like I was in grad school until my lease expires in June and I retreat to Texas. Plenty school districts there offer alternative teacher certification programs similar to Teachers for Chicago. Maybe they will take me.

I submit my letter to the time clock supervisor. The guy looks up and grunts like an aging, slurry-speeched light heavyweight in a made-for-TV movie.

On unit, I inform Attendant Edison too that I am quitting. He has returned after nearly a month. His mother passed. "I just couldn't do it," he describes battling to open his front door each day and leave for work. He mentions an estranged sister, whom he and other family members believe neglected mom, affecting her death. My quitting seems to offend Attendant Edison because he is cocking his head away from me. Normally, we talk pupils to pupils. I feel good about my resignation because I want to reject most of the juveniles—they're rejecting me. I also love the idea of punishing Assistant Superintendent Davis for misleading me with his spiel about it being possible to just "sit and watch the kids" and not have hell on your hands. I feel bad about my resignation because Attendant Walton and Attendant Edison have done everything to help me endure, and I am not.

In a week I'm angrier that Darren is about to ruin my résumé than I am about how challenging he renders my life on 3G if Attendant Edison isn't here. Leaving after nine months will embarrass me with family and friends after the upbeat way I spoke about my volunteer experience. The only way to take revenge on Kenneth, Darren, and every other inmate who won't act like Hector is to last a full year. That was my goal on day one. To let kids foil my plan would mean I'm no longer a man. Only a kid would lose a battle with another kid.

I rescind my resignation and volunteer for overtime to convince myself and any juvenile who sees me remaining at the console after 10:00 P.M. that I'm not beaten. Into the A.M. hours, I wander along the cell row and stop to stare through Darren's window. I want to rip open his door and kick his sleeping torso with such force that the sun will rise before he can fade from consciousness again. He ruined my mission and decimated my belief that simply wanting to help unfortunate young men like him had made me an adult male before even setting foot on a cellblock. I want to ruin what I can of his mission, if only for this night.

25

To have someone like Edison backing me during the six hours our shifts overlap is a lifeline. The third-floor floor manager just summoned me to her office. The fiftyish black woman informed me that an unnamed 3G inmate has informed a caseworker that he overheard me say to a white inmate (the shaggy-haired level four turned pot smuggler/smoker): "I hate niggers and spicks!" I left with her smiling and thanking me for stopping by. Almost apologetic, she closed the matter. Attendant Edison then tells me about the rumor and fingers Jaytwan—"Little Mike," as the other 3G boys call him because he resembles a miniature Mike Tyson, squeaky voice and balled deltoids and biceps included, but sans any Mickey Mouse or Chairman Mao tattoos. Edison also lectures 3G hard and long about believing everything they hear. "Always consider the source," he warns, pointing his head down the cell row toward Jaytwan behind Plexiglas in Confinement. I'd locked him up after he cursed at me in the rec yard when I jogged to home plate from the pitcher's area to demand the softball bat after he lined out to centerfield but insisted on another set of balls and strikes. I repeated that he was out. Jaytwan slammed our bat into the concrete. The 8–4 attendant zipped over from the bench and cut him off from charging me and then escorted him inside. I wrote a report after we finished the game.

Besides Attendant Edison's sobering effect on inmates like Kenneth, Darren, and Little Mike, I missed our conversations about God and race and America while he tended to his mother and her death. He has even disclosed why he won't smoke KOOL cigarettes—the overlapping O's on the wrapper resemble slave manacles. His lectures to juveniles with tattoos also fascinate. To him, tattooed black people recreate the slave trade because slave sellers branded their stock like ranchers their cattle. I enjoy none of this stimulation when Attendant Rollins is the 4–12. I must be ready to monitor, redirect, and discipline all shift long.

Edison buried his mother a few weeks ago. Right now we face our juveniles lined along the cell fronts. We're back from gym time. Attendant Edison directs the spot search. No contraband flutters or clangs to the floor, but he doesn't dismiss the boys to the TV area and ping-pong or card tables. "How many of you been in here before?"

At least half the young men lift a hand. I leave his flank for the console behind him and plunk down. Since his mother's passing, everything about Attendant Edison is more "militant"—his walk, his talk, his dishing up the dinner plates, the way he begins questions with an emphatic "D," and then never turns his head or moves his eyes off me until I complete my answer.

"Any of you ever been to the zoo?"

A smattering of hands fly up. A greater number of heads nod.

"Have you ever seen a lion or a tiger locked in one of those cages? What's the look in the lion's eyes?"

"It looks scared," a fifteen-year-old calls out.

"Exactly. You see fear in its eyes." Attendant Edison shakes his chin side-to-side and paces down the row toward the bathroom area. He stops. "And what does it do when they throw that piece of meat in the cage?" Before anyone replies: "It gets all excited to get some shit to eat! And if you open the cage, it won't even run out! It'll just sit there, happy to be locked up! Now tell me this, if you took a lion or a tiger back to the jungles of Africa, would it ever want to come back to the zoo in America?"

"No way! Heeell no!" the juveniles chime together.

"So if an animal that sees freedom won't come back to the zoo, why do you guys keep comin' back to this bitch? Do you like it better here than at home?" Edison is strutting toward the TV area now, his hands and chin wagging.

The line of male adolescents erupts into a louder "Hell no!" chorus.

"Or maybe you're like that lion that's so used to being locked up that even when the cage door is wide open, it doesn't run out!

They let you go, but you're programmed to come right back." Attendant Edison has never interrogated the inmates like this.

The recidivism record, I'm told, is a boy freed at morning court but re-arrested and returned to his original cellblock in time for lunch. In my children's attendant career, I count seventy-four kids whom I know were released, but then days or months later, return for more cardboard hamburgers and drying off with pillowcases instead of towels. When I recognize a face, I scribble his name down. Some faces I've seen four, five, and six times.

Everyone is silent for a few seconds until a spongy-haired sixteen-year-old moves a foot forward and says, "Tupac had a song called *White Man's World*. I listened to it and it sounds pretty real to me." A felony drug charge has detained him for two months.

"Check this out," Edison waves a hand in front of his own chest. "In South Africa there are four million whites and twenty million blacks. But for years, the blacks were oppressed. To me that's not a white man's world. There were five times as many of us as there were of them! To me, that's a lion conditioned to like being locked up. Even if the cage door is wide open, it won't run out. They were so used to being exploited that it took them a long-ass motherfuckin' time to finally revolt!"

The boys idle in position as if they'd love to holler out in agreement but are incensed that they have been duped as such.

"The same thing happened here," Attendant Edison rests his feet and breathes in after pacing until now. "After World War II, the beast, the Illuminati, which is really the American government, decided to put all the guns and drugs in our communities. It was jealous of the little progress we made in the Civil Rights Movement, which was really a lot of bullshit! Wweee shaaall ooovercomme," he sings. "Man, buuulllsshhit! What did we overcome? We're still poor and oppressed, and a lot of us are locked up! So they started puttin' guns and drugs into our neighborhoods. Then they got a bunch of us on welfare. Then they went to the gang leaders and told them how they could control all the guns and drugs. But then they started lockin' 'em up for it! Man, where the fuck are Jeff Fort and Larry Hoover right now?"

Without pause, several juveniles chant, "In jail."

Fort and Hoover, incarcerated for the entire lives of these 3G boys, are legends to many of them. In the 1960s, Jeff Fort chartered the Black Peace Stone Rangers, a street gang morphing into today's Black P Stone Nation. Fort projected himself and associates as community activist humanitarians to obtain federal funds. Authorities soon raided his command center and arrested him, contending that their millions had subsidized criminal ends. Larry Hoover engineered the concurrent rise of the thirty-thousand-member Black Gangster Disciple Nation, triggering a bloodied enmity with Fort. Hoover is serving a two-hundred-year sentence for a 1973 drug loot murder. Recently he was transferred to the federal prison in Terre Haute, Indiana, where Timothy McVeigh awaits execution. A local rap group called the Ghetto Boys heralds Hoover as a political prisoner, crowning him "the Nelson Mandela of the United States." Most Chicago gangs still pledge allegiance to fight and die for Fort or Hoover's umbrella organizations—*People* or *Folks*.

Attendant Edison's arms and hands slash the air. He roves halfway down the inmate line, stops, and stares at the boys, then spins on a heel to pace toward the other end. It's like what he has to say is so important that he must move while saying it.

"So the beast got the leaders to put their gangs against each other, fighting over drug deals. That way the government could build more prisons and make money off lockin' us all up. Look, even if you weren't out gang-bangin' and selling drugs, they'd still find a way to come and lock yo' black asses up!"

I'm still hunkered at the console behind him as inmate faces and torsos blank in and out of view with Edison's motion. Police were the good guys in my boyhood. They smiled. They waved. But now in my adulthood, skin color mutates everything.

Attendant Edison is far from finished with the young men lining our brick wall. His legs in shorts churn and arms fly around beyond his plain T-shirt in front of the boys—some nearly our size. Most rivet their eyes on him, following his track side-to-side up and down the row. "When are we gonna unite! We got the GDs at war with the Vice Lords! We got the Black P Stones at war with the Mickey Cobras! When are we gonna motherfuckin' unite! When they come kick down your door and take your mom off to concentration camp number eight and your sister to concentration camp number nine and your dad to concentration camp number ten!"

Attendant Edison doesn't call his audience niggers, but it seems like he believes the boys have an identity problem. "So why do you guys keep comin' back? Why do you keep doing what the beast wants you to do?" Attendant Edison asks in a lower volume, his legs and feet slowing. Half a dozen kids have slid to the floor.

From a still standing sixteen-year-old comes, "I ain't fixin' to work at no McDonald's for no four dollars an hour when I can sell five bags in about a hour and make a hundred." No verbal reaction from Attendant Edison. His head points straight at the kid, already miffed at him, a kid we've nailed repeatedly with wall time. He doesn't know that he is God's chosen, one of the "true Israelites," and should act differently.

Illinois workers younger than eighteen years old earn at least $4.65 an hour, but I doubt the kid is lying about never having toiled for minimum wage. This is his eighth stay here. The Audy Home is his home. My first wage was $3.35 per hour, filling paper bags with Granny Smith apples and cellophane-wrapped mounds of ground chuck. Had someone assured me a century-note in sixty minutes, I had too much to risk by jettisoning my grocer's apron and black polyester-blend pants to do something that might change where I slept at night. This kid though must have little to gamble by peddling drugs. Maybe that is why police have arrested him eight times—we take better care of him than anyone else. Not a visitation period that I've worked 3G has anyone looked in on this young man.

Another inmate raises a hand. "Go ahead, man." Attendant Edison nods at him and inches backward to rest against the console a couple feet from me.

"At my age, I can't see far enough ahead to think about working a regular job for honest money. Right now, all I can see is the easy money to get whatever merch I want." The kid dons a pair of $150.00 white and red Air Jordan sneakers—merchandise.

"But see that's exactly what they want you to think." Attendant Edison re-elevates onto the balls of his feet and steps in toward our sitting and standing bunch. "'That's the only way for me to make money'—selling drugs and stealin' shit. 'I'm black. I'm poor. That's all I can do is sell drugs and steal.' Pretty soon you'll be just like that lion that won't run outta the cage when the door's wide open. Some of you are there already. The lion gets all excited when the zoo worker throws it some meat because that's all it knows. It thinks livin' behind bars and having someone bring it food is the best life possible. That way the lion keeps eating the meat, people keep coming to the zoo, and the zoo owner keeps making money. Just like you guys keep making more money and more jobs for the government when you keep stealing and keep selling drugs, and they keep locking you up over and over and over. That's exactly what they want."

Attendant Edison's theories sound asinine until I visit another library to look up demographics. Cook County is only 26 percent black.[1] I'm working in a three-quarters black jail in a one-quarter black county. Immediately, I quit caring about the Garden of Eden's location or if Jesus's skin was a hundred shades darker than mine or whether the Illuminati exists. "Nigger" remains a non-word for me. And I dread being white in America when God sends us to our Egypt. Our Constitution-writing founding fathers quickly forgot who they were too.

26

After Attendant Edison's lecture on zoo lions, Africa's lions, narcotics, gangs, concentration camps, and welfare, someone wins the shift bid for 3G's 2–10. I'm floating again. I miss the rap sessions with Edison, his provocative questions and my sketchy answers prompting more provocative questions, and his coal eyes glaring the inmates into near perfect behavior.

Supervisor Mitchell returns me to 5D. Attendant Marcus has won a different shift bid. Chance and Donnell are already transferred to 26th and California. I recognize only one inmate, a strapping but mellow kid I'd met in Medical. The TV area chairs are eerily rearranged; some line the glass partition and the sidewall instead of all facing the screen, to keep visual wars from erupting into physical wars. A four-foot wide floor-to-ceiling section of partition glass between steel columns is empty—that flying chair I'd heard about in training. This is not October's 5D.

Attendant Courtney, slightly younger than me, whom I've already seen in the halls, has been doing 4–12 for a couple weeks. Taller than me and with a gold Egyptian emperor head hung on a thin chain around his neck, he makes a decent first visual impression. Courtney's short Afro is frizzed, in a way that looks deliberate, almost like he visits a salon but in no way is feminine. He's not suburban and white like me and looks a thousand times hipper than short, bookish Attendant Jensen. This will be easy like with Attendant Marcus.

I'm manning the TV area when he arrives. Emell, an AT with a forty-inch waist, vaults up from a card table to the console, where Attendant Courtney sets his bag and fumbles for the logbook. Emell throws out a hand. Courtney lifts one of his and lets this twenty-five-year-old-looking teen massage his palm through three or four pec-level gestures and then bump their wrapped palms against both chests, as if homeys saluting on the corner. Bad second impression. *Here comes a long shift.* I traded handshakes with plenty of juveniles when a volunteer. But no more. By shift's end, we've confined four or five and several are banging their doors after lights-out. Furious at Courtney, I ignore it. This is his unit. The banging is his fault.

It's our second shift together. Attendant Courtney arrives. We direct all the inmates into the TV area—the card tables were throbbing with cackles and shouts. Noisily, everyone lands in a seat. From the bodies jostling and chairs squeaking on the hard floor, I hear Lafredrick, another AT with a puffy Afro and beltline nearly as broad as Emell's, mouth off to Courtney—*Attention 5D, Mr. Courtney can't make me be quiet in the TV area because he's a weak ass punk!*

Half the inmates laugh in agreement.

Attendant Courtney sinks into a seat along the glass partition. I stay upright near the back row, the cell door windows behind me. I used to be Attendant Courtney.

"Young man, step to your room!" I butt in. Screw wall time.

The TV area blanks silent like a ringmaster just clanged a bell for the fight to begin. Lafredrick rises and heads down the aisle between the glass partition and chairs toward me.

I hold my eyes on him. After a few steps, his eyes hit mine. Being an AT, if convicted, Lafredrick could do twenty or thirty or forty years. His plod quickens, as if the closer Lafredrick advances, the more defiance he exhibits as opposed to remaining seated and aloof.

"Stop!" Our chests will bump if he doesn't. Lafredrick halts a couple paces in front of me. Our irises, mine hazel and his black, meet. Our shoulders are level. His as wide as mine. More hush. Every eye beats on us. Attendant Courtney is a part of his chair, apparently leaving me to battle Lafredrick solo if he lunges and others fly in to assist.

"Where's your room?"

"Right there," Lafredrick points through me to door number sixteen behind us.

How did this asshole score a cell in front of the TV*?* I hedge backwards, careful not to show Lafredrick my back and the back of my head. Swiveled sideways, I key open his cell and ease aside.

"Take your shoes off."

He does and moves past me, his arm brushing the hair on my arm, to enter the cell.

I lock the door.

Success—mine after eleven months of dreading whether I can back down a nasty hulk of a juvenile without an attendant like Edison or Pruitt or Marcus monitoring nearby. Because of me, this asshole hasn't fully mocked a grown naïve man without consequence—the grown naïve man I once was. I saved black Attendant Courtney from black kid thug Lafredrick, who watches us through his Plexiglas the rest of the evening. He never pounds his door. I write no report to explain his idling in a cell before and after dinner and all the way to lights-out. I hear no one else mouth off to Attendant Courtney. Spades games are quieter too.

27

I submit another quitting notice a few days after staring Lafredrick into his cell. This one takes me to a full year of attending children at the Audy Home. I relocate to my native Texas and apply to Houston's equivalent of Teachers for Chicago. I continue logging on to the *Tribune* website, though. I still need news about Chicago's kids. Removing myself from the tumult has abated my exasperation with strip searches, ripping fighters apart, peeling eyes for gang hand signs, supervising group showers, stressing over who will be my coworker on what cellblock, and strategizing how best to checkmate two dozen juveniles into silent and peaceful formations while traversing long drab hallways or sequestering them on hard chairs in a bricked television corner. Once again I'm thinking about troubled children's lives outside and inside that jail. Time is recycling itself.

Several nights after my first Christmas back in Texas, I crouch over my laptop computer and read: "Teens Charged with Slashing Guard's Throat: 2 Allegedly Tried to Escape Audy Home." I click on the headline and a text appears. A week ago, minutes after midnight, an attendant, "guard," noticed a sixteen-year-old "inmate" outside his cell and "confronted" him. The teen wielded "a box-cutting razor" and slashed the man's hands, forearms, and the right side of his neck. Using the bleeding attendant's keys, the kid released another sixteen-year-old from his cell. The two then dragged their collapsed victim into one of their vacated cells. The attendant was working the 12–8 shift solo because his block had no overflows. Next the boys keyed open an equipment cabinet and with its softball bat pounded at one of their cell's streetside windows. Perhaps they had already knotted sheets, blankets, and pillowcases together for anchoring to a commode and rappelling down the building's exterior like one inmate had during the early 1980s. Attendants from adjacent cellblocks heard this latest wee hour upheaval, abandoned their posts, subdued the bat-brandishing pair without incident, and contacted police. One inmate already carries a first-degree murder case. Now both are charged with attempted first-degree murder and attempted escape.

"We've never had anything of this magnitude take place here in my six years," Superintendent Doyle explains to the *Tribune*. "Most of our children are well-behaved. This is an anomaly in our history." Doyle adds more to agitate me, "We have a very good staff here who receive 160 hours of training in their first year and have worked with troubled youths before. We have a lot of troubled children in here for a lot of serious offenses, but we keep problems to a minimum."[1] In my children's attendant year and three days, I sat in training for 124 hours, not 160, and no session taught me how to thwart a razor-wielding teen from blading my throat. Superintendent Doyle, if you ensured that front desk staff inspected care packages and their shampoo bottles, maybe cellophane-wrapped cigarettes and matches, and now box-cutting tools, wouldn't infiltrate the cellblocks to slice up your "very good staff."

I phone Attendant Simons on his day off. He still works the cellblock with steel-doored chambers where Tiny Timmy spent countless nights and days. "Yeah they're here on 3B. Behind the steel." Simons has listened to them snickering off the incident through their adjoining cell wall as "no big deal." He relays a description of the inmates' victim—darker skin, square-faced, and a placid disposition. I think for a moment and then remember him: a trainer about forty or forty-five years old reporting to the basement classroom, coffee in one hand, having done his regular 12–8 upstairs. I ask Simons how the inmates obtained their weapon. No one knows, or administration won't disclose. The first kid escaped his cell either when the 4–12 left it unlocked, or despite his decade-plus experience and endorsement from Doyle and Davis to teach and train the rest of us, the now hospitalized man opened the cell while alone on the block. My Texas friends hear about this near murder from my mouth, but never will my parents learn of Chicago's gash-throated children's attendant. While felony suspects potentially swinging razors no longer menace me, I'll perpetuate their ignorance of my former dangers, emotional and physical. I won't allow Mom and Dad to envision what could have been me crumpling to a dull floor, my blood seeping across cellblock floor tiles, filling the tiny crevices between them, and then sneakers kicking me into a brick and steel catacomb.

The Houston school district accepts my college degrees and me the next spring. I pass the certification exams and complete my internship and rookie teaching year. I have a new career. To reward myself, I vacation in Cozumel, Mexico, as well in Wisconsin and northern Illinois. On a day when the friend I'm staying with near La Grange is at work, I board the same Metra train I used to take. For a better perspective of the city, I climb the metal staircase to the second level and sit adjacent the north-facing windows. Unlike most passengers who read or chat or chart their upcoming footpaths to the Art Institute or the lakefront, the increasingly gritty cityscape once we pass through Brookfield and Riverside concentrates my full stare out the train windows. As we approach Western Avenue, the view half a mile north above freight yards, squat brick factories, and tar-roofed tenement flats is clear enough for the Audy Home's top floors to peak above everything. My stare out the train's second-deck windows at the jail feels listless, like Tiny Timmy's trance out of the jail looked that visitation day with his mother. My stare melts into that collective year of listless juvenile stares at me and I'm tempted to brand the entire endeavor idiocy. Then I wonder if, as I've suppressed certain facts from my parents, I've done likewise with myself. My mission was somewhat succeeding. Darren and Lafredrick entered their cells. I even directed a decent 3G with Attendant Avalon. Another year or two or three, and perhaps I could have evolved into Edison, Pruitt, Hammonds, Marcus, and Tucker—even somewhere else than 3F. Instinct and attitude and insight, not skin color and size, are everything for the children's attendant. But with two college degrees, other options enticed, and I bailed. I quit rather than endure and discover that if once I established consistent order and respect, most inmates didn't start to "eat out of my hand," as one veteran promised they would. Maybe then I could have, for a few, nurtured and mentored.

The commuter transport hisses to its scheduled halt on the grungy 18th Street trestle over Western Avenue. North, above all the browns and grays, above all the blacks of the tarred roofs, I observe more of the sleek jail, its symmetrical tinted window rows—dark dashes set off by the white steel of the exterior walls. Every window represents a kid, a kid whose life I once idealized that the days and weeks and years and heartbeats of my career would change. Since leaving, I've dreamed monthly that it is me who is locked up inside the Audy Home. I'm a juvenile. In every dream, it is night and only night, and I'm always in my cell but never lie down on my green mattress. Rather, I linger upright studying the sky outside my rear wall window with the cellblock's blue light penetrating my door's Plexiglas behind me.

One or two passengers stand and leave. The train revs up again. Minutes later we snake into Union Station nestled in the Loop's gleaming labyrinth of skyscrapers. I stand up here with everyone else. We descend the grooved steps to track-level and file out. Then we march up a ramp and staircase to street-level and into full daylight. A Chicago of conventions, parades, and postcards surrounds me.

ACKNOWLEDGMENTS

Critique and encouragement from readers at various stages enabled this book. The professionals—Jon Billman, Sarah Burnes, Jennifer Carlson, Chris Parris-Lamb, and Sandi Wisenberg. Those as helpful as the professionals—Scott Dakin, Nate Dickerson, Robert Edwards, Beth Feest, Joseph Feest, Pete Fischer, Phuc Luu, Lou Markos, Pierre Matta, Ken Olsen, and J. Mark Price. Thank you as well to Deborah King and Julie Thomas at The Chicago Historical Society. Personal essay classes with Emily Fox Gordon and Amy Storrow at Inprint in Houston provided valuable insight into the craft of narrative writing, as did a nonfiction class with Anthony Swofford at the Tin House Summer Writers Workshop in Portland, Oregon. Thank you to everyone in those classes. Many thanks to *Ascent*, *Cimarron Review*, *Southern Indiana Review*, and *The Summerset Review* for input on the published excerpts. Thank you to everyone at the Cardinal Beran Library, nestled amongst the pine and live oaks along Memorial Drive, for the hospitality and writing solitude. Uncle Brent, thanks for the "Other" subtitle! For Elisabeth Chretien in Iowa City: Thank You for an entire Creative Nonfiction-MFA in thirty-two single-spaced pages and all the subsequent cyber-ink! With all matters technical, thanks to Will Tyler and Charlotte Wright. I stand in great debt to my former fellow children's attendants (impossible to mention everyone) and certain caseworkers and supervisors. My deepest gratitude is to Attendants Childress, House, Ordonez, Price, and Tanner for their warmth and assistance in a universe far more familiar to them than to me. To Alejandro, Christopher, Corey, Darrell, Derris, Devon, Heriberto, Jermal, Juan, Robert, and Taroderick—your real names, I did what I could, I think and hope. If only it could have been more. And to Jerome and Terry from before. Wherever all of you might be now, may you reach some new place.

NOTES

Chapter 1

1 Alex Kotlowitz, *There Are No Children Here: The Story of Two Boys Growing Up in the Other America* (New York: Doubleday, 1991): x.

2 Kotlowitz, *There Are No Children Here*, 268.

Chapter 2

1 "Administration and Management—General Administration and Mission Statement," *Participant Guide: Juvenile Careworkers Training Curriculum* (Chicago: Cook County Juvenile Temporary Detention Center, 1997): 1.1.

Chapter 5

1 *Holy Bible: English Version for the Deaf* (Grand Rapids, Michigan: Baker Book House, 1992): 2–3. Most contemporary English Bible translations employ "Cush" instead of "Ethiopia," which is likely why the association with Africa surprised me. Some biblical scholars suggest that the area referenced, ancient Nubia, may correspond to the region south of Egypt in modern Sudan, as opposed to Ethiopia.

2 *Holy Bible: English Version for the Deaf*: 962.

3 *Holy Bible: English Version for the Deaf*: 218.

Chapter 6

1 The American Correctional Association, Commission on Accreditation for Corrections, *Standards Compliance Reaccreditation Audit*, conducted at the Cook County Juvenile Temporary Detention Center on June 9–11, 1997.

2 American Correctional Association, *Standards Compliance Reaccreditation Audit*, June 9–11, 1997.

Chapter 8

1 Meg O'Connor, "New Home, Philosophy at Audy," *Chicago Tribune*, 3 May 1973, Metro/West.

2 Another story I heard soon after being hired.

3 "Rules and Discipline—Rule Violation reports," *Participant Guide: Juvenile Careworkers Training Curriculum* (Chicago: Cook County Juvenile Temporary Detention Center, 1997), 211.

4 "Rules and Discipline—Rule Violation reports," 207–209.

5 "Security and Control—Mechanical Restraints," *Participant Guide*, 158–60.

6 "Juvenile Rights—Grievance Procedures," *Participant Guide*, 225.

7 "Juvenile Rights—Grievance Procedures," 226–27.

8 Doyle quoted in Larry Engelmann and Jim Szantor, "Faces in 1994," *Chicago Tribune Magazine*, 1 January 1995, http://articles.chicagotribune.com/1995-01-01/features/9501010249_1_billy-joel-actor-gary-oldman-tickets.

Chapter 9

1 Maria Pappas, "Can't Give Up on Problem Youth," *Chicago Tribune*, 25 February 1997. Ms. Pappas published this essay as a 10th District Cook County Commissioner and chaired the Cook County Board of Commissioners' Committee on Law Enforcement and Corrections.

Chapter 10

1 Gary Marx, "Panel Uncovers Security Leaks at Juvenile Jail," *Chicago Tribune*, 2 March 1998, 1.

Chapter 13

1 "Security and Control—Music, Video, Literature," *Participant Guide*, 200.

2 Gary Marx, "3 Boys Found Guilty in Gang-Rape of Boy, 10," *Chicago Tribune*, 26 January 1995.

Chapter 14

1 The American Correctional Association. *Commission On Accreditation For Corrections: Standards Compliance Reaccreditation Audit*. Conducted at the Cook County Juvenile Temporary Detention Center on June 9–11, 1997.

2 "Behavior Management Program," *Participant Guide* supplement, 1–3.

3 *Trends and Issues 1997* (Chicago: Illinois Criminal Justice Information Authority, 1997), 167; *Illinois Juvenile Law And Practice 1997* (Springfield: Illinois Institute for Continuing Legal Education, 1997), 3.1, 3.26.

4 Dionee Searcey, "Sixteen-year-old Charged in Fatal Shooting at Liquor Store," *Chicago Tribune*, 6 April 1997; "Teen Charged in 2nd Man's Death," *Chicago Tribune*, 7 April 1997.

Chapter 18

1 "Juvenile Rights—Resident Abuse/DCFS Mandated Reporting," *Participant Guide*, 231–34.

2 "Security and Control—Mechanical Restraints," 158–60.

3 "Security and Control—Mechanical Restraints," 158–60.

Chapter 20

1 Caseworker Hampton clipped the blurb and taped it to his office door.

Chapter 21

1 He is also a trainer. How he hit four hundred pounds, I am not sure. He bottomed out after returning from Vietnam, living on the streets, almost drinking himself to death. Once sober, he started attending children at the Audy Home and worked his way up to a supervisor and trainer. "Not bad for someone with only a high school diploma," he boasts.

2 *National Juvenile Detention Directory 1997–1999* (Lanham, MD: American Correctional Association, 1997), 49.

Chapter 22

1 "Security and Control—Resident/Room/Living Area/Body Cavity Searches," *Participant Guide*, 176.

2 David E. Reed, Wendy Perimutter, and Jennifer Gill. Children and Family Justice Center, *Juvenile Court Trends 1996* (Chicago: Northwestern University School of Law, March 1997), 15.

3 O'Connor, "New Home, Philosophy at Audy," 1.

4 "Security and Control—Resident/Room/Living Area/Body Cavity Searches," 168–69.

Chapter 23

1 Steve Mills and Diego Buñuel, "Not Yet 13—and a Murder Suspect: Boy Charged in Killing of 2 Teens," *Chicago Tribune*, 4 February 1998.

2 Steve Mills, "A Life on a Collision Course: Young Murder Suspect Fell to Gangs' Lure." *Chicago Tribune*, 5 February 1998.

3 Gary Marx and Steve Mills, "Cracks Develop in South Side Double Killing," *Chicago Tribune*, 5 February 1998.

4 John Chase, "Boy Convicted of Killing 2 Teens," *Chicago Tribune*, 3 February 1999; Gary Marx, "Boy Gets 5 Years in Double Murder," *Chicago Tribune*, 17 February 1999.

Chapter 25

1 Deirdre A. Gaquin and Mark S. Littman, eds., *1998 County and City Extra: Annual Metro, City, and County Data Book* (Lanham, MD: Bernan Press, 1998), 152.

Chapter 27

1 John Chase, "Teens Charged with Slashing Guard's Throat: 2 Allegedly Tried to Escape Audy Home," *Chicago Tribune*, 24 December 1998.

CRIMINOLOGY / CURRENT EVENTS $19.00

"Although Dostert writes vividly of the gangs, brawls, and sadnesses of children who enter incarceration lost and without hope (and the staff who must cope with them every day), it is his moral sense, his unsentimental view into their underlying humanity and the system that keeps them locked inside, that is truly memorable. . . . Sure, *Up in Here* is a harrowing book, but it is also deeply humane and very beautiful."— **Kevin Prufer**, author, *National Anthem* and *Churches*

"*Up in Here* is a fine book in the spirit of Ted Conover's *Newjack*. Dostert, who writes heartbreaking sketches of his juvenile charges, charts his evolution as a 'children's attendant' in Chicago's Audy Home, brightly illuminating the irony of a correctional system that too often shapes all connected to it for the worse."— **Alexander Parsons**, author, *Leaving Disneyland* and *In the Shadows of the Sun*

"Americans watch news reports and reality TV shows about Chicago's hard streets and wonder how these tragedies happen. If you want to understand more, if you want to hear the beating heart, the laments, and the hopes of children at the epicenter of these tales, you must read Mark Dostert's haunting book."
— **Luis Alberto Urrea**, author, *The Devil's Highway*, a finalist for the Pulitzer Prize

"Utterly unprepared for the Hobbesian world he encounters at Chicago's juvenile jail, Mark Dostert soon realizes that any hesitation or uncertainty on his part could let all hell break loose. *Up in Here* is the ruthlessly honest and touching story of his struggle to become the essential male authority that he needs to [be to] keep himself and the boys safe. "— **Emily Fox Gordon**, author, *Mockingbird Years: A Life in and out of Therapy* and *Book of Days*

Mark Dostert holds degrees from Moody Bible Institute in Chicago and University of North Texas. His writing has appeared in *Ascent*, *Cimarron Review*, *Houston Chronicle*, *Southern Indiana Review*, and *The Summerset Review*, and been cited as notable in *The Best American Nonrequired Reading 2011*, *The Best American Essays 2011*, and *The Best American Essays 2013*. Presently, he teaches English Language Arts in the Houston Independent School District.

UNIVERSITY OF IOWA PRESS
www.uiowapress.org

Cover photo © Richard Ross, www.juvenile-in-justice.com

ISBN-13: 978-1-60938-270-4